Fashioning the Bourgeoisie

A HISTORY OF CLOTHING IN

THE NINETEENTH

CENTURY

by

Philippe Perrot

Translated by Richard Bienvenu

PRINCETON UNIVERSITY PRESS · PRINCETON, NEW JERSEY

Library of Congress Cataloging-in-Publication Data

Perrot, Philippe.
[Dessus et les dessous de la bourgeoisie. English]
Fashioning the bourgeoisie : a history of clothing in the
nineteenth century / Philippe Perrot ; translated by Richard
Bienvenu.
p.   cm.
Includes bibliographical references and index.
ISBN 0-691-03383-8
ISBN 0-691-00081-6 (pbk.)
1. Middle class—France—Costume—History—19th century.
2. Costume—France—History—19th century. I. Title.
GT871.P3913   1994
391'.024'0944—DC20   93-40094

This book has been composed in Adobe Janson

Princeton University Press books are printed
on acid-free paper and meet the guidelines
for permanence and durability of the Committee
on Production Guidelines for Book Longevity
of the Council on Library Resources

Second printing, and first paperback printing, 1996

Printed in the United States of America
by Princeton Academic Press

3 5 7 9 10 8 6 4 2

Contents

List of Illustrations

With the exception of "The three dominant dress types, 1760–1930," on p. 22, and "Fashionable ladies, 1800–1900," on p. 28, all illustrations are from the Bibliothèque Nationale, Paris.

Preface

WHEN IT FIRST APPEARED in 1981, Philippe Perrot's *Fashioning The Bourgeoisie: A History of Clothing in the Nineteenth Century*—or, in the original French, *Les Dessus et les Dessous de la bourgeoisie*—exploded, as Perrot intended, the myth that it is futile for historians to study inconsequential things, or things that *seem* inconsequential and trivial. The inconsequential things in this case were, of course, clothes—underpants, petticoats, neckties, dresses, shawls, corsets, and socks—which all of us, whether we admit it or not, take rather seriously in our personal lives. But are they worthy of serious historical consideration? Perrot's path-breaking book, as well as a number of studies that have appeared in the intervening years, has answered that question resoundingly.

Perrot did not claim, of course, that clothing, and especially fashion, had been completely neglected by writers. He did insist that most "fashion history" either cataloged geometrical changes in dress forms and material—lengths, breadths, and volumes, silk, linen, or cotton—or that it was concerned with aesthetic appreciations that celebrated designers of "genius," as though they drove the process and exhausted the meaning of fashion. The serious intellectual work on clothing was, as he points out, done by sociologists or economists, such as Spencer, Veblen, and Sombart, or later, by semioticians like Barthes, whereas novelists from Balzac on provided brilliant if impressionistic observations. But the sociologists were not particularly interested in history (that is, change over time in specific societies), and semioticians such as Barthes were concerned with how fashion had been written about rather than with how and why men and women in a particular society dressed the way they did and what that meant.

Perrot's book helped to initiate and energize a discussion of clothing's *historical* (the word must be emphasized) significance. In this country the preferred rubric for his undertaking would probably be cultural history, but Perrot conceives of his work as historical sociology or, to use the expansive and yet more precise term that H. Stuart Hughes used to describe the work of Marc Bloch, Lucien Febvre, and their successors, the *Annales* historians, as *retrospective cultural anthropology*. For, if Perrot handsomely acknowledges his debts to Veblen and Barthes and treats clothing as a system of signs, his work can also be seen as belonging to that large and ever-growing body of cross-disciplinary historical study that is based on the assumption that few, if any, human artifacts are without meaning, in that they first are created by humans and then more-or-less profoundly shape the way we live. As the quotation from Fernard Braudel with which Perrot closes his introduction notes, habitat, food, and clothing are a realm of material "things," but they exist in a "world of 'things and words,'" that is, "languages with everything that man contributes or insinuates into them, . . . as he makes himself their unconscious prisoner."

Les Dessus et les Dessous de la Bourgeoisie was much discussed and widely read in France (it quickly became a mass-market *Livre de Poche*) and was translated into both Italian and Japanese. Curiously, though, it seems to have escaped American attention even in the principal academic journals whose reviewers one would expect to take notice of what the French judged an important book not only for nineteenth-century French cultural and social history but also for the history of the nineteenth-century bourgeoisie throughout Europe and the United States. Perhaps this revealing oversight can be explained by the persistence here of what Perrot called the "myth of the futile."

Or perhaps the editors of these and other journals assumed from the subtitle that Philippe Perrot's was not real history but just another book about hemlines, crinoline volumes, cravat knots, or the creations of the designer-geniuses of haute-couture. In fact, it may be necessary to emphasize that this is not a work of "costume history" but a social and cultural history, specifically a cultural history informed by both semiotics and certain concepts from the social sciences (including ethnology and anthropology) of crucial and only superficially trivial or even embarrassing aspects of the history of the nineteenth-century French bourgeoisie: not only *how* they dressed—that is, how they appeared (*les dessus*)—but also *why* they dressed as they did, how they behaved in their clothes, and how their clothing both reflected and embodied their values, aspirations, and anxieties (*les dessous*).

Thus, "fashion," *la mode*, and "style" are considered by Perrot only when they are relevant to the major themes of his inquiry. For example, in the important chapters "The Imperatives of Propriety" and "Invisible Clothing" (on underwear and night clothes), he deals not with "fashion" but rather with rules of behavior, conduct, propriety, and self-presentation that were either effortlessly inherited or else painfully, and probably always ineptly, copied from the flood of *savoir-faire* manuals that appeared and reappeared in the nineteenth century, written by authors who sported unlikely "aristocratic" noms de plume, such as the Countess Dash, or the pseudonymous cravat-knot adviser who called himself the Baron de l'Empesé, or "Baron of the Starched."

From the outset Philippe Perrot and I have considered this translation a collaboration and are presenting it as a revised English-language edition rather than a mere translation. And our purpose was to make it available, approachable, and useful to as wide a range of readers as possible. Thus, we have felt it unnecessary to indicate where we have inserted references to new works on some of the subjects discussed in this book or where we have corrected a few slips in the French version. It is my pleasure and duty as translator to add that I am very grateful for Philippe Perrot's help, guidance, and friendship throughout a long project. I remember with special fondness the hours we spent in an upper-story Paris apartment on the rue Tiquetonne discussing whether or not something was "impossible to translate" while across that narrow medieval street, for more hours than were probably legal, a man ironed, steamed, and quickly smoothed out identical renditions of a ready-to-wear and probably not-inexpensive woman's garment, which he then hung on a coat rack—a compelling image of one of the many ways in which, as Perrot puts it at the close of this book, the "nineteenth century still insidiously haunts our armoires."

—RICHARD BIENVENU

Fashioning the Bourgeoisie

Introduction

NOTHING APPEARS LESS SERIOUS than a pair of underpants or more laughable than a necktie or a sock.

Current historical research prides itself on encompassing the most diverse approaches and the most varied subject matter. Yet it seems unable to escape from the myth that it is futile to study inconsequential things, for it largely skirts the domain of clothing, just as it once ignored the body as too trivial a topic.

There are, of course, histories of dress. But they are too often limited to descriptive chronicles or aesthetic judgments;[1] and consequently they do not venture into the terrain of gestures, anatomy, sexuality, hygiene, economics, signs, rituals, morality and law—the very subjects that would illuminate our dress behavior.[2]

Indeed, except for the stimulating but impressionistic contributions of novelists,[3] it has been primarily Anglo-Saxon and German sociologists and economists—notably Spencer, Veblen, Sumner, Simmel, and Sombart—who since the end of the nineteenth century have perceived and analyzed in depth the social aspect of clothing.[4]

This social dimension is even more obvious, suggestive, and inescapable today, because the growing homogeneity seemingly characteristic of modern, standardized bourgeois clothing has been accompanied by the proliferation of secondary, subtle differences. Any moderately informed observer can read differentiating messages in the flood of generic jackets, dresses, and blue jeans that covers us all. In 1830 Balzac could point to "the new suit of the dandy, the tweed of the rentier, the short frock coat of the unlicensed stockbroker, the dress coat with cast gold buttons of the unfashionable provincial from Lyon, the filthy spencer of the miser."[5] We point to the soft, close-fitting English flannel jacket of the top-ranking civil servant, the garish plaid sport jacket of the Texas tourist, the somewhat stiff blue-gray polyester suit of the Communist deputy, the yuppie tweed of the residents of the Avenue Victor-Hugo or the Avenue de La-Bourdonnais, the slightly shabby corduroy suit of the left-wing intellectual, or the painfully studied three-piece suit of the white-collar worker. Details of cut, choice of material, nuances of shade, degree of wear, placement of buttons, style—in short, the many ways we experience our own wrappings suffice to distinguish our clothes from the nearly similar garb that others wear.

This book describes the early manifestations, stages, and consequences of this dual trend toward differentiation and similarity. To understand contemporary dress we must study the nineteenth century, the century that pushed to the fore the individual and the anonymous crowd, dandyism and uniformity, distinctiveness and conformism. It is particularly important to examine the Second Empire, this crucial period of technical, industrial, and commercial innovation that broke with clothing's ancien régime in fact as well as in principle and that did so in a general fashion rather than just sporadically.

The rapid growth of the textile industry, the sizeable development of the ready-made industry, the unprecedented impact of the department stores that distributed the product of that industry, the parallel decline of the centuries-old trade in used clothes, and the improvement in living standards made possible the process that eventually made everyone look like a bourgeois.

The leveling process that threatened groups who were until then "distinguished" had to be warded off. Consequently, there emerged increasingly sophisticated standards of appropriateness and increasingly strict criteria for elegantly tailored men's wear. There appeared "high fashion" designers who gained international reputations. At the same time, the diffusion, circulation, and transformation of fashion accelerated even more.

Paris, of course, remained the supreme reference point for chic and good taste, the favored space for fashion rivalries, and the magical place for launching new fashions. The mythic aura that had long surrounded it was perpetuated by the new dominant social classes through the splendors of the *fête impériale*, lavish displays at the Longchamp Races, brilliant promenades in the Bois de Boulogne, dazzling Universal Expositions, and the sumptuous creations of the couturier Worth. But Paris also became a fashion manufacturing and marketing center that multiplied these rare assets by copying models and, infringing on their exclusivity, popularized them to the point of spreading and imposing, in diverse and inescapable ways, the norms and forms of bourgeois dress on a mutating society.

This study is not, therefore, restricted to the clothing of the Parisian bourgeoisie. It is also concerned with bourgeois clothing in general, with the behaviors it implied and the upheavals it provoked. This style of dressing defines itself in opposition to popular clothing, worn by workers or peasants; aristocratic garb, fossilized and obsolete; official, clerical, or military uniforms that were proliferating; specialized costumes such as those of children or those associated with specific occupations; and finally occasional attire, as for weddings or mourning.

Obviously these practices cannot be observed directly. We know them only through what was said or shown about them. This material forms a complex source that is difficult to decode, one rich in information and yet deceptive[6] insofar as its images and discourse, often normative, cannot restore without distortion an experience that they affected profoundly at the time. As Fernand Braudel points out, "Our investigation takes us at this point not simply into the realm of material 'things' but into a world of 'things and words'—interpreting the last term in a wider sense than usual, to mean *languages* with everything that man contributes or insinuates into them, as in the course of his everyday life he makes himself their unconscious prisoner."[7]

Toward a History of Appearances

PENIS-CASE OR THREE-PIECE SUIT, jellaba or Chanel suit, blue jeans or jerkin, ball gown or swimsuit: clothing is ever-present, an investment both monetary and symbolic. But why does a particular society dress as it does? Because values and constraints such as custom, cost, taste, and propriety prescribe or proscribe certain practices and tolerate or encourage certain behaviors. Dictating both the use and the selection of articles of clothing, this set of values expresses a veritable ethic of clothing protected by a series of sanctions. These range from mere ridicule to legal penalties, such as those once imposed by sumptuary laws, or prescribed today by laws prohibiting transvestism or forbidding civilians to wear military uniforms and laymen to don ecclesiastical or judicial costumes,[1] thus guaranteeing that certain signals vital to the social order are clear.

Clothing oneself is not a matter of freely assembling elements drawn from a wide range of possibilities but rather one of arranging components chosen from a limited pool according to certain rules. It is thus a personal act. But at the same time, there is nothing more social than clothing. This dual nature of clothing reflects the dialectic of structure and event. On the one hand, there is the weight of *la longue durée*, the inertia of an organized society with its customs, proprieties, and institutions. On the other, there is the group or the individual who obeys the rules but occasionally transgresses or innovates, either bringing about a marked change or becoming the topic of a banal anecdote depending on whether this crystallizes a tendency and leads to a transformation of the clothing code. During the course of the nineteenth century, for example, soldiers who had been wearing their two-cornered hats parallel to the body gradually turned them to a perpendicular position because of developments in shooting techniques. This is of fundamental interest for the history of the hat. On the other hand, the fact that Louis XI concealed his protuberant ears with the cloth cap that has become associated with him may be an important biographical detail, but for the history of the hat it matters not a whit.

This distinction makes it possible to keep in mind two facets of clothing history. There are broad strands that require conceptualization, and there are vicissitudes that call for narrative history and perhaps psychological analysis. But the social and legal dimension of a system of dress must be clarified before establishing a "vestignomy." We must define and explain clothing's social and legal dimensions, its ideological basis, the factors of its evolution, the conflicts that it engenders or reflects. Clothing, like language, always happens somewhere in geographical and social space. In its form, color, material, construction, and function—and because of the behavior it implies—clothing displays obvious signs, attenuated markings or residual traces of struggles,[2] cross-cultural contacts, borrowings, exchanges between economic regions or cultural areas[3] as well as among groups within a single society. Thus the ancient world can be divided into two broad systems of dress: humanity sewn and humanity draped. The former—for example, the Mongols, or the Gauls with their breeches— wore fitted clothing. The latter—the peoples along the Mediterranean and as far as India—were clothed in ample draperies like the toga or the peplum. Little by little, sewn clothing, barbarian clothing, prevailed in Europe. In the nineteenth century the triumph of the bourgeoisie spread its clothing across classes and oceans as the middle class progressively imposed its economic, political, and moral order and, along with it, its system of dress with its commercial and ideological implications.

Because Western clothing is symbolically charged, its adoption or rejection can be a crucial governmental decision. Once elected President in 1923, Mustapha Kemal forbade wearing the yashmak under penalty of hanging in his attempt to modernize Turkey. Today the imposition of the chador contributes to the restoration of Iran's Islamic identity.[4] In Europe fossilized vestiges of former pomp do persist within small groups or in exceptional circumstances such as court dress, the robes of judges and academicians, the uniforms of church vergers. Everywhere else bourgeois norms inevitably prevail. No one can evade the clothing trade's distribution channels except the autarkic followers of Lanza del Vasto, who wear booties knit from the hair of their own goats.

CLOTHING AS SIGN

Discussions on the origin of clothing recall those on the origin of language: the same unknowns and the same perplexities arise before these two exclusively human phenomena, speech and dress.

The development of the different functions of clothing is no better established than that of language. Generally, protection is invoked as clothing's prime and universal purpose, to which are added modesty and adornment. This simplistic functionalism, however, presents the serious danger of viewing clothing only in terms of "natural" needs, and endowing it with a basically utilitarian status, secondarily influenced by other functions. This substantialist concept of needs condemns us to remain at the most superficial level of manifest discourse. To put the history of clothing on track we must follow the signposts of a conceptualization that takes us into the unconscious or unacknowledged social discourse beneath practical rationalizations and aesthetic alibis. We must attempt to glimpse what determines vestimentary forms and behavior at the deepest level.

It is difficult to establish the existence of a physiological need for minimal clothing. The natives of Tierra del Fuego, for example, remain nude to hunt guanaco in the snow.[5] This makes one ask whether clothing is ever truly necessary. Yet every group has a historically and culturally determined minimum of body covering, without which the individual disintegrates socially and even biologically. For women in our society, good grooming and modish hairstyles can function as a sign of identity and become indispensable for psychic survival. It has been suggested that some deported women died on arrival at the concentration camps from having their hair sheared, an outrage that they experienced as the final spoliation.[6]

What we need, require, and desire from dress doubtless expresses a logic of use-value. More than any other fabricated object, clothing has meanings that are not exhausted by a study of its explicit uses and its traditionally admitted functions of protection, modesty, and adornment. Basically, it is first through dress that groups and individuals give themselves meaning. Mutual recognition, through which one exists in the eyes of others, is an omnipresent function. One would tend to agree with Maurice Leenhard that "neither cold nor nudity led man to clothe himself, but the desire for what would help him toward self-affirmation and self-realization."[7]

Because clothing oneself is an act of differentiation, it is essentially an act of signification. It manifests through symbols or convention, together or separately, essence, seniority, tradition, prerogative, heritage, caste, lineage, ethnic group, generation, religion, geographical origin, marital status, social position, economic role, political belief, and ideological affiliation. Sign or symbol, clothing affirms and reveals cleavages, hierarchies, and solidarities according to a code guaranteed and perpetuated by society and its institutions.

The nineteenth-century bourgeoisie worked out an elaborate system of appearance, which reveals the importance it attached to clothing's signifying role as opposed to its functional role. This concern extended even to the most disadvantaged segments of the middle class who needed to distance themselves from the workers precisely because they were themselves so close to working-class. An ideology of profit and comfort permeated bourgeois society, yet its conception of prestigious clothing (inherited in part from the ancien régime) contradicted the notion of functionality. What discomfort it endured, what efforts it deployed, what risks of mortal illnesses it accepted, bundled in stiff collars, tormented by starched shirtfronts, and tortured in corsets, all to give itself meaning and justify its existence!

With the acceleration of material progress and social mobility, and with the advent—principally under the Second Empire—of new kinds of consumption by new strata of consumers, a strict social mechanism began to regulate the relationship between class and dress. Clothes became organized as significative differences within a code and as status symbols within a hierarchy. When this began to affect minds more or less alienated, "intention" and "motivation" in the matter of dress choice and behavior became a problem complicated by the universal semanticization of "utilitarian" objects and by the inevitable intermingling of use-values and sign-values. This phenomenon, first pointed out by Veblen in his analysis of conspicuous consumption, was further developed by Merton's notion of latent function[8] and by Barthes's concept of function-sign.[9]

The manifest purpose of an automobile is to transport and that of food to nourish, but they signify as well as function. We cannot use an overcoat as protection against the cold or rain without making it, knowingly or not, willingly or not, enter into a system of significations. The overcoat integrates a function-sign into its practical function and does so by means of the practical function; it protects and, by protecting, signifies. Everywhere, behind the practical rationality of consumption and behavior in dress, lurk meaning and social values. Because of inertia, this semantic content participates in the survival phenomenon where the sign of a decaying function lives on as a prestigious holdover. Articles of clothing that originally fulfilled real functions in war, hunting, or work have degenerated into pure signification. Today, for example, a "sports" outfit no longer serves a useful function in sports, though it still parades the qualities and signs of "sportiness." Similarly, the martingale used by horsemen to tuck up or gather their greatcoats' flaps has lost its original use-value and now connotes only a vague aristocratic aura. The original function of certain items of clothing can sometimes be found in the etymology of their names. The term *redingote* (1725) comes from the English "riding coat"; *chandail*, or sweater, which appeared at the end of the nineteenth century, derives from the popular abbreviation of *marchand d'ail*, or garlic merchant; and the *cravate* (1651) may trace its origin to a band of cloth that Croatian horsemen wore around their necks.[10] In a short article, George Darwin, Charles Darwin's son,[11] suggested that living beings and clothing develop in the same way: clothing, like men, evolves in terms of genetic inheritance, natural selection, and the imperceptible degradation of organic forms. This analogy illuminates the transition from the pure function-sign, the signifying "useful," to the ornamental "useless": the necktie, the notch on coat collars, the buttons along the sleeve, or the rivets on blue jeans[12] seem to be the homologues in clothes of the appendix or tonsils in people, and equally devoid of use-value.

The interdependence and the plurality of clothing's functions—manifest or latent, real or imaginary—can be used profitably, particular commercial discourse. Since the practical and aesthetic functions of cl ing are inseparably linked to its sexual function—modesty or seductio and to its social function—prestige and distinction—commercial discou selectively overemphasizes some functions the better to conceal others tl are less admissible, expedient, or persuasive.

In the strongly hierarchical society of the ancien régime vestimentar signs distributed in a set way guaranteed the social order. Aristocratic clothing in its magnificence functioned as a sign of both lineage and essence; it needed no mendacious justification or apologetic rationalization. Aristocratic dress openly performed a sociopolitical function—self-affirmation for some and subordination for the others—freezing everyone in their places by signaling the place of everyone.[13]

Then came democracy and a puritanical, utilitarian orientation of consumption. The bourgeois clothing code, now legally free from sumptuary regulations, established itself as legitimate by hiding behind practical alibis and moral or aesthetic pretexts, as if to exculpate itself of the charge of gratuitousness. Still recognized in the nineteenth century, signs of prestige with their aristocratic connotations are blurred today by an ingenious discourse that claims that a hat, a silk scarf, or a fur protect and embellish, instead of admitting openly that they actually function as distinguishing markers and status symbols, like wigs or red heels in earlier times.

BEAUTY IN CLOTHING

A new social and commercial aesthetic proposes justifications instead of imposing norms. Created by the discourse on fashion, it serves as the guarantee and the symbolic tool of a class. Through its tailors, dressmakers, and milliners, this aesthetic produces and reproduces a distinguishable product by systematically rejecting—and debasing—the formerly "beautiful"—declared "out of style"—so as to praise today's "beautiful"—dubbed "in." The point is to create values, thus scarcity, but never a definitive, consummate beauty that would terminate the process and its profitability. Everyone admires, desires, and deems beautiful—elegant, chic, distinguished—what they think is admired, desired, and deemed beautiful by those whom they acknowledge as competent to designate the canons of beauty, even though these will eventually be repudiated—endlessly and profitably.

We can distance ourselves from fashion by looking at rural societies where celebrations are accompanied by a display of costumes free from mercantile parasitism. We can then identify the conjunctures, tendencies, and styles within which the hasty and fickle tempo of fashion moves. These relate to an aesthetic that operates at a deeper level, an aesthetic less garrulous and studied, which histories of costume,[14] often closer to art history than to the history of techniques, occasionally record.

The aesthetic function of clothing also fits within a *rélative durée*, closely tied to the moderate tempo that in the West governs the variations as to what parts, postures, or forms of the body will be singled out. Erogenous or sexually desirable zones of the body have varied through time, as has how much one could expose, a process with profound consequences for clothing.[15] This variation is exemplified by the ostentatious prominence of women's abdomens in the Middle Ages, the flat, muscled stomachs of contemporary cover girls, the legendary décolleté at the court of Louis XV, the flattened bosoms of the flappers, the chesty, callipygian figures of Hollywood stars, the protuberant rumps of nineteenth-century bourgeois women, and the bare legs and hands that appeared after World War I.

In less mobile societies this aesthetic and erotic topology undergoes only slight changes. Geographically, however, the disparities are extreme: from the Muslim woman totally hidden by ample draperies to the Brazilian Indians or Australian aborigines nude but for their decorated epidermis.[16]

Within relatively stable ethnic or national groups in the West,[17] the changes in stances and body parts considered sexually arousing are closely related to seduction strategies. They have focused at various times and for various lengths of time on shoulders, bust, waist, hips, buttocks, legs, arms, height, and weight. This process recalls that of fashion, though it takes place more slowly; and like fashion aims to endow the individual with a new identity, realized through new forms of expression.[18] Exploiting various techniques and artifices, this elaboration of and on the body multiplies its real or factitious aspects over time, always holding back from a complete revelation to maximize partial glimpses, concealing what had been displayed while uncovering what had been concealed. In the nineteenth century, female bosoms and behinds were emphasized, but legs were completely hidden, distilling into the lacy foam of underwear an erotic capital, the returns on which could be gauged by the cult of the calf and by the arousal caused by the glimpse of an ankle.

When legs were finally revealed in the early twenties, after centuries of reclusion—except for a few years during the French Revolution—they became an object of enthusiastic examination and overt fetishism. This interest, briefly revived after 1965 by the miniskirt, has apparently waned in contemporary society. In much the same way, the egregious postwar bustiness exemplified by Jayne Mansfield, Sophia Loren, and Elizabeth Taylor enjoyed only a brief burst of popularity.[19] The abdomen, long restrained by the corset then tightened by exercise, may one day regain prominence in the morphology of female beauty; or the hips may again broaden to produce ample, majestic posteriors.

Whatever the case, clothing is inextricably bound to morphological constructs such as fashion, which embody new definitions of physical beauty; but at the same time, the clothes aesthetic implied in the new fashion can become a veritable anatomical mold.

CLOTHING AS SCREEN

Clothing is ambivalent. It reveals as it veils, and showcases the sexually charged body parts it conceals. Thus it becomes a crucial tool in seduction and yet constitutes the ultimate obstacle to desire. The very modesty for which it vouches suggests the fascination of what it covers. "Why do women," asked Montaigne, "cover with so many impediments, one on top of the other, the parts in which our desire and theirs principally dwells? And what is the use of those great bastions with which our women have taken to arming their flanks except to entice our appetite and to attract us to them by keeping us at a distance?"[20]

Just as blushing calls attention to the embarrassment one would like to hide, so does modesty sharpen the amorous desire it is supposed to ease. Regulating intimacy is tantamount to regulating feelings. In *Penguin Island* Anatole France mischievously relates the consequences of a saintly missionary's decision to cover the nudity of his newly converted female penguins. He clothes one of them, who is instantly pursued by all of the suddenly aroused male population, so much "does modesty communicate an invincible attraction to women."[21] The more sexually charged features are hidden from sight and kept out of discussion, the more they invade, populate, and haunt the imagination. As Georges Bataille points out, "The appeal of a beautiful face or a beautiful garment is effective insofar as the face suggests what the garment hides."[22] Nineteenth-century prudery was so obsessed with sex that it clothed piano legs in pantaloons. Because of its modesty function, clothing fulfills best its erotic function at the point where it gapes, tucks up, and acts as a potential brake, defense, obstacle, or delay.

CLOTHING AND CONDUCT

Clothing always affects the body, and the body always affects dress. The functions of clothing condition its forms, and these forms in turn condition behavior, posture, gait, and gestures, which in turn sometimes condition clothing and its functions in a kind of circular causality. In short, one does not walk the same way in a fustanella as in trousers, in high heels as in thighboots. One does not stand or act the same way with or without a corset, with or without a tie.[23]

The forms and functions of dress vary according to circumstances, sex, class, or social role, and consequently everything influenced by these factors varies in the same way. Thus in the Middle Ages the opposition between ample and fitted clothes, long and short robes—respectively impeding or facilitating movement—mirrored the rift between nobles and bourgeois on the one hand and peasants and urban lower classes on the other. The position of the upper classes was reaffirmed by ceremonious slowness of movement, whereas the lively gait of the lower orders underscored their abasement.[24] Nevertheless, dress evolved toward shorter, more fitted forms until the twentieth century made functionality prestigious. Full, cumbersome robes such as those of churchmen,[25] physicians,[26] judges,[27] and professors[28] persist in solemn circumstances because the hindrance they impose upon swift motion, the constraint they place upon posture and bearing, the distance they require between arms and body correspond symbolically to calm, majesty, gravity, and decorum.

Clothing helps to model a body trained for a particular activity (it can be a veritable tool) or for a particular sociosomatic model (the atrophied feet of Chinese women, the wasp waist of European women).[29] It can also dictate particular gestures. Consequently, it influences attitudes, creates dispositions, and both emphasizes and reflects preferences. Metaphorical expressions such as *faire jabot* (to pout) or *être collet monté* (to be stiff-necked, literally "high collar") illustrate these correspondences. Buffon, legend has it, ensured that his style would be noble by wearing a court costume to write. Dress forms are standards that, depending on their functions, can act as reminders of strict ethical or aesthetic requirements or as persistent invitations to relaxation. Wearing masks encourages license, guarantees impunity, and provokes excitement and so exposes *a contrario* the restrictions of everyday clothes and the limitations they impose on play, desire, daring, or insouciance: "Give a child a false nose and he will assault with confetti or paper streamers the adult he normally fears. And a mask allows one to weave amorous intrigues in a language liberated from the usual conventions."[30] Geoffrey Gorer's studies on swaddling in Russia suggest that the clothes that wrap an infant might even determine basic personality traits.[31] In any case, clothing produces patent signs of socialization and acculturation. The first pair of long pants or the first formal gown punctuates the crucial moments in life, for these changes in one's appearance mark passages and symbolize conditions that are socially recognized, as does the first communion dress or the bridal veil. Accepted and legitimate clothing functions as a powerful element of political domination and social regulation: it induces the individual to merge with the group, participate in its rituals and ceremonies, share its norms and values, properly occupy his or her position, and correctly act his or her role. In the West, bourgeois models such as shirts or trousers need not be prescribed legally because they impose themselves imperatively. The only differences are interpretations, themselves codified more or less tightly according to one's social standing. In the mid-nineteenth century Henri-Frédéric Amiel suffered an early—but comparatively mild—attack of the malaise an individual can experience when he believes himself outside the pale of proper attire:

> My boots hurt, my suit wrinkles, my hat does not fit: a general disgrace. And this is irritating. This outfit looks as though I had worn it on a dare. Besides, one does not like to be uncomfortable or disfigured. Ugliness and imposed discomfort oppress in a revolting manner. They insult personal dignity, which secretly takes offense. One feels out of luck, duped, wronged, ill-served though one has paid well, and worse served than others for no good reason. Rivalry is added to discontent, and one's self-esteem protests as does one's taste. As a consequence, one's freedom, sense of justice, instinct for elegance, and feeling for the appropriate are called into question. And one foresees an entire season of repeated annoyances, the distress of displaying oneself and of feeling cheapened in appearance and being.[32]

Functional analysis breaks down and itemizes the missions assigned to clothing. It must take into account economics, aesthetics, signification, sexuality, and politics and establish a hierarchy among them for each society. But because of its finalism, functionalism too often tends to explain things by what they are. Seeking to define the function of sleeve buttons, Clyde Kluckhohn writes that "they subserve the 'function' of preserving the familiar, of maintaining a tradition," for "people are in general more comfortable if they feel a continuity of behavior, if they feel themselves as following out the orthodox and socially approved forms of behavior."[33] This tautological or at least circular logic, based merely on the notion of continuity, is certainly inadequate as a historical explanation.

Clothing's Old And New Regimes

FROM LAWS TO NORMS

DURING THE ANCIEN RÉGIME, the form, fabric, and color of a garment announced a person's condition, quality, and estate. It did so juridically, clearly, unabashedly, and without justifications.

"Sumptuary laws" and "vestimentary ordinances" were continually issued in Europe. They were instruments of political, social, and economic regulation. For the aristocracy they were protectionist measures; and more important, they kept social ranks visible and proclaimed the nobles' monopoly of luxury that distinguished them from rising classes. By codifying cut, materials, and colors, aristocratic clothing guaranteed the exclusivity of vestimentary marks of power. Brocades, linings, furs, feathers, lace, gold and silver trimming, and expensive dyes intensified the brilliance of clothes and proclaimed one's right to wear them.[1]

Inertias

Ancien régime clothing therefore classified its wearer in society along strict lines, themselves determined by material constraints. "For signs, transparency and cruelty go hand in hand," writes Jean Baudrillard.[2] During the Middle Ages in particular, there reigned a ferocious system of identification that required that the marks of infamy, exclusion, and proscription be worn as conspicuously as the aristocrats displayed their marks of honor and privilege. Lepers were identified by the wearing of black-hooded mantles or red robes and by the shaking of a rattle or clapper. The outcast Cagots of southern France wore on their chests a goosefoot made of crimson cloth. Jews were often set apart by a yellow or red round patch and occasionally by a yellow conical hat. The Albigensians, the Cathars, or the Vaudois were recognized by one or more crosses of yellow felt sewn on their clothing. Green was the color of the insane. Prostitutes, Saracens, perjurers, necromancers, and conjurers wore marks that signaled the anathema that they evoked.[3] Clothing reveals aspects of the structure and functioning of societies because it both supports and proclaims the hierarchization, regulation, rigidity—or mobility—of social groups. The study of clothing can help explain the cathartic release of the witches' Sabbath or carnival, in which the signs of power and legality are temporarily reversed.

Immobility in the distribution of vestimentary signs always corresponds to immobility in social structures. For centuries in China, as Braudel reminds us, "Simple robes were assigned to common people, distinguished people might wear belted robes, while the mandarins sported robes with distinguishing marks: two gold embroidered squares, one on the breast, the other on the back."[4] In the West, a long stability similar to that which reigned in China, India, or Islamic countries prevailed until the beginning of the twelfth century. Then one perceives a few slow mutations, at first principally among the rich. In fourteenth-century France men and women alike wore a long surcoat, a sort of beltless pleated smock that reached to the ankles. Little by little men abandoned it: their dress became shorter,[5] freeing their legs and fitting close to the body, so that they were differentiated from women who continued to wear long robes. Childhood, as Philippe Ariès has shown, did not really exist until the end of the sixteenth century. Hence, "The Middle Ages dressed every age indiscriminately, taking care only to maintain the visible vestiary signs of the social hierarchy. Nothing in medieval dress distinguished the child from the adult."[6] Clothing thus reveals a society's image of itself, its social divisions, its anthropological specifications, and its sexual differentiations.

Accelerations

Before the Renaissance, social roles and status were patently immutable. During the entire epoch, the individual's power was limited by entitlement, and one could not desire what one knew was beyond reach. With the rise of the bourgeoisie, the decline of feudalism, and the correlative slow but perceptible emergence of fashion, there appeared the preconditions for what would become the endless race between desires and signs. The numbers involved remained quite small, but one detects a nearly imperceptible increase in the flouting of codes, the transformation of etiquette and the debasing of vestimentary rituals. They would cease to be reliable measures of social and political organization.

Sumptuary laws and court decorum tried to stem this inflationary movement.[7] During the reign of Louis XIV (1643–1715), for example, even such details as gold braid and buttons[8] were minutely regulated according to estate, rank, season, and circumstances. But the violent struggles and bitter rivalries over clothing still mattered, mostly among courtiers for whom

appearance conditioned being. As they challenged themselves and one another, their ostentatious expenditures served royal absolutism, which was
enhanced by this splendid display.[9]

During the eighteenth century, changes escalated. Court rivalries progressively escaped the sovereign's control. And fashion, which since the
Renaissance had evolved slowly over centuries and within a closely regulated social space, acquired around 1700 its modern definition of "something adopted temporarily, on a basis of collective but ephemeral preferences."[10] It also took on unprecedented scope, sway, and pace. Fashion
crafts, shops, and journals proliferated, fueling an extraordinary acceleration of fashion production. The Marquis de Caraccioli echoed this in his
Voyage de la Raison:

> To be in Paris without seeing fashions is to have one's eyes closed. Squares,
> streets, and shops, horse fittings, clothes, and persons—everything displays
> fashion. . . . A fifteen-day-old outfit is already very out of date among the
> well-dressed. Fashionable people want new materials, the latest publications,
> modern ideas, and trendy friends. When a new fashion hatches, the Capital
> becomes infatuated, and no one dares appear unless decked out in the new
> finery.[11]

Aristocrats were the indisputable leaders for styles that still originated at
the court, but they viewed fashion as both agent and symptom of the polit-

Court dress

ical decline of the class it served, the very class that promoted its creation. An expanding commercial economy gradually dispossessed the aristocracy of its traditional social roles by eliminating a way of life tied to feudal organization. Fashion triumphed in the eighteenth century as the dying aristocracy definitively lost its sociological legitimacy. The repudiations, apostasies, and increasingly unbridled mutability of fashion[12] hastened the crumbling of the older clothing code, forcing it to abdicate. Fashion multiplied differentiating characteristics—the beauty or ugliness, elegance or absurdity of a garment now depended on its adherence to modish tempi. But by so doing, it questioned hereditary vestimentary signs, stressed their arbitrariness, and in a way denied past custom and tradition. For the Church and the monarchy it was of utmost importance that their ancestral signals of power be preserved intact. The frenetic ups and downs of fashion, on the contrary, aimed at novelty, even when it mimicked the past— Greek or oriental, for example.

Originally a prerogative of birth and rank but increasingly claimed by all, fashion spread in a simplified and frequently coarsened version into many strata of the rising bourgeoisie now untrammeled by sumptuary laws.[13] "Today luxury is widespread, and because money rules," noted the attorney Barbier in 1745, "everything is topsy-turvy in Paris—the comfortable artisans and rich merchants rise above their estate and no longer number themselves among the people."[14]

This was in fact a time when barbers, printers, tailors, shop assistants, and shop clerks wore powdered wigs and thick layers of pomade, and strutted about with swords even when this practice was waning at court. This was also the age of *petits-maîtres*,[15] fops who displayed extravagant vests with buttons of aromatic wood or mother-of-pearl, encrusted with gemstones or decorated with miniatures under glass, while the pockets bulged with gold watchcases and gold chains. During the second half of the century, critics systematically and harshly attacked the sophisticated and affected manners and dress of the young, wealthy bourgeois—financiers, lawyers, or magistrates—who aped aristocratic courtly ways.[16] In his *Année merveilleuse*, the abbé Coyer tells the following story:

> I needed to talk to a twenty-five-year-old judge. I wanted a private audience, but he was being dressed. I suffered a Spectacle that consumed more time than I required to state my business. I thought he had been summoned to the side of a duchess for a hairstyle and perfume competition. . . . We should not wonder when earring-bedecked male individuals do crewelwork, receive guests at noon while still abed, interrupt a serious discussion to converse with a dog, speak to their own images in the mirror, stroke their laces, become furious over a broken Chinese magot, faint over a sick parakeet, in a word borrow the mincing ways of the opposite sex.[17]

As its vestimentary prerogatives declined, the aristocracy was no longer copied in the clumsy, attenuated way of Molière's Monsieur Jourdain or admired respectfully by people who fully acknowledged their lower stations. Now the wealthy bourgeoisie envied the splendid display of an aristocracy increasingly forced into ruinous expenditures to maintain its station.[18] At the same time, the aristocracy was increasingly reviled by the partisans of egalitarian ideology and rational bookkeeping who were completely at odds with the indecent magnificence of aristocratic dress that manifested unwarranted privileges, improper gallantry, idleness, and waste. Moreover, as the Revolution approached, the sober, discreet bourgeois clothing, earlier codified and imposed by the régime, became a symbol flaunted by its wearers, a kind of increasingly vocal expression of their legitimacy. This attitude was reflected in the psychological shock produced in May 1789 at the first meeting of the Estates General by the confrontation between the dark, plain suits of the Third Estate representatives and the suits of the other orders, whose lavishness was deemed improper.[19]

The toilet of the prosecutor's clerk (Carle Vernet)

As significant as they were, these sudden upheavals took place only among the wealthy, urban dwellers. On the eve of the French Revolution all the inertia of a centuries-old code still weighed down the rural folk and markedly differentiated the urban aristocrats, bourgeois, and masses from the denizens of the countryside. In the rural world people had not changed clothes, so to speak, for a couple of centuries. They were still poorly or scantily clad, in hempen or linen cloth, canvas, or rough homespun, virtually without underwear, heads always covered but feet often bare. The urban lower classes gladly outfitted themselves in used-clothes shops. Wearing the used clothes of more prosperous classes, they were therefore less obviously set apart from the bourgeoisie. Most of the middle class, still of modest condition, dressed in coarse cloth, woolen twill, serge, or barrakan, in dark, plain colors. Women wore gray, brown, or green plain cloth made of linen or wool, unadorned by embroidery, ribbons, or lace; but all sported hooped skirts, though less full than those of the aristocracy.

"Freedom of Dress"

On 8 Brumaire, Year II (29 October 1793), the Convention issued a decree that epitomized the rupture with former vestimentary codes: "No person of either sex can force any citizen, male or female, to dress in a particular way, under penalty of being considered a suspect, treated as such, and prosecuted as a disturber of the peace; everyone is free to wear the garment or garb suitable to his or her sex that he or she pleases."[20]

Thus did the Revolution radically and legally overturn clothing's hierarchical and statutory signs. In fact, it allowed the transition to a system of differentiation and management of signs determined not by law but by social norms. This new "freedom of dress," it should be noted, did not extend to transvestism; and on 16 Brumaire, Year IX (7 November 1800), a police ordinance expressly forbade Parisian women to wear trousers without special dispensation.[21] This ordinance has never been abrogated, so that today any woman who wears pants does so in violation of the law.

Little by little the bourgeoisie would affirm its dominance over clothing and appearance. This would be done by elaborating a complex system of dress including aesthetics, hygiene, fashion, and propriety. It thus produced a capital fund of symbols along with social strategies and a moral ideology of good taste, good manners, distinction, modesty, respectability, and "self control." Concurrently a new institution appeared in the marketplace during the nineteenth century: consumption in the modern sense; that is, consumption whose distinctive function was founded no longer simply on juridical and economic discrimination—purchasing power—but also on the social and cultural ability to discriminate—purchasing know-how.

RHYTHMS AND OSCILLATIONS

Forms

The normative relationships between clothing forms and wearers are determined exogenously and sociohistorically. Yet though we have many histories of dress, it is difficult to find systematic connections between dress styles and the chronology of politics. Changes of regime, ideological upheavals, and transformations in mores sometimes superficially influence the pace and content of fashion, but these variations take place within slow oscillations analogous to the deeper tendencies that economists perceive beneath rapid day-to-day price movements. The regular evolution of these tendencies is rarely disturbed by historical events. In fact, like economic history, cultural history marches to a different drummer. The history of the beard unfolds in century-long variations. It vanished under Louis XIV and rose again during the Romantic period, only to disappear again after World War I. Yet the enthralling story of the rise and fall of facial hair remains to be told.[22]

The anthropologists Alfred L. Kroeber and J. Richardson[23] quantitatively analyzed body measurements in women's fashion plates from 1605 to 1936 and identified three principal periods in their evolution. At the base, forming a pedestal, lies a basic pattern of archetypical forms extending over large areas: in the West, close-fitting garments; elsewhere, the Mexican poncho, the Japanese kimono, or classical draperies. These basic patterns resemble Braudel's structural, almost immobile conception of time.[24] Within these patterns, wide oscillations occur, modifying the silhouette in cycles lasting roughly a hundred years. It is within this shorter duration that fashion, properly speaking, unfolds. Its variations alternate between two principal types: a permanent, relatively stable transformation that takes place over several decades and an aberrant type that is rarer and far more unstable.

Short-term fashion is the object of most discussion and interest, yet it only rarely affects the general evolution. A whole mythology of spontaneity and creativity in dress, perpetuated by fashion journalism, argues that the abrupt yearly about-faces in design prove the unfettered innovation and profuse inventiveness of the designers. This mythology cannot stand up to analysis. The serialization of quantitative data corrects our myopia and illuminates the deceptively brief durations of fashion by situating them in century-long tendencies and broad predictable rhythms. Real trends emerge—the position and girth of waists, the width and depth of necklines, the length and fullness of skirts—trends similar to those governing anatomical forms, each of course influencing the other.[25]

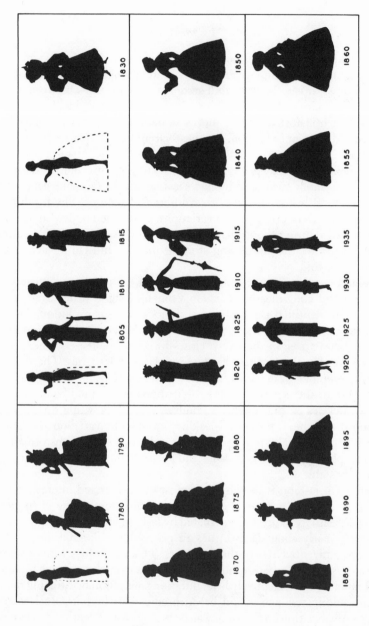

The three dominant dress types, 1760–1930. From Agnes B. Young, *Recurring Cycles of Fashion* (New York, 1966)

Agnes Young has refined and enriched the analysis. She studied clothing forms from 1760 to 1937 and noted not only changes in dimensions within the same system but also changes in the organization of forms around the body—the "contour."[26] She cataloged three types of dresses that reigned cyclically for several decades over a period of 178 years: bustled, tubular, and bell-shaped.

Though more difficult to measure, it would be just as pertinent to analyze the evolution that hides or reveals certain aspects of clothing, ruling them intimate underwear, or allowing them as visible outerwear, such as shifts, bodices, underskirts, stockings, vests, and pantaloons.

The establishment of all of these cycles within a basic Western pattern serves as a database that demonstrates that a form cannot be systematically related to its historical context. A finite number of forms[27] rotate or alternate in combinations that are limited by technical incompatibilities. The crinoline and the miniskirt are not the genetic or analogous products of a political regime or political upheavals but the result of a relatively autonomous evolution in clothes, wherein they stand at opposite extremes. But what relationship (other than chronological) can be established between the long, full dress and the Second Empire, between the short, narrow skirt and the sixties? Certainly, the former signals a society more rigid and prudish than the latter, but exposing the legs does not indicate "sexual liberation" for women any more than long hair in men indicates feminization. Neither in clothes nor in hairstyles does any trait dictated by nature permit such inferences. Skirts became short because they had been long; hair grew long because it had been short. Fashion's distinguishing values arise from this short-lived rejection of the past and those who stagnate in it. Nevertheless, there sometimes arise new representative forms, such as the child in the eighteenth century, new practices, such as bicycle riding at the end of the nineteenth century, or new social situations, such as working women in the twentieth century. These changes bring about new silhouettes and imply new forms with an obvious historical origin and evolution.[28] The French Revolution transformed men's clothing in the long run but did not really affect feminine dress, which continued to evolve along its predictable course without reacting significantly to historical shocks. The "new look" of 1947 emphasized the waistline, padded the hips, lengthened the dress, widened it with ruffles of stiff taffeta, and contrasted the billowing skirt with a tightly fitted bodice. Yet this fashion revolution was nothing more than a reincarnation of the farthingale, pannier, and crinoline of earlier centuries. The "new look" was not a particular response to political or social developments.

The alternation in styles is imposed by the limited number of forms and their limited possible combinations. But this should not take us into the cyclical monosemy of the mystics who believe in a vestimentary "eternal return,"[29] when, for example, they see similarities between the "two-piece" of Pompeian frescoes and the Miami Beach bikini. Forms return along Vico's spiral rather than Spengler's wheel, so that their meanings are never the same. Each recurring form is enmeshed in specific social configurations and subject to always-differing oppositions.

The diachronic study of clothing transformations from one period to another, or from one society to another, must be complemented by a synchronic study of the relationships and functions of forms within each period and each society. Their social significations would then appear in the details that differentiated them and in the opposition of their distinctive traits. During the Second Empire the relative size of a crinoline classified a woman as effectively as her speech: parvenus and tarts displayed exaggerated, showy skirts; proper ladies wore moderate, elegant crinolines; while working girls in their Sunday best donned modest, inexpensive skirts.

The evolution of the materials for these clothes is linked to technical developments and geocommercial changes in textiles and dyes. During the ancien régime, scarcity was as important as sumptuary laws in fixing meanings and use over long periods. Materials precious because they were rare, colors bright because expensive—like purple, which remained for ages the exclusive attribute of cardinals or princes of the blood—necessarily accrued to the nobility. For centuries somber colors and simple cloths were assigned to the middle class. This tradition of sober clothing for men remains ubiquitous; but since the nineteenth century, developments in textiles and artificial dyes have increased the choices for women's wear in a world where the sense of sight plays an increasingly important role.[30] It should be noted, however, that supply does not always meet demand; neither does it always predict or create it. The invention and commercialization of a new color or material can be decisive in determining new aesthetic canons, but a protectionist trade policy might also have the inverse effect— such as Anglomania during the Napoleonic empire or Westernism in the formal Soviet Union—so that some products become all the more prized for being unavailable.

Fashion

Fashion is only one aspect of the phenomenon of dress, a transitory modality operating within an intermediate time period that can be likened to style, which it occasionally modifies or transforms. Yet material, social, or political conjunctures do effect this multilevel history, which encompasses other histories, internal and systemic, each evolving at its own rate and in its own time, yet all interwoven like a braid. These conjunctures can disturb the regular tempo of evolution by slowing it down or speeding it up.

Without a modicum of prosperity, no change in fashion is possible: the fundamental costume of the Chinese peasant hardly changed over time, whereas the French peasant did acquire a few new articles, such as underwear, which came into use in the twelfth century, or the woolens that became common in the eighteenth century. Paintings of rural life in a particular region reveal long-term changes in clothing that are imperceptible in the short term but nevertheless follow the slow rhythm that marks transformations in ecclesiastical vestments or guild costumes. But neither does wealth automatically bring transformations, as the centuries-long immutability of the mandarin's gown attests. Wealth must circulate within a changing social structure to affect the pace in clothing change and to subvert at times the vestimentary system of prestige and power signals. Because elegance is an important symbolic prize, clothing becomes a field for rivalry in every society with some mobility, some possibility of wanting what others desire.

In the West from the twelfth century to the twentieth, fashion trickled down from the affluent to the poor through used-clothing dealers and thus affected dress at all levels of society that material progress, evolving social relationships, and acculturation had opened to economic, social, and cultural change. With the coming of industrial society, changes in fashion that had occurred at a rapid but disorderly pace became organized as commercial outlets took charge of distribution. To accelerate production while moving a large volume rapidly, and to increase demand, it was necessary to limit the physical life of a garment (built-in obsolescence of its use-value) and its social life (built-in obsolescence of its sign-value.)

Fashion rhythms thus became institutionalized so that the official changes occurred annually and seasonally. Repeated breaks with last year's canon, constant celebrations of the latest styles, tireless reproduction of the good and the beautiful spread fashion to ever-larger audiences through a formidable publicity system with a specialized press that chronicled fashion and published fashion plates. These publications now played a decisive role in both the creation of fashion and its demise, propelling it along from innovation to imitation, from originality to conformism, from distinction to sameness, from the Other to the Same: in short, what was coveted by everyone soon became revealed to all.

The Vestimentary Landscape of
the Nineteenth Century

WOMEN'S CLOTHING: A SMOOTH EVOLUTION

APPLYING ALFRED KROEBER's methodology to a body of exclusively Parisian fashion plates, we can establish series for certain forms of bourgeois feminine clothing and abandon traditional descriptions of the chronology of dress to focus on a slowly changing silhouette. We thus step back in both space and time, ignoring the annual or seasonal details of clothing change to focus on long-term developments.

Once the different forms of clothing that emerged during the Second Empire are viewed within their own time frame, continuities and real originalities appear, at least in fashion magazine representations. We should remember that between plates and clothes as actually worn, there always existed the inevitable time lag between invention and interpretation. Nevertheless, random samplings in the fashion iconography of certain specialized journals such as *La Mode*, *La Sylphide*, or *Le Follet*, between 1830 and 1914, enable us to measure the volume and length of dresses. These illustrations represent an "ideal" fashion, probably overdone as far as social proprieties were concerned, yet reflecting long-range tendencies and evolutions.

Surprising dates, mysterious continuities, unexpected peaks suddenly appear. From 1837 to 1913—that is, for seventy-six years—dresses remained steadfastly at a length that made it difficult to glimpse the tips of the high-buttoned shoes. On the other hand, the period from 1830 to 1836 concluded a thirty-year phase during which even the calf was exposed, and 1914 ushered in a pronounced trend toward a spectacular rise in hemlines.

The width of dresses varied more frequently. Imperceptibly after the Restoration of 1815, more noticeably around 1830, and very decidedly after 1854, dresses grew fuller and more flower-shaped. After 1862 they flattened out in front, to assume a no-less-cumbersome oval shape lengthened by the addition of a train. In 1859 came the apogee of the circular crinoline, and in 1866 that of the ovoid crinoline. The latter shrank gradually and gave way around 1868 to the bustle. The pouf, a prominent padding of the rear, magnified the train, which disappeared around 1880. The bustle itself did not vanish until the early 1890s, after it had suffered an initial eclipse between roughly 1878 and 1884. The last decade of the century saw dresses puff out once more. Then, around 1898, they took on the aspect of an inverted lily, hugging the hips and flaring out below to become spindle-shaped.

The waist, on the other hand, placed high during the Consulate and the Empire, resumed its more customary position after 1824. It fell until 1833, then rose imperceptibly, until it reached a high point in 1874, finally descending again until 1920, when it reached the small of the back, a position as far removed as possible from the one it had occupied more than a century before.

Wandering the length of the torso, the waist fluctuated in size for obvious anatomical reasons. Thickened at the beginning of the century when placed below the breasts, it was then constricted, becoming for more than ninety years the most attractive feature of the female body. During the reign of the crinoline and of the earlier tournure, however, the voluminous hips and behind allowed the waist some slight widening. There was also a great regularity, despite some new tendencies, in the width and depth of necklines, although the pace of change accelerated around 1874, and the area exposed became larger. Princess Bibesco described the recurrences of forms and the cycles of fashion in terms recalling a time-lapse film of flowers opening and closing:

> The peony blossomed with the panniers of Marie-Antoinette; it lost its petals in the winds of the Revolution; and the shrinking feminine corolla contracted until, under the Directory and the Empire, it was little more than an envelope, a sword scabbard, the spiral of a half-opened iris. Under the Empress Marie-Louise, sleeves grew larger, and the Restoration filled out skirts. With Marie Amélie they grew larger, billowing out until Empress Eugenie displaced as much air when she walked in her crinoline as Marie-Antoinette in her panniers. The year 1871 returned to more modest proportions, until 1900 again opened the upturned calices of skirts and sleeves. This pace of expansion and contraction has some regularity; it must correspond to star movements and celestial seasons as yet uncalendared.[1]

Such a "calendar" is all the more difficult to establish because it is neither independent of historical vicissitudes nor correlated to them. The fact that hemlines rose early in 1914 appears to be neither a simple secular reiteration—a hundred years later—of the changes that occurred around 1810 nor an economic consequence of the Great War. It resurrected and crystallized, with a vengeance, a practice forgotten for nearly a thousand years, namely exposing the leg. Shorter dresses constituted a new representation

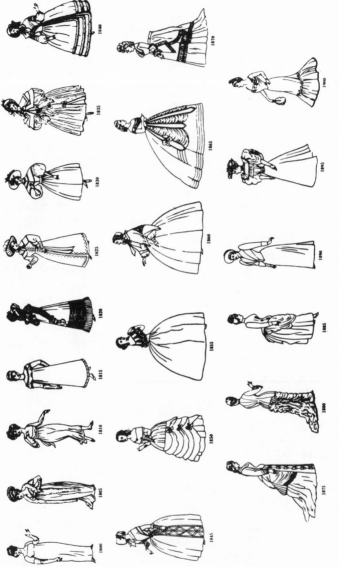

Fashionable ladies, 1800–1900. From Charles H. Gibbs-Smith,
The Fashionable Lady in the 19th Century (London, 1960)

of woman, called for new behaviors on her part, and resulted in a true cultural mutation as well as a new erotic behavior toward her. Similarly, the waist (once again constrained by the corset after the interlude between 1790 and 1810) could not have freed itself irreversibly in 1914 (after descending from the breasts to the small of the back) unless a profound sociohistorical phenomenon rather than a mechanical, cyclical phenomenon was involved.

On the other hand, the explanatory variables for the long-term ballooning of dresses remain largely unknown, and no one has accepted Alfred Franklin's challenge to define them:

> It would be rather interesting to discover the origins of the passion women have for full dresses, for those exaggerated skirts called *vertugale*, or *vertugade*, in the sixteenth century, which became *vertugadin* in the seventeenth, and took the name of "pannier" in the eighteenth and "crinoline" in the nineteenth. This voluminous attire has been abandoned occasionally because it seemed ridiculous to wear the same costume all the time, but never for very long, and an invincible force restored it repeatedly.[2]

All vestimentary practices thus require the study of form in two senses of the word: form as silhouette, which evolves more or less autonomously over time, even though the pieces that can be combined are limited for technical reasons; and form as norm, closely interwoven with historical circumstances with their own semantic restraints. Unlike the twentieth century, when in both these aspects of form the appearance of the legs, the abandonment of the corset, and the adoption of trousers profoundly transformed women's attire, the nineteenth century recorded no striking break or basic discontinuity with the tradition bequeathed by the ancien régime. In the final analysis, the tradition remained intact. The French Revolution paved the way for a revolution in men's clothing, the triumph of austerity, but no great changes in the color, cut, or materials of dresses, except insofar as technology and rapid stylistic innovations brought a new abundance and radically modified the habitual cycles and the ritual wastefulness of former times. Nevertheless, as we will see later, this asymmetry in male and female appearance imposed different behaviors on women and assigned new functions to their dress.

MEN'S CLOTHING: THE TRIUMPH OF BLACK

Changes in men's clothing during this period are difficult to measure. This difficulty stems not so much from the regularity of superficial changes as from the continuity of general lines over the *moyenne durée*, or medium run:

Take a good look [suggests the *Journal des modes d'hommes*] at the very elegant
gentleman, wearing his short sack coat as befits the taste of our times. Examine carefully the parts of his costume, beginning at the base: two straight pipes
containing the legs disappear into a main pipe, from which emerge two ap-
pendages, also in the form of pipes in which the arms are enclosed. To crown
the edifice there is another pipe, a gutter pipe this time, which we have
dubbed "hat."[3]

This undistinguished collection of pipes seemed permanently frozen. Its
adoption, along with the gradual replacement of brilliant, precious, elaborate fabrics like brocades, silk, velvet, and lace by plain cloth, and the sub-
stitution of solid, dark colors for bright, variegated ones reversed previous
tendencies, and the nineteenth century bourgeois founded a morality of
clothing.

The stiffness, austerity, and asceticism of his attire would thereafter totally differentiate male from female. The bourgeois drew these elements
from an ancient tradition, which can perhaps be traced back to the tightly
buttoned, strict dress that appeared at the Spanish court under Charles V
and Philip II, then spread to Flanders after the sixteenth century. Adopted
by Protestant reformers, by Cromwell's followers, by Puritans and Quak-
ers,[4] it became a point of reference and a symbol for the English bourgeoisie as it elaborated its system of dress. After destroying royal absolutism
and winning the right to sit in Parliament, the bourgeoisie espoused this
elimination of color to repudiate the multicolored splendor of fabrics and
finery identified with aristocratic idleness and sumptuousness. Dark
greens, blues, grays, and especially black denied color, and with it the distinctions that color emphasized. The extinction of color was a political
signal that a new social order had come into being. It also signaled the
onset of a new ethic based on will, self-denial, thrift, and merit.[5]

In France the Revolution of 1789 gave rise once again to dazzling chromatic conflicts.[6] Public opinion was finally liberated, and it expressed itself
through insignia, cocades, fabrics,[7] forms of dress, and accessories[8] still
largely derived from the ancien régime. Aristocratic refinement and the
brilliant array of colors outlived the aristocracy. The sans-culottes' striped
trousers, the meridional workers' blue woolen carmagnole jacket, the
phrygian cap, and the low, two-cornered hat originated in the lower
classes, hence their mythic value. Nevertheless, the political heavyweights
of the day, like Robespierre, Saint-Just, or Hérault de Séchelles, were powdered and bewigged, and affected or tried for the elegance of the fallen
class, just as did certain politically moderate bourgeois. The revolutionary
clubs did attempt to level pretension in clothing by proposing a variety of
national costumes, but they never caught on.[9] Quickly and naturally, bourgeois republican clothing, as far removed from the stigmatized aristocratic

dress as from the overly plebeian carmagnole, sought its models and standards in England. There, a century earlier, the triumph of the bourgeois led to such a generalization of their dress that it even infected North American fashions between 1770 and 1789. It spread to European countries: Goethe's Werther, for example (1774), already dressed in the English manner—blue frock coat, yellow vest, and trousers. Both aristocrat and bourgeois in France during the same period—foreshadowing future upheavals—adopted the same style for their day or country wear.

The sumptuously clad aristocrat was soon supplanted as an ideal by the "proper" gentleman austerely dressed in dark or discreetly striped fabrics. Of the revolutionary costume only the trousers survived. These would long be considered subversive, but gradually they were admitted into the bourgeois wardrobe and tolerated in the salons. After 1830, under the July Monarchy, knee-breeches were worn only for official ceremonies. Trousers, therefore, constituted one of the rare nineteenth-century examples of a fashion moving all the way up the social scale.[10] Napoleon I, Charles X, and Napoleon III vainly attempted to reinstitute aristocratic court dress, but the finery of the ancien régime survived only in a few fossilized examples like knee-breeches, two-cornered hats, and wigs, relegated to minor roles or occasional displays: valets, magistrates, or church vergers.

Bourgeois dress, 1831

This austerity, which descended upon men's clothing and affected it all the way down to shoe buckles—replaced by laces—aroused the chauvinistic indignation of nostalgic aesthetes and clientless tailors. They were quick to point out its foreign provenance and irreversible character:

> One wonders how the French people, who long dazzled the world by the richness, brilliance, and variety of their national dress, could end up with—as a result of progress—this threadbare, puritan, and austere attire, so out of character with its lively wit and gay disposition, this black attire inflicted upon everyone, the schoolboy as well as the old man, the man rushing to a ball as well as one going to a funeral. Had anyone told the fine eighteenth-century gentlemen that their descendants would one day exchange their brilliant toilettes for this piece of black cloth bereft of decoration, they would have protested against this mistake in fashion and this contempt for color. And yet, this is what we have come to, little by little. Spangles, braids, ribbons, and lace have all in turn disappeared and given way to a severe costume that makes us look like seminarians or penitents. The sun's rays have disappeared, giving way to the lugubrious shadows in which our tailors envelop us.[11]

The abandonment of display and color was more than mere Anglomania. The new dress embodied the ideological justification for and social legitimacy of the bourgeois. Clothing reaffirmed the concepts of modesty, effort, propriety, reserve, and "self-control," which were the basis of bourgeois "respectability." They combined a moral rejection with their political rejection of color. "The world of colors," writes Jean Baudrillard, "is seen as opposed to that of values. 'Chic' effaces appearance so that being might stand revealed. Black, white, and grey, the very negation of color, were the paradigm of dignity, control, and morality."[12] Ideally, the bourgeois' rather stiff black suit, like that of a clergyman, disguised or effaced his body, allowing the wearer to distance himself from it, abandon it, and forget its embarrassing or inopportune presence. It became, as Théophile Gauthier pointed out, "a sort of skin that no man will shed under any pretext. It sticks to him like the pelt of an animal, so that nowadays the real form of the body has fallen into oblivion."[13]

The aristocrat had enjoyed a positive image of his body; the bourgeois did not. Disasters threatened it: sickness, ugliness, and blemishes[14] that even his triumphant portliness could not obliterate from the mind. The body was not as emphatic as before. Gestures became reserved and poses ridiculous.[15] Lace, jewels, ruffles, snuffboxes, swords, garter belts, and shoe buckles disappeared along with teachers of comportment.[16] With hats, canes, and gloves left in the cloakroom, no accessories remained to give a gesture grace, to occupy a hand, or to sustain the required sober bearing.

In this morality of discretion and inwardness, the use of colors other than somber, neutral ones was always dangerous, and often unseemly, suggesting the subversive world of artists[17] or the suspect one of pederasts. Yet bright colors did not totally desert the masculine wardrobe. Shamefacedly, they hid under collars, coattails, and lapels, or on linings still made of "noble" and brilliant materials—furs, satin, silk, velvet, and moiré. They survived in the vest, which, barely glimpsed under the coat, tolerated novelty cloth.[18] And they appeared in dressing gowns, obviously confined to private life. The ambiguities of bourgeois clothing did not oppose aristocratic dress in every detail but maintained certain hidden similarities with it. It reflects perfectly the divided feelings the bourgeoisie experienced toward the aristocracy it had displaced but continued to admire. These bright colors that the bourgeois concealed and still preserved as prestigious souvenirs, these many fine details that were esteemed because they were exposed to view only surreptitiously, were what the nineteenth-century bourgeoisie cultivated on the sly as old aristocratic attributes of wastefulness and idleness even as they upheld the ideal of functional and hygienic dress, supposedly designed to celebrate thrift and work.

Artfully tied cravats, bright yellow gloves, glossy silk hats, detachable collars, immaculate cuffs, starched shirt fronts, dress coats that smoothly outlined the waist, and trousers pulled down by understraps to make the foot seem smaller acted as obstacles to utilitarian efforts. They imitated the earlier aristocratic elegance, which proclaimed the wearer as a consumer, not a producer. Formally "democratic" and "egalitarian," this attire did not make its wearers look alike. On the contrary, it promoted a new value: distinction.

The prestige of the "gentleman" would depend on the fact that his puritanical elegance represented a subtle compromise between a work ethic that rejected external pleasure in favor of amassing wealth and a leisure ethic that required that wealth be squandered. Tailors complained in their publications that the cost of bourgeois clothing and its upkeep would never reach the fabulous amounts once spent by courtiers. As an anonymous author wrote in the *Écho des tailleurs* in 1858,

> What explains the sterility of contemporary men's fashion is the rarity, indeed the virtual absence, of clients of high estate and great wealth who can impart an impetus to fashion. Great fortunes are certainly not lacking; they breed and multiply more than ever. But where is the taste, where is the imagination, where is the love of art? Formerly, they could be found among our great lords and wealthy financiers, though they were not as rich as today. For some sixty years we have alas followed in the wake of an England that graciously lavished upon us its redingote, its gaiters, its paletot, its greatcoat, its mackintosh, and its silk hat.[19]

The utter confusion of powerless indignant tailors who tried in vain after the July Monarchy to reverse the trends reveals how profound were the forces that spread the new code and set the new comportments. As one of them wrote in 1862, "When will we be delivered once and for all from this costume that lends itself only to insignificant modifications that do not permit our art to display its genius? With each new season we hope for the fall of this somber drawing-room tyrant. In the end, however, it always triumphs, and seems to leave the battleground stronger than ever."[20]

Obsessed by the demise of the black suit—which never came but which they always awaited—the tailors regularly delivered its funeral oration, as if to cast a spell, as though the premature announcement of its death, finally believed and heard, could bring it about:

> O, black-lined black suit, so tight it does not button, borrowed from perfidious Albion who inflicts it on every rank from a Peer of the Three Kingdoms to a Street Sweeper! Livery of Wealth and Poverty alike, of baptisms and weddings, of burials and visits of condolence, of tears and laughter, good for everything, same for everyone! Modern adornment of the undertaker and the guest, the conquering hero and the supplicant; black suit of my first communion and my last visit, suit that presides over what little I am, and over everything I seek. What a great blow you received, you inevitable castoffs that never cost over fifty écus, even to the worst spendthrift, even if he frenetically loaded the collar with velvet, the tails with satin, and the lapels with moiré! I won't miss you, dull, banal black suit that everyone wears on every occasion. May you disappear forever. May you emigrate with an export subsidy, go away threadbare, and, giving up the ghost through your broken buttons, may you metamorphose into a tabard on the back of a London cabby or on the rump of a Congolese or Zanzibarian as black as you, since each year we send them a carnival of cast-off fashions. The black suit is dying; . . . the black suit is dead![21]

No conspiracy, disapproval, or suggestion could hinder the inexorable tendency toward somberness and severity that led men to give up the fashion game and accentuate sexual dimorphism as never before.

WOMAN, THE MARQUEE OF MAN

"What does a man look like next to his wife? He in a simple black suit, dull, smelling of his cigar; she pink, elegant, brilliant, exuding the ambergris scent of her face powder. Doesn't he look like her chef in his Sunday best?"[22]

In fact, bourgeois men displayed their glory or power in an oblique way, not through what they were but through what they owned. Men's abandonment of sumptuous appearance and acceptance of exile from their bodies endowed women with a new function. The unchanged splendor of their toilettes and the opulence of their flesh signified the social status and the monetary power of their fathers, husbands, or lovers, who amassed wealth but did not exhibit it. Veblen[23] has given a most subtle interpretation of this vicarious consumption, which condemned a woman to wear the livery of the man who kept her, and to serve him as a foil. As signs of wealth and ornamental objects, women replaced the lace and jewels banished from men's clothing by the Revolution. Following an aristocratic tradition that never really died, women would fulfill the role of spendthrift, a role that they had to play doubly now that they assumed it alone. "As long as men battled for wealth," writes Octave Uzanne, "women's sole resource was to spend their financial conquests."[24] In fact, they did go out to show off finery that was all the more brilliant now that male attire served as its foil. In the name of thrift and equality, men replaced embroideries, lace and feathers, knee-breeches and bright colors with a frock coat suitable for all occasions and affordable by everyone.

> While men accepted these sacrifices in the name of economy and equality, our intractable better halves dolled themselves à la Grecque, à la Turque, à la Chinoise, à la Mary Stuart, à la Medici, or dressed as Watteau shepherdesses or as Louis XV marquises, so that in today's households the wife, beribboned, bestarred, triumphantly wrapped in an invisible Venus-like aura that wafts around her, stands beside a husband who is resigned, somber, dull, and insipid.[25]

In the same manner, the bourgeois child who wore feminine, very sophisticated outfits and the footman[26] who disguised himself as an ancien régime courtier stand out in this sea of black: they too exhibited the prosperity of the master of the house, and they too figured in his social shop window.[27]

Traditional Trades and the Rise of
Ready-Made Clothing

AGE-OLD PRACTICES

During the ancien régime, the making and selling of clothing was confined to specific channels determined by the guilds' complex and meticulous regulatory apparatus. To have a suit made, one bought material from the draper and accessories or ornaments from the mercer and brought it all to the tailor.[1] He took the measurements, and then set to work according to the norms dictated by his customer's status and the rules set down by his guild for cutting cloth.

"Makers of suits," for example, were prohibited from stocking or selling cloth, just as drapers were forbidden to make suits from their own goods.[2] Ordinarily in this economic system small-scale retail trade merged with artisanal production—the artisan was a merchant, and vice versa. In the clothing trades, however, the supplier was sharply separated from the producer, a division secured by regulations so meticulous that they clearly indicated an ongoing struggle between the different crafts, each severely restricted yet jealously protecting itself against the encroachment of rivals.[3] Their history is marked by legal quarrels, protests against the monopolies enjoyed by others, and denunciations of illegal sales. There were critical moments in that history, as in 1675, when dressmakers were authorized to form a guild, "considering," said the Royal Edict, "that it was appropriate and becoming to the modesty of Women and Girls that they be dressed by persons of their own sex."[4] Not until the seventeenth century was it felt that for modesty's sake there were disadvantages in having men dress women. Yet until 1781, the making of "bodices for women and children" remained the privilege of the powerful tailors guild, whose propriety was always distrusted by males. A special intimacy, a diffuse eroticism fluttered about these shops because the tailor could see and touch the bodies of his customers. As a representative of the husband or lover who possessed these rights, the bodice-maker identified with him so as to become the discreet artisan of enhancements, concealments, and adornments.

Indispensable associates of feminine pulchritude and loyal accomplices in seduction, the bodice-makers gained a privilege that was all the more precious because since the sixteenth century nudity had been increasingly less frequently displayed.[5] Speaking of the tailors who dressed and undressed one's mistress, adjusting slips and undergarments, Brantôme reported the comment of a prince whose wife was being so handled: "Could this man have been my rival? Yes! I do think so, because strip my rank away from me, and he gets the better of me."[6]

The relationships between aristocrats and their servants were marked by such mutual contemptuous indifference that a noble woman was in no way ashamed to appear naked before a lackey. Longchamp, valet to the Marquise de Châtelet, relates two significant anecdotes:

> While my sister was preparing a shift, Madame du Châtelet, standing before me, let slip the one she had on and stood there naked, like a marble statue. . . . A few days later, she was bathing and told me to get a kettle set on the hearth and add hot water to her bath because it was cooling off. Drawing near, I saw that she was naked and that because there was no oil in the bath, the water was clear and limpid. Madame spread her legs so that I could pour more conveniently and not hurt her with the boiling water I had brought. As I began the task, my eye fell on that which I was trying not to see. Ashamed, I averted my head as far as possible. My hand shook and I poured the water haphazardly: "Be careful," she said abruptly in a loud voice, "you are going to scald me." Despite myself, I was forced to keep my eyes on my task longer than I wished.

Fitting a corset (A. Wille)

I can indeed say that great ladies look upon their lackeys as mere automatons. I am convinced that Madame du Châtelet did not see the slightest indecency in ordering me to serve her in her bath, and that in her eyes I mattered no more or no less than the kettle I carried.[7]

As far as tailors were concerned, however, the jealousy that men felt toward them indicated that they were perceived not as automatons or kettles but as sexual beings, often pictured in engravings because of the amusing ambiguity of their gestures.

Yet restricted to their specialty, paralyzed by their traditions, and subjected to royal ordinances and ancestral guild regulations, tailors—even the tiny fraction of this industrious world that supplied the court or the wealthier bourgeoisie—remained obscure and anonymous. Costumes are sometimes described in correspondence or memoirs, but the names of their makers, who might have enjoyed some reflected glory from their products, are hardly ever mentioned before the eighteenth century.[8] The slow merging of the clothing crafts[9] and the lifting of obsolete guild regulations finally made it possible for creations to be signed.

Until then, the tailors, dressmakers, and milliners—newly emerged from the mercers' guild—had merely executed designs or given advice. They now became confidants whose counsel was increasingly sought on every aspect of clothing. Some became famous and even legendary. Rumors were spread, anecdotes swapped, and ratings set about Léonard, the hairdresser; Rose Bertin, the impertinent dressmaker; Mme Éloffe, the exclusive seamstress; or the ferociously competitive Beaulard—all purveyors to Marie-Antoinette—as well as Sarazin, Lemaire, and Pamard—who dressed the noblest of lords.[10]

Inaugurated by the high aristocracy, the unbridled pursuit of fashion that characterized the eighteenth century moved imperceptibly from the court to the city, where it hurled its decrees, issued forth from the best workshops and boutiques of the rue Saint-Honoré—Pompée's, Alexandrine's, Labille's, Fredier's, Quentin's, Lenoir's, and other magical names before "designer brands" existed, which now glorified both artists and their works. "I forgot to mention," wrote Louis-Sébastien Mercier in 1783, "that fashion is an art: a valued, triumphant art that in this century receives honors and awards. This art penetrates the palaces of kings, where it encounters a flattering reception."[11] This new promotion of fashion trades, which affected perhaps one in fifty of its practitioners,[12] was partly responsible, as we have seen, for the declining prestige of the courtly label and courtly sartorial prerogatives. Yet the producers of prestigious signs contributed to the increasingly rapid obsolescence of these signs while gaining an insidious control of their renewal. Meanwhile, they became increasingly conscious of their legitimacy, merit, and importance—gains based as much on the bourgeois virtues of talent and work as on the capacity to invent and create.[13]

Surviving the Revolution, which suppressed the guilds and might have emancipated their industry, mercers, dressmakers, and tailors remained for years steeped in antiquated principles and paralyzed by tradition. The most respected served the new masters. The many obscure second- or third-raters carried on their more or less profitable labors[14] for an avidly sought clientele to whom they extended long-term, ruinous credit. "The lower courts know how many whippersnappers there are, not only wrapped but well wrapped, who haven't paid for their wrappers," noted Mercier.[15] But owing one's tailor was more traditional than ever in the nineteenth century, and clothiers continued hearing their debtors reply cynically that "a tailor earns a living only as long as he need not be paid" or that "it is unheard of to pay a tailor except in one's will."[16]

Louis Huart provides the following statistics about men's tailors: in 1840 there were 3,000 shops in Paris, of which 200 were good, 500 to 600 mediocre, and the rest detestable.[17] Paris had a population of about 800,000. Subtracting 400,000 women and 50,000 children leaves 350,000 males living in the capital, "at least 100,000 of whom, were doomed for life to the worker's blue, wearing nothing but overalls or plain smocks."[18] The 3,000 master tailors and their 30,000 workers therefore shared a market of some 250,000 persons.[19]

Nevertheless, the myth of Parisian chic increased this clientele by attracting visitors from the provinces and from Berlin, Madrid, and St. Petersburg. Having a suit made was part of the ritual. In an 1842 monograph, Roger de Beauvoir stressed the enormous disparity between the mass of anonymous artisans, themselves hierarchically classified according to the quality of their products and of their customers, and the few celebrated tailors whose names were the talk of the town:

> Who is this poor creature, skinny as Harlequin's bat, yellow, so sickly that he scares you, whose sunken chest is arc-shaped, whose skinny legs form an X? A wisp of a beard trimmed à la Don Quixote grays on his chin; a magician's or alchemist's eyeglasses pinch his nose. When he sees you turn his corner and climb up to his fourth floor, he drops his scissors in a transport of joy. You knock at his door and he receives you with the utmost humility, offering you his best chair. He has no valet, only a wife, a Chinese figurine who bows her head at your least command and whose fixed smile begins on New Year's Day and ends on New Year's Eve. A provincial who saw you climbing up to see a man lodged on the top floor in a noxious cage between a plucked parrot and a woman reeking of cooking odors would think that you were bringing alms.

You leave and he accompanies you, his black silk bonnet in hand, down twenty or thirty steps. Is he a usurer? His condition is too modest. A landlord? Perhaps, but would he be so poorly lodged? An author? Possibly. But look up at the sign and learn his trade: he is a tailor.

What about this gentleman in a black frock coat who, borne on the soft seats of an elegant cabriolet, liveried black man at his side, holds the reins with yellow gloves and need not shout "Watch out!" even on the most crowded streets? The fittings are in the latest style; his horse came from Crémieux's stables. He bought a black servant because blacks are fashionable for carriages. His carriage wheels brush you as they go by, and nearly crush you. . . . "Who is that insolent fellow?" you ask the knowledgeable corner porter, and the answer comes: "He's a tailor."[20]

A similar gulf separated dressmakers. Talent was a pretty slim asset unless it was associated with a reputation, a name at first mentioned here and there, and then spread in praiseful echoes from salon to salon. A dressmaker or a tailor could become a means of social prestige whose ministrations had to be acquired at any price to gain elegance, style, distinction— markings that became symbolic capital, commercially profitable.

During the Directory and the Empire, Louis Hyppolite Leroy was one of these *maîtres d'élégance* singled out by public opinion who maintained their fashionable image by sending bills as exorbitant as their pretensions.[21] He was sought by Mme Tallien, Joséphine de Beauharnais, Queen Hortense, the duchess of Bassano, Lady Wellington, and the queens of Spain, Bavaria, and Sweden as well as by other celebrities. He even made the costumes designed by the painter Isabey for Napoleon's coronation. When the Bourbons returned, this man—who had until then dressed only parvenus—easily became tailor to the old nobility and supplied the court and the toilettes for the coronation of Charles X.

Like Mesdames Vignon and Palmyre, Victorine belonged to the new generation of great dressmakers who served fashion during the July Monarchy. Praised by Stendahl in his *Souvenirs d'égotisme*,[22] she also dressed several heroines of Balzac's *Comédie Humaine*.[23] This intrusion of literature into an already-mythic domain helped to make reputations. Thus Straub, "the great Straub" who was forever famous, Straub who first thought of cutting a suit lapel to sew it back on so as to get a more graceful shape, "a smoother fold,"[24] was tailor not just to the Count d'Orsay but also to Stendahl's Julien Sorel and Balzac's Rubempré. Balzac notoriously specialized in this insidious kind of advertising, from which he derived some advantages. His tailor, Buisson, for example, who was for a time his landlord at 108, rue de Richelieu and tailor to members of the Jockey Club, may have remitted a quarter's rent or sewed him a new vest in exchange for the enthusiastic mention in the *Physiology of Marriage*.[25] In the 1830s masculine bourgeois elegance matured, and many other sartorial talents appeared, such as Humann, Dusautoy, Renard, Véronique, Lafitte, Pomadère, Blain, and Chevreuil,[26] some of whom continued their careers into the Second Empire. Shirt and glove making also expanded. Among the great couturières, Mlle Palmyre and Mme Vignon—who were mortal enemies—enjoyed reputations that lasted into the second half of the century since they presided—separately—over the making of the trousseau and wedding dress of Empress Eugénie.

The reign of Charles-Frederic Worth revived the tradition of tailoring for women—which had been lost again after Leroy—and, during the 1860s, laid down the foundations of high fashion. Yet great couturières like Mmes Roger, Laferière, and Pingat, and Mlles Félicie and Laure still retained their prestige, as did milliners like Mmes Virot, Rebout, and Braudès. They faithfully supplied the court and "high society" with articles representing supreme elegance and the acme of taste. Yet the most durable reputations were those of mercers and drapers. The disciple of a great tailor was not necessarily destined for glory, but a great house could survive its founder. Its lineage could be displayed like a coat of arms. Gagelin-Opigez's mantelets, Doucet's lingerie, Lemonnier's hats, Perry's gloves, Verdier's canes, Bodier's cravats, and Sakowski's boots gained reputations maintained from father to son, or father to son-in-law, for in such enterprises "shop-sign nobility" had to be earned.

The sale and production of luxury clothing favored certain locations and adopted zones of influence that reinforced their prestige. High-class stores and workshops, concentrated along the rue Saint-Honoré during the Regency (1715–25), spread during the course of the first half of the nineteenth century to the rue de Richelieu and surrounding neighborhood[27] and then moved in the 1860s to the rue de la Paix and its vicinity. Certain names and addresses had a magnetic aura, whereas others connoted a prosaic world of inferior products. The shops in the rue Saint-Denis, for example, produced lower middle-class but respectable fashion, while the galleries of the Palais Royal sheltered a flashy trade in which looks replaced quality. There, tailors specialized in new clothes, ready-to-wear instead of made-to-order, a kind of artisanal production for the "provincials who came through Paris without even spending the night, who wanted to take back home some samples of the great city's fashions."[28] In each neighborhood one found swarms of small-time dressmakers and tailors[29] working to order. They disappeared only gradually, smothered by ready-made clothing. They often combined a position such as concierge with their trade, receiving clients in their lodge—"well-off laborers, bourgeois who freshened up a worn-out suit with a velvet collar or new buttons, or mothers who entrusted them with their son's first communion suit,"[30] in short, local, small-scale business.

Going eastward from the rues de Richelieu, Vivienne, or Saint-Denis, one reaches the Temple neighborhood, where the Parisian used-clothes trade occupied most of its denizens from cellar to attic.[31] A universe unto itself, teeming and picturesque, it has now vanished; but Eugène Sue in *Les Mystères de Paris* and Paul Féval in *Le Fils du diable* described some of its aspects. In the nineteenth century it handled a considerable volume of business and supplied large numbers of people. Its size made it an important market; and its mores, a most peculiar one.

The guild of fripperers who supplied the majority of the city's dwellers with secondhand clothes had been in existence since the beginning of the thirteenth century. It quarreled endlessly with the other clothing trades and competed, often illegally, with them. Originally its statutes gave it the exclusive right to repair and resell old clothing. But the boundaries distinguishing new from used were hazy, like those between fabrication and repair, so that abuses were possible and used-clothes dealers expanded their activities in many ways. In 1430 the guild obtained a decree permitting it to work with new material, provided its value did not exceed twelve *sols parisis*. Statutes of 1554 authorized them to use a range of materials priced at forty-eight *sols* or, in 1618, ordinary fabrics costing no more than two *écus* an ell. In 1664 it was allowed to make new garments, but not to measure. It could also make infant clothing, up to ten *livres* an ell. Despite obstructions and restrictions demanded by the master tailors, frippery became a real clothing trade, enlarging its selection if not its clientele. The eighteenth century further liberalized the profession—the shopkeeping dealers merged in 1776 with the guild of tailors and gained the exclusive right to sell repaired clothing, dominos, and fancy dress for costume balls; to clean and dye fabrics; and to supply funeral garb. The itinerant fripperers—mainly women—were left to buy, sell, and exchange old clothes in the streets or in the markets.

Until the Revolution most of the fripperers worked in small shops, under the arcades of open-air markets known as the Halles de la Tonnellerie (on the future rue Baltard). They occupied thirty of these spaces and nursed an ongoing rivalry with the cobblers established under the seventeen others.[32] Some also kept shop in the now-vanished Place du Louvre. Louis-Sébastien Mercier waxed indignant in describing their unusual trade:

> Before this superb colonnade—admired by all foreigners—one sees old clothes, a hideous display that hangs on strings and turns in the wind. This frippery seems both dirty and indecent. There, shop clerks, masons, and porters scavenge for obviously worn breeches. New ones are contraband. Of every kind, every color, every degree of wear, they hang exposed to the chaste glances of the sun and of pretty women.[33]

The used-clothing trade had always been suspect because of its wares, sometimes stolen or fenced,[34] because of its merchants, who were often Jews,[35] and because of its dubious practices. As Mercier wrote,

> One must expect fripperers to practice deceit and take advantage of the credulous passer-by who enters the shop and is fooled by a semidarkness intended to hide the defects of the garment he bargains for. The baseness to which the Jewish race has descended through its daily practice of knavish tricks is enough to forewarn the buyer and to keep him from being duped.[36]

Later we shall see this threatening, dirty world of corruption reinterpreted in hygienic terms as a breeding ground of infection. During the Revolution it came under tighter control. During the Consulate it was provisionally moved to the Halle aux Veaux and to the Carreau des Innocents. A decree of the First Consul issued on 29 Vendémiaire, Year XI (21 October 1802), and later supplemented by an Imperial decree of 16 March 1807, permanently assigned the trade in "old linen, old clothing, and rags" to a plot within the Temple enclosure. Women's and children's frippery until then sold in the Place de Grève on Monday—the day no executions were carried out—also moved to the Temple.

Four open sheds constructed between 1809 and 1811 on plans by the architect Molinos occupied 10,831 square meters enclosed between the now-vanished Place de la Rotonde and the present-day rues du Temple, Dupetit-Thouars, and Perrée. Their size attested to the social and economic importance of this flourishing business as well as to the government's determination to control a space still deemed dangerous. A chief inspector, twelve policemen, three security agents, and a deputy sergeant supervised a market where 1,888 stalls, each 2.62 meters square, were allotted to 870 merchants for twenty centimes a day.

The sheds were separated by two passageways that intersected at right angles. Each shed offered specific objects intended for a distinct kind of customer. The *carré* du Palais Royal ranked first in this pandemonium. It occupied the place of honor and owed its pompous name to the wonders occasionally unearthed by its well-to-do merchants, who were often wholesalers and owners of nearby stores. The display of carpets, silks, Valenciennes, Venetian and English point, ribbons, cashmere shawls, gloves, feathers, Saxony linens, moiré corsets, paste jewelry, still-smart hats, and evening dresses that had been worn only once aroused suspicions that they kept in reserve even more precious treasures that had been snatched from ruined aristocrats or redeemed from pawn shops. Chambermaids or grisettes looking for something showy, actresses performing a new role, and "needy Parisian princesses who made a purchase and flitted away like frightened birds"—they all converged on this part of the market.[37] Gestures here were furtive, and transactions done on the sly: "Sometimes, in a shop with modern clothes, one catches a glimpse of an elegant woman slipping into the shadows and disappearing behind a serge curtain. She is a customer. The mantilla that hangs from a string will be worn at the opera tonight."[38] In fact, for people with social ambitions, to be seen at the Temple meant exposure of financial misfortunes or a fictitious status. For the would-be dandies who flocked there, the Temple signified bourgeois parsimony. Yet sometimes a rare or unusual object surfaced there. "Women—and I mean the most posh—go there in the morning searching for lace and baubles they cannot find elsewhere," notes the shrewd observer Edmond Texier.[39]

The *carré* de Flore, less fashionable and more utilitarian, specialized in bedding, sheets, household linens, curtains, layettes, napkins, calico dresses, and workers' smocks. These castoffs, offered to the poor seeking warmth or a minimal decency of appearance, were seldom in good condition, no easily freshened items or barely faded luxuries among them. Here, one gladly paid fifty centimes—the cost of laundering—to change a dirty shirt for a clean one.

The Palais-Royal *carré*

In the "Pou-volant" *carré* (literally "The Flying Louse"), filthy old clothes were heaped up with assorted metal scraps. It was nearly impossible to distinguish the shapeless, expiring used garments from the rags also sold there. Only the merchant knew their respective genealogies, which he learned from his nocturnal supplier, the rag-picker.

The Forêt noire *carré* sheltered leather flotsam and jetsam: dilapidated shoes, down-at-the-heel boots, fossilized purses. A fetid, smoke-filled atmosphere emanated from the rancid grease that covered them thickly. In fact, these merchants were called "caulkers," because "public opinion accused them of caulking the merchandise that they were supposed to mend; that is, of hiding damage and holes with a coating of black grease or some coloring material."[40]

Characteristic of this ancien régime business, which perpetuated a century-old tradition, was the obsfucation of both shop windows and commercial relations. Merchants lied or exaggerated. The bright light of day was replaced by semidarkness;[41] the magic gaslight that would illuminate goods in the department stores was replaced by magical words that attributed thousands of invisible qualities to the merchandise.

We should, however, distinguish between the "red series" (the first two sheds) and the "black series" (the other two). The red series practiced the same commercial strategy as other shops of the time: as long as customers

"Women . . . cling to your legs, your neck, your clothes—
whatever they can grab."

only looked in the shop window they were left alone, but they were subjected to an inescapable stream of haggling as soon as they stepped over the
threshold. The "black series," on the other hand, practiced a systematic
touting as professionals harassed and pestered passers-by forced to choose
between a quick purchase and a shower of insults:

> At the least hesitation, the least inquiring glance that identifies you as a poten-
> tial customer, twenty or thirty voices assault your ears, murdering every note
> of the scale, creating an infernal charivari. Women, dogs, brats, *tutti quanti*
> leave their respective *ayons*[42] and cling to your legs, your neck, your clothes—
> whatever they can grab. Once entangled in this trap, you're lost. In two flicks
> of the wrist you have been propelled into the inextricable labyrinth of the
> market's innards. You look for a way out and find a thousand, winding perfidi-
> ously to draw you deeper and ever deeper into the heart of this chaos. At each
> step crooked fingers reach out and grapple you, and a shrill voice intones,
> without skipping a single item, the long litany of the "like-new" objects
> heaped at your feet.[43]

Beyond the four pavillons there was a curious building, the Rotonde du
Temple, whose arcades sheltered still more shops. These specialized in
military clothing as well as costumes for small theaters and traveling cir-
cuses. They displayed "cheap finery, cast-off clothing, hussars' jackets,
spangled carnival costumes, National Guard tunics, red-gallooned suits,
strange outfits, and peculiar overcoats."[44] Built in 1788 by Perrard de Mon-
treuil, the Rotonde served for a few years as a refuge for insolvent debtors

The Temple Rotunda

and bankrupts, who could not be arrested within its confines. Rents for shops and apartments were extremely high, and tradesmen, freed from guild restrictions, enjoyed an exceptional freedom. There, a ruined merchant could rebuild his fortune rapidly. It became an integral part of the market in 1811, and prosperous fripperers lived on the second floor, those who set the day's quotation for torn trousers or cast-off paletots.

In the market, an open space situated between the Rotonde and the sheds, there functioned from 11:00 A.M. to 2:00 P.M. a clothing exchange that obeyed the rigorous law of supply and demand. Amid an agitated pack of illicit brokers stood the dominating figure of the wholesaler who could make the market rise or fall by depleting or flooding it, by massive buying or selling of entire shop inventories, batches from the morgue, or remainders relinquished by tailors for minor defects. "One has seen," writes Marc Fournier, "overalls fall and goat-hair vests rise to incredible rates. In 1830, after the July Revolution, court dress sold for a hundred sous, including the blue cordon of the Order of St. Louis. Two weeks later, their price rose sky-high, and none were to be had. . . . There were scandalous profits and frightful bankruptcies."[45] Edmond Texier adds: "Make no mistake, speculation there is as deadly as at the Casino or on the floor of the Bourse. Stocks of breeches and overripe clothing are traded on margin exactly like state bonds, oil, coal, gas, and spirits. There are Rothschilds also at the Bourse du Temple."[46]

Supply and demand were not always based on deceit, nor were the rise and fall of prices always artificial. The market and exchange rates were controlled by the nature, quantity, and pace of supply; that is, they were controlled by the productive activity of a very peculiar group—nomadic clothing merchants, wardrobe dealers, and rag-pickers who scoured the streets and buildings of Paris daily, tracking down and flushing out nails, leathers, tattered rags, or sparkling coats, depending on the territory and their prey. To itinerant middlemen on the path that led to the Temple market they tirelessly fed this immense stream of used clothing.

The rag-pickers were as hierarchically arranged as the fripperers. Only the *chineur* actually went to the Temple. The *piqueur*, or runner, "wandered through the streets, basket on his back, lantern and hook in hand, contending with starving dogs over the loathsome things he deals in."[47] His nocturnal rounds brought him face to face with dead cats, cabbage cores, bones, crusts of bread, tin cans, corks, broken crockery, glass shards, cardboard scraps, and towel scraps rather than with actual clothing. Nevertheless, he might chance upon worn-out footwear, from which cobblers extracted what they called the "soul" of the shoe: "A piece of leather . . . could be used between ten and twelve times to make new shoes. Leather was used until it literally disappeared out of existence."[48] His finds, however derisory, could all be recycled: "The vile debris from the trash heap were chrysalides, which science will endow with elegant forms and diaphanous wings."[49] Everything was picked up, nothing was lost, "even empty, crushed sardine cans, which in skilled hands could become toys: trumpets, cut-out soldiers, lilliputian families."[50]

The *placier* occupied a better position. As the name suggests, he possessed a place, a veritable office transmitted from father to son, which allowed him—with the agreement of a building's concierge—to take out and collect the garbage, to ransack it and haul away his pickings in a horse-drawn cart. The *piqueurs* and the *placiers* sold their booty, whenever it resembled cloth, to either the wardrobe dealer or the *chineur*, a privileged middleman, less a ragman than a "roving" clothes merchant. He, too, scoured Paris in all directions, but he did not crawl along the gutters by night to collect what the city threw away by day, nor did he anxiously search through household garbage. He belonged to the great and venerable family of criers. And he bought. Glancing at housefronts, he could spot the discreet gesture inviting him up, usually to the upper stories. During his long, slow ascent, he knew that need or poverty awaited him. These made the client docile and the transaction favorable. Systematically disdainful or deprecatory about the proffered objects, the *chineur* had mastered the art of enlarging a stain or a worn spot to slash by a quarter or a third the price anticipated by the seller. Once home, he knew all the ways of rejuvenating castoffs. "The garment that you would not give to your janitor he could clean, brushing it with a thistle so as to give it a silky nap. And after he stitched in a new lining and ran the barb of an inked feather over stitches bleached by wear, any worker would think himself lucky to pay twenty times its worth to show it off in the dance halls beyond the city gates."[51]

The wardrobe dealer functioned in a different register. Like the *chineur*, she tramped up and down sidewalks and stairs from morning to night, but her methods were more gentle, more secretive and persuasive, aimed at a female clientele whose confidante or procuress she often was and whose vanity she knew how to exploit. Her craft "required infinite tact, a Machiavellianism tempered with finesse, good humor and directness, audacity, pliability, in other words, high diplomacy."[52] She sold (dearly and on credit) as much as she bought (cheaply and for cash), and her traveling storehouse—a large cardboard box—often harbored splendid things. Moreover, "She had entrée to society women whose taste for variety she could satisfy,"[53] and she cultivated numerous contacts. According to Countess Dash, "High-society Parisian chambermaids are better dressed than rich bourgeoises. . . . They wear cashmere shawls from India, jewels, and lace because they levy a tithe on household suppliers, the wardrobe dealers with whom they exchange their mistresses' old garments."[54]

LE MARCHAND D'HABITS.

chand d'ha . bits marchand   ha . bits ha . bits   mar .

. chand   a . vez . vous   de vieux ha . bits   à   vendr

Roving clothes merchant

But the wardrobe dealer traded most with kept women. She extended long-term credit—at 15 or 20 percent—to the less affluent and even lent clothes if this might help her client find a more generous protector. For she knew that the credit she offered would bring her double—as lender and as supplier. "These merchants," writes Arnould Frémy, "are the indefatigable, satanic counselors who prey pitilessly on the weaker side of women—their vanity and desire to impress. They ensnare their clients, envelop them in irresistible nets, and daily catch them on new fishhooks. It is usually spending for usurious cashmeres, lace, and gewgaws that leads a woman imperceptibly to the last pied-à-terre of vice and sorrow, the poorhouse, whose foundress and porteress ought to be by rights the richest and best-known wardrobe dealer."[55]

These harpies occupied different positions in the hierarchy of used clothes, depending on whether they roamed the city or established a fixed place of business. Sedentary at the Temple and cut off from their network of exchange and deals, they lost status:

> Dressed in rags and tatters with some remains of pretension, carrying large
> baskets overflowing with mysterious contents, wearing ancient hats sugges-

Wardrobe dealer

tive of an earlier opulence, and especially wearing faces as rough as their voices, bent fingers, and lips shrunken into purse clasps, they resembled occult genies who would predict the future for this ignoble, intimate commerce, these speculations based on prodigality or poverty![56]

The Temple was a lower-class market that supplied the most deprived strata of the city with clothing. Yet because of its ramifications it was nevertheless a fundamental link in the distribution of bourgeois clothing. It was a stage in the life of middle-class garments, almost always the last one. "Unloading dock for all past glories, . . . the Amphritites of all sunrises,"[57] it drew from the middle class a motley stock in which "satin slippers and wooden clogs, marabou feather bouquets, calico coiffs, ball gowns, and charcoal-burner's vests hang from the same hook or lie on the same table."[58]

A Straub suit, for example, would make the rounds of the salons and theaters on elegant shoulders until a stain, a tear, or simply wear forced its purchaser to cede it to a servant or janitor. The new owner would then sell it to the *marchand d'habits*, who would in turn peddle it at the Temple Market. There, the tailor-fripperer would clean, mend, dye, and refinish it, giving the garment a second life and the possibility of a second career, one less brilliant but still honorable. It would probably clothe that fringe group often poorer than artisans or skilled workers who needed this simulacrum, however pathetic, of bourgeois respectability to be anything at all: debt-ridden students, low-level bureaucrats, small shopkeepers, impoverished private tutors, or captains of industry in bad straits. Once threadbare, it would wend its way back to the Temple, though not necessarily under a death sentence. Reinforced with heavy materials and enlarged by alterations, it might again be incarnated as a worker's Sunday best, unless its dilapidated condition classified it as a rag headed for a radical transformation at the paper mill.[59]

Clothing passed thus from one class, as it wore down and was mended, through cycles whose length was determined both by social imperatives and by material availability. But soon it would circulate through the social structure along new paths. In the meantime, used clothing remained the principal source of sartorial supplies and the only opportunity of elegance for those who could not afford the services of a tailor or dressmaker:

> A whole class of young women who love to haunt the Temple Market: chambermaids, maids, cooks, cleaning women earning fifty *écus* a year. . . . Poor creatures, who work day and night, eat poorly, sleep on hard beds, and always have Madame or her eldest daughter on their heels! But on Sunday, after a week of labor and privation, they have two hours of freedom: and they seize the chance to dress up a bit. . . . Fabrics are expensive, and they have no time to cut and sew a dress. Hence they rush to the Temple and buy a five-franc

calico peignoir, a cheap *barrège fichu*, or a tulle bonnet with pink ribbons. The poor girl has never had anything so pretty; she runs up her six flights, dresses before a mirror the size of her hand, and as pleased as a great lady goes to a dance hall beyond the city gates.[60]

And there was also the poor workman who, feeling winter's bite, tells his wife:

Take seven and a half francs; go to the Temple and buy me a coachman's coat. They're out of style this year and sell for a song. The porter across the way sold his because he claims they're old-fashioned. . . . What nonsense! Nothing like a carrick to make a man look good! Get one with five collars: they're rich, they keep you warm. . . . Get one in mignonette green, a strong one, a first-rate one. Thérèse, Thérèse, while I think of it, . . . please be careful to hold it up to the light to see if it has holes. They're clever, these fripperers; they're tricksters who deceive everybody. They fill up tears with wax, mend boots with lickable glue. Be careful, Thérèse, be careful: for seven and a half francs, wife, you can get something neat.[61]

BRAND-NEW BUT CHEAP

Many people bought secondhand clothing to equip themselves cheaply but decently with worn garments that had the advantage of being ready-to-wear. Their existence inspired the idea of mass-producing new clothes that were ready-made and modestly priced.

Until the Revolution legal obstacles prevented any serious development of such an industry.[62] Afterward, some garments made in advance, such as paletots, vests, redingotes, and dressing gowns were sold in the galleries of the Palais-Royal by tailors known for attracting, as was mentioned earlier, provincials and foreigners with limited time. But these shops did not try to draw customers by offering bargains, nor were they comparable in scope to the store, La Belle Jardinière, that the mercer Pierre Parissot opened in 1824 on the Quai aux Fleurs, near the Temple. Neither a large capitalization nor cheap textiles nor mechanized sewing techniques—to come later—were available to him, but he made the manufacturing process more rational through a subdivision of manual labor and the simultaneous cutting of several thicknesses of cloth. As a merchant he innovated by being among the first to adopt fixed, stable prices that were clearly marked, and he appealed to the lower classes, whom he supplied with fabrics and with specialized work clothes that did not need a precisely fitted cut. In the face of increased demand, however, he quickly diversified his production and began to make bourgeois clothes along with smocks, overalls, aprons, and duck-cloth trousers. The tailors objected and boycotted him for a while, forcing him to recruit his laborers from prison workshops to satisfy his already substantial clientele as well as to keep his prices low. For five francs, seventy-five centimes he sold a full, well-made suit barely more expensive than a used one. Around 1830, he bought buildings adjoining his shop and, continuously expanding, had by 1856 annexed the twenty-five houses forming the whole block wherein he had started out in a stall twelve meters square.[63]

His great success led to imitation. Around 1830 Ternaux, a cloth dealer who pioneered the domestication of Tibetan goats in France, opened a store at the sign of the Bonhomme Richard, at 9, Place des Victoires. His establishment offered clothing made with fabric he manufactured. At the same time, the house of Coutard was set up at 21, rue Croix-des-Petits-Champs, its founder having "understood that the ready-made industry not only could benefit the working class but could also serve elegant and distinguished customers."[64] Moreover, the reorganization of the National Guard made it necessary for the army to stockpile finished uniforms classified by size.[65] These military workshops were in fact the first large-scale companies to produce ready-made clothing. Their production would be increased later by orders for foreign uniforms.

The 1840s saw the real takeoff of ready-made civilian clothing, not because of industrial concentration—useless in the absence of mechanization—but because of improved cutting and sewing techniques and an increasingly rational division of labor. The crafts involved in producing ready-to-wear remained artisanal insofar as they were manual. Little by little, however, they organized a system of "sweat shops" that gathered together tailors or seamstresses, cutters, and assemblers in a single workshop where cloth was cut and the pieces assembled. Linings, decorations, and buttons—in other words, the finishings—were done by men and women working at home. Describing their labor, Jules Simon notes that "working from seven in the morning to eight at night, and stopping only to eat, a skilled seamstress could make three paletots in two days, and earn two francs a day. Try to imagine sewing for thirteen hours without getting up, without looking up, without resting one's hands a second. Add to that cold feet and at least five hours of bad light in the winter."[66]

The ready-to-wear industry began among the popular classes whom it supplied with work clothes and everyday wear, then later with Sunday best. As it improved, ready-to-wear caught on with the lower middle classes. Thanks to a sophisticated system of sizes, patterns, and forms as well as a skillfully graduated scale of measurements, it succeeded in fitting the body and reproducing the elegance and chic of custom-made clothing. As its share of the market increased, it enabled customers to save: manufacturing costs were substantially reduced and stabilized because fabrics were bought in bulk and the work force employed throughout the year. It also enabled them to save time by eliminating endless fittings and alterations. In short, ready-to-wear stripped away from the acquisition of clothing its solemn, ritualized character.[67]

Tailors expressed their disdain for this kind of clothing but noted its numerous advantages as they found themselves slowly, but dangerously, challenged by it.

Ready-made may have taken over a large segment of the buying public—in 1847 Paris had 233 ready-to-wear manufacturers with more than 7,000 workers[68]—but it could not, so believed the upper classes, attain the "artistic" excellence of the great tailor who would long remain an indispensable artificer for the well-dresssed man. On the eve of the Second Empire, the *Journal des Tailleurs* summed up the situation: "The purchasers of ready-to-wear belong to two groups, laborers who have never bought and never will buy anything from a tailor, and people who are well off or of moderate means. A few years ago the latter constituted half of the tailors' clientele. But they have given up owing tailors and now pay cash in ready-to-wear shops."[69] The technical progress and lower production costs of a clothing trade in the process of industrialization threatened the small jobbing tailors, those humble but independent neighborhood artisans. Competition from the ready-to-wear industry spared only the most prestigious custom-made tailoring.[70]

Ready-made wear for women appeared later, around 1845. Unlike men's ready-made, which appealed essentially to the working class, the women's market attracted a substantial bourgeois clientele. Some companies had long made short cloaks (crispins), spencers, or mantlets. But, retailed only by a few "fancy goods stores" or shipped to the provinces and abroad, they did not constitute a major branch of business.[71] After 1847, Paris had 225 dressmakers and seamstresses working in women's ready-to-wear. Together they employed over 1,300 female workers.[72] Some of them made only cloaks, coats, and pelisses, ample garments that did not need to be fitted; others provided custom clothes, as well as ready-made dresses, aprons, peignoirs, slips, or children's clothing. Some worked primarily for the "fancy goods stores," and others for their own customers, making fine ready-to-wear clothing from fabrics they supplied. These women later gave Worth the idea of realizing triple profits by buying directly from the manufacturer, selling the cloth, and making several models of a garment.[73]

The "fancy goods stores" specialized in millinery, notions, and rather ordinary ready-to-wear articles, but because of their size and commercial practices, they anticipated the department stores of the Second Empire. They were the new kind of stores that appeared here and there in Paris after the Revolution,[74] alongside the dark, low-ceilinged, and stuffy holdovers from the ancien régime, shops with fronts almost devoid of glass, whose fabrics were haphazardly piled up, and whose business practices were numbed by centuries-old habits.[75] In the new stores light replaced darkness, and space was substituted for exiguity, neat displays for piled-up goods, marked prices for haggling, and cash payment for usurious credit. Family businesses, once transmitted from one generation to another like the venal offices of the ancien régime, took on new dimensions, bought directly from factories, stocked large inventories, multiplied their "counters," and hired battalions of clerks. They no longer sought to keep overhead as low as possible to increase profit margins but strove to reduce the profit on single items while increasing the volume of sales by attracting customers with low prices, appealing displays, and wide choices. "Fabrics of all kinds roll, stream, froth in the displays: taffeta, levantine silk, cashmere, brocaded muslin, pink crepe, chine silk, peckinets, Naples silk, marbled satin, Valenciennes lace, Mechlin lace, woolen muslin, cotton muslin, and so on—all of it numbered and marked down, sparing nothing to fire feminine imaginations."[76]

Fancy goods store

Spurred on by competition, these stores were the first to use advertising in the modern way—through posters and handbills.[77] As Auguste Luchet wrote in 1834,

> Throughout the city was waged a strange battle of facades, displays, and store signs. Mercantile vanity accomplished miracles. Buildings were decked out with flags from top to bottom, like ships on holidays. Inscriptions proclaiming "Department Stores with Set Prices" ran along facades, repeated at every level from the first floor to the chimneys. The address number was written in figures three feet high, on the right, on the left, above, below, in front, in back, and everywhere. Two or three hundred ells of cloth were sacrificed to festoon the displays; the shop signs became oil paintings, painted on canvas and costing up to a thousand écus.[78]

Ensnared by this insistence, a customer entered the store where her eyes were pleased and her desire to buy aroused by an elegant decor and a stagy presentation of goods. Paul de Kock describes one such store:

> On the ground floor spacious galleries, elegantly, luxuriously decorated; counters done up in Renaissance taste, mirrors everywhere; a colorful floor, waxed and polished, with carpets stretched along the aisles where one walks. You believe yourself mistaken, you must be at Versailles, and you would not dare enter this palace to buy a flannel vest or fabric for a camisole did you not see a flock of clerks and employees, coming and going, folding and unfolding, measuring and piling up cloth, shawls, scarves, dresses, silk handkerchiefs, fichus, cravats, and a flock of people of all classes, looking, admiring, buying.[79]

This description would fit the future department store, which developed on a different scale. The "fancy goods stores" were handicapped by the backward, archaic practices of a country that was still artisanal (though it had begun to concentrate industry, especially in the textile sector),[80] a pre-capitalist country where loans were hard to secure, a country too large for its expensive, rudimentary means of transportation, and a Paris divided into autonomous neighborhoods for lack of wide traffic arteries. Most novelty shops did not survive the economic and social shocks of 1848. Le Diable boiteux, La Fille mal gardée, Les Vêpres siciliennes, Le Juif errant, Le Masque de fer, Le Coin de la rue, La Mansarde des artistes, La Fille d'honneur, Le Vampire, and Le Page inconstant, all shops drawing their singular names from the titles of popular operas, ballets, operettas, and vaudevilles, had appeared too early. Neither French society nor economic conjunctures provided the conditions under which they might have prospered. Some, like Le Tapis rouge, Le Siège de Corinthe, Le Phare de la Bastille, Le Pauvre Diable, and the Gagne-Petit, survived, but the department stores for which they had prepared the way[81] would become the ones that, because of their size, stimulated the production and distribution of ready-made clothing and inaugurated a new kind of consumption.

A Short Lexicon of the Secondhand Clothes Trade

Ayon: shop, street stall
Bausse, baussesse: boss
Bibeloter ses frusques: to sell one's clothing
Décrochez-moi-ça: woman's hat, on sale
Galifard: porter who delivers purchases to the buyer
Gonce: passer-by
Limace: shirt
Mastiqueur: clerk who camouflages holes in shoes with a greasy material
Niolle: patched-up hat
Niolleur: old-hats merchant
Pantalzar: pants
Pelure: suit or riding coat
Raleuse: female tout who works on *gonces*
Refaçonneur or *Rebouiseur*: specialist who raises the nap on worn cloth
Roulant or *chineur*: itinerant clothing merchant
Se renfrusquiner: to dress oneself

The Department Store and the Spread
of Bourgeois Clothing

Soon there will be only one kind of dress
in the West, South, and North: ours.
This is becoming increasingly obvious.
—*Fashion-Théorie* (February 1863)

THE DEPARTMENT STORE came into existence because it could bring together two equally important groups: products and buyers. Its development required two sets of factors: audacious innovations and favorable
economic conditions, which combined in the second half of the century to
produce a commercial revolution.[1]

THE TAKEOFF

Department stores or *grands magasins* were established during the Second
Empire,[2] but not all were born *grands*, nor were they all substantially capi-
talized. Their founders often started out as lowly employees. Aristide Boucicaut began as a sales clerk at the Petit-Saint-Thomas before creating the
Bon Marché in 1852. Alfred Chauchard started at the Pauvre Diable before promoting the Louvre in 1854. Ernest Cognacq clerked at the Gagne-
Petit before launching the Samaritaine in 1869. The Bazar de l'Hôtel-de-
Ville was born in 1856, on the initiative of the street peddler Ruel, whereas
the Printemps was founded in 1865 by Jules Jaluzot, a former department
head from the Bon Marché.

Some of these exemplary "self-made men"—Chauchard, for one—attracted investment capital immediately;[3] but most started out small, in-
vesting their wives' dowries or forming partnerships with owners of small
shops.[4] They achieved their expansion by inventing commercial strategies
and profiting from favorable economic conditions. Capital duly followed,
and confirmed the relevance of the innovations. Only then did the *grand*

magasin merit its name. Actually, only La Belle Jardinière (which crossed the river in 1866 to occupy a grander establishment on the Quai de la Mégisserie) and a few prosperous "fancy goods stores"[5] ever became department stores thanks to the substantial assets they had already acquired and the large amount of capital they were able to attract.

The first principle and absolute rule of department stores was the reduction of gross profit margins offset by rapid turnover of stock and capital. The large-scale application of this concept required a radical transformation of production techniques, a transformation that could take place only if the textile industry expanded[6] and ready-made articles multiplied. Mass production, which involves both an industrial multiplication of standardized, identical units and the consumerism that would create the "department store" life-style, appeared with large-scale production of finished products during the last third of the nineteenth century.

Department stores were thus born of the textile industry, the cutting edge of French industry and the major purveyor of fabrics and ready-to-wear, but they expanded as mass production developed and diversified. A survey of department store catalogs reveals the correlation between the increasing choices of goods and services and the evolution of industry. Until the 1870s the catalogs advertise only household linens, fancy goods, lingerie, clothes, lace, furs, mourning clothes, headgear, accessories, carpets, and bed furnishings. Then they expanded to include furniture, china, knickknacks, and toys—the large choice we now expect from department stores.

Like other large companies, the department store exemplified the concentration of capital and labor, and it then based this concentration on internal specialization: each department within the store had a head and an army of clerks,[7] and each functioned like an autonomous store. The profitability of this immense merchandise depot also depended on attracting legions of buyers. Essential to that development were increasing urban concentration, Haussmann's transformation of Paris, and the improvement of public transportation in the capital. In 1855, 347 omnibuses carried 36 million passengers; in 1865, 664 vehicles conveyed 107 million passengers.[8] These figures indicate clearly that neighborhoods opened up and that mobility progressed in a city that doubled its population by annexing many suburbs in 1860.

SETTING THE TRAP

It was the responsibility of the department stores to lure these hitherto fluid masses from the traditional shopping channels and attract them by offering not only the advantage and ease of modern commerce but also an unprecedented spectacle of permanent temptation. Marked prices and *entrée libre*, or "no obligation to buy," played a decisive role in this shift: they did away with wearisome bargaining and the moral obligation to buy.

The shops described by Balzac—where once a shopper crossed the fatal threshold and entered the confining, obscure space, there was no turning back—had not yet disappeared. Instantly assaulted, the customer was forced into tiresome haggling. The inevitable and age-old struggle developed between those unequal adversaries, a distrustful but ignorant buyer and a seller comfortably established on his own turf. The latter could decipher the code on labels that bore a double price: one the asking price and the other the minimum amount acceptable. To foil deceptive strategies, evaluate quality and quantity, make a final choice, and fight for a reasonable price, the customer needed to muster all his attention and aggressiveness.

Marked prices had already been tried in the "fancy goods stores," but these establishments had not linked them to *entrée libre* so that they did not reap all the benefit they could have. As Arnould Frémy wrote in 1841, "The poor girl can contemplate these luxurious treasures only through the magic prism of the shop windows! Unlike the great lady, she cannot have everything laid out and heaped on the counter merely because a green-liveried footman attends her and gray-dappled horses prance and foam before the door. Only the rich have the right to buy nothing."[9]

The department store broke with these restrictive practices. Instead of engaging in economic discrimination, or considering the buyer as an enemy to be fleeced whose indecision had to be forcefully overcome, the department store sought to seduce, to satisfy and secure the confidence and loyalty of the many by proving its honesty[10] and softening the too-obvious mercantile relationship. Store clerks[11] were required to be invariably pleasant, present unfurrowed brows, speak gently, and be restrained but solicitous, whoever the buyer, whatever the purchase. Making modest customers feel reassured and the rich ones feel safe, this novel courtesy gave people freedom to finger, heft, turn over, try on the merchandise profusely displayed, to wander among the counters, to lose themselves along the galleries, and to be treated everywhere with equal deference by an anonymous, eager staff. Everything was done to arouse desire and de-dramatize buying. Piles of choice goods overflowing everywhere denied scarcity and affirmed abundance. "It was a giant fairground spread of hawker's wares, as if the shop were bursting and throwing its surplus into the street," wrote Zola in *Au Bonheur des Dames*.[12]

Drawing increasingly dense crowds and amassing a growing volume of transactions,[13] these miraculous stores spawned impressive edifices whose display and ostentation made them look like cathedrals dedicated to the glory of the age. The "Hausmannization" of Paris both inspired and facilitated their expansion.[14] Wide storefronts with plate-glass windows attracted boulevard strollers, subjugated by carefully studied appeal. Like fashion plates and catalogs, store windows become the best place to school and train the public about its appearance. Inside, the clever arrangement of departments and the stagy display of goods aroused further excitements.

Octave Mouret, in Zola's *Au Bonheur des Dames*, was a "revolutionary window dresser." He created the school of "brutal and colossal" window dressing, the perfect incarnation of the new business tactics: "He wanted cascades of goods, looking as though they had fallen by chance from broken racks, and he wanted his displays to blaze with fiery colors that intensified one another. When the customers left the store, he said, their eyes should hurt."[15] In fact, with these conflagrations of fabric, orgies of gaslight,[16] flashing chandeliers, splendor of domes, gilded candelabras, and mirrors to reflect everything a hundred times, the department store and its counters sparkled like the sun. The fascinating modernity of the spiraling iron staircases and upholstered elevators dazzled the eye and the mind. But comfort was not forgotten: a reading and writing room stocked with newspapers and magazines, pens, ink, and stationery was available gratis to visitors, while a buffet served grenadine to children.

Peasant and mannequins

The public was not admitted behind the scenery. Backstage were found administration, accounting, correspondence, delivery, advertising, maintenance, lighting, heating, the staff restaurant, and the workshops where the *poignards*, or alterations, were done.

The stores' bargain prices, and the advertising that announced them everywhere, appealed to the buyers' "economic reasonableness." But "reason" was overwhelmed by many powerful devices calculated to make spending blameless and guiltless. In 1852, Boucicaut, the pioneering department-store owner, instituted the practice of accepting returns, which quickly became general, pledging to take back at its original price any article that did not satisfy the customer. Despite many abuses—women bought a headpiece or a mantle for an evening and returned it the next day, swearing they never had worn it—the acceptance of returns long remained a commercially profitable psychological gambit, a way of postponing the buyer's decision by making it revocable. "Dresses have been exchanged for other dresses; money has been returned to persons suddenly bereaved. Poorly fitting garments have been altered, and others taken back. Our promises are true," proclaimed a Printemps advertisement.[17]

To hasten the process, commissions were instituted to give employees a financial stake in sales volume, and a calendar of events was established in the form of monthly promotions. Each department was featured in turn: white goods in January, laces and gloves in February, coats and day wear in March, summer clothes in May, floor coverings in September, and winter wear in December. These drew crowds almost as large as for the sales, another invention that liquidated inventory at season's end. The department store could not tolerate deserted corners or dead spots. If necessary, crowds and bustle were simulated—just as abundance was—by planned overcrowding.

"Everywhere he insisted upon noise, crowds, life," writes Zola of his Octave Mouret:

> First of all there should be a crush at the entrance, it should seem to people in the street as if a riot were taking place in the shop; and he caused this crush by putting remnants in the entrance, shelves and baskets overflowing with articles at very low prices, so that working-class people accumulated, barring the threshold, and gave the impression that the shop was bursting with people, when often it was only half-full. . . . If he could have found a way of making the street run right through his shop, he would have done so.[18]

In this brave, new world where customers, their distrust allayed, were drawn only by the display, choice, and bargain prices of products, shopping became a random, dreamlike, or impulsive activity. Its objectives became vaguer and amenable to influence, and its course was strewn with unexpected suggestions and sudden decisions. For people who were short of money because they did not intend to spend that much, another serv-ice—home delivery—further reduced hesitation: one paid at home, later. In the *Coquet*, Henriette d'Orvalle ironically notes that the delivery serv-ices that traversed Paris in every direction were uniquely suitable for noisy advertisement: "Vans like the chariot of the sun, postilions in braided uni-forms, high-spirited horses such as only the Perche can produce, ringing bells, deliverymen busily handling the three or four packages contained within the immense vehicle, high speeds that didn't endanger pedestrians thanks to the skill and responsibility of the drivers, and above it all, the miraculous advertisement in golden letters: '*Grand Magasin de l'Obélisque*—the largest store in the world' (along with many others)."[19]

TRAPPED WOMEN, THIEVING WOMEN

Women, whose appearance and clothes henceforth signified their hus-bands' status, women, who increasingly managed the family budget, women, who were both delegates and managers, became the prime target of the new business practices. For them the department stores multiplied the snares and seductions that both enslaved and exalted them simultane-ously. "A woman must be the queen of the store; she must feel that she is in a temple raised for her glory, her enjoyment, and her triumph," Zola had noted in the outlines for his novel. "The omnipotence of woman, the scent of woman dominates the whole store. That is Octave's commercial credo, more or less conscious and open."[20] His success ordained him as the high priest of a

> new religion that converted a rational browser into an unbridled coquette. . . .
> Churches, which were little by little being deserted by those of wavering faith,
> were being replaced by his bazaar. Woman came to spend her hours of idle-
> ness in his shop, the thrilling, disturbing hours which in the past she had spent
> in the depths of a chapel. . . . If he closed the doors, there would have been a
> rising in the street, a desperate outcry from the devout, whose confessional
> and altar he would have abolished.[21]

One year before Zola, Pierre Giffard had said much the same thing: "Eve's daughter enters this hell of temptation like a mouse into a trap. . . . In this abyss, whirlwinds are strewn with mirages each one more dangerous than the other. As if from Charybdis to Scylla, she glides from counter to counter, dazzled and overpowered."[22] The more daring of these stores pre-sented a topography diabolically calculated to draw captivated customers into a labyrinth, keep them wandering, prolong their browsing routes, and enlarge the shopping space by a network of counters so arranged as to destroy any sense of symmetry or any geometrical frame of reference.[23]

The product of a meticulous and controlled design, the apparent jumbled disorder of merchandise proffered unexpected suggestions and aroused unsuspected temptations. At a time of relative increase in buying power the department store induced the psychological "takeoff" of modern consumerism, this increasingly socially dictated definition of needs. With this development came acute frustrations and culpable transgressions. Now unleashed, the shopping spree revealed its sexual component: "The customers, despoiled and violated, were going away disheveled, their sensual desires satisfied and with the secret shame of having yielded to temptation in some shady hotel."[24]

This palace "offered" a provocative abundance, and theft made it possible to experience the new euphoria of acquisition without the agony of payment. Shoplifting introduced the gratuitous into a system where everything had a market value, without short-circuiting the commercial mechanisms. Its statistically computed cost was figured into the pricing structure. Nevertheless, because bargain prices were a decisive selling point, floorwalkers were assigned to keep an eye on the counters. It then became apparent that these arenas, in which people, goods, and money circulated frenetically, engendered or brought out aberrant behaviors that attracted the attention of psychiatrists and forensic physicians. Along with commonplace thefts, there were others that were singularly specific to the department stores, committed without apparent motive by affluent

Ready-to-wear salon

women. It is difficult to fathom the motivation of a wealthy middle-class woman who snatched in one fell swoop three hundred ties from a display stand and whose house disclosed to a police search "two hundred and forty-eight pairs of pink gloves, stolen from all over Paris."[25] Another one was caught stealing a sponge worth 60 centimes after having spent 200 francs. This kind of behavior, which defied explanations based on utility or economic rationality,[26] became the subject of a psychiatric literature that accounted for such crimes by invoking "hysterical" and "menstrual" causality.[27] These studies led to more general investigations of the pathogenesis of department store theft—*apéritifs du crime*—and of the neuroses that they induced or revealed.[28]

This peculiar climate—compulsive, feverish, sensual—caused by a tide of women examining, fingering, and caressing the fabrics with desire and delight, also attracted an odd male population, which the floorwalkers spotted out of the corners of their eyes and cataloged:

> Here is one, slovenly dressed, with a polka-dot tie. He is alone. . . . What is he, looking for in this display, which reeks of woman? . . .
>
> He is happy amidst the undulating movements of these women, who give off emanations and odors that excite him sensually. He is a demented, emotionally unbalanced individual, who gets intoxicated by the natural and artificial scents of women. He lets himself be carried along by the crowd that squeezes him, surrounds him, and takes him three steps forward and five steps back. He lives and breathes in this feminine element as easily as a fish in water. . . .
>
> Such unfortunates always end up among those who indulge in loathsome maneuvers against the fair sex. Driven by their passion, they sometimes sink so low as to forget themselves before passers-by. . . .
>
> First come the "gropers," casual and haphazard, not yet fully corrupted; they slip into crowds and manage to run their hands over the breasts and curves of pretty girls. . . .
>
> Somewhat worse are the "frotteurs", easily recognized by their glances from top to bottom, directed primarily toward women's necklines and bosoms. Once they have chosen the target of their obscene intentions, they brush against her and pester her for hours, inflaming and sustaining their desire by rumpling her dress.
>
> A subgroup of "frotteurs" is even more audacious and shameless. They take advantage of the crowds to indulge themselves in surreptitious touching. They then go away satisfied, having sullied a woman's clothing.
>
> A young girl complained to her mother of having been literally assaulted by an individual whose wild eyes rolled in their sockets. "Let's get out of here," she said. "I can hardly breathe, and that man frightens me. He's crazy; you see, he just spat on me."

Unfortunately, this is not an isolated case. Far worse yet is a curious category of emotional deviants who go from crowd to crowd, hesitating and lingering before stopping. Once they've made a choice, they throw themselves upon the targeted woman, madly kiss the curls on her nape, then vanish as if by magic, clucking their tongues and licking their lips to savor the perfume left by the "ringlets" of their preferred color. . . .

Another class of specialists, the most singular of them all, can be called the "destroyers." These maniacs use scissors to cut women's dresses and coats, carefully storing the pieces they take with them in drawers. Each trophy is identified by a label which bears the date, the name of the store, the woman's description, and the degree of satisfaction experienced. . . .

After the "dress destroyers" come the "hair cutters." I interviewed one of these souvenir-collectors. He would go up to ten- to twelve-year-old girls who wore braids or shoulder-length hair. Armed with scissors, he would mutilate their silken hair, shortening it by half.

To conclude this pitiful catalog, we have the handkerchief-collectors. These at least have a purpose in mind, a hardly admissible purpose, . . . one difficult to discuss, a purpose that is hidden, it is true, until they're arrested. Then we find this item, the most indispensable one in your wardrobe, wrapped around a part of their body.[29]

THE TRIUMPH OF DISTRIBUTION

The department store was denounced from all quarters. It was a plague[30] that instigated baseness, corrupted people, prostituted women, broke up marriages, devoured small businesses,[31] and made products ugly. Yet it expanded unflinchingly, sure of its strength and its future. Some stores died because they tried to grow too quickly.[32] Others, more prudently intrepid, diversified the choice, quality, and price of their merchandise to attract a more diverse clientele. The middle class shopped at the department stores in great numbers, but the stores sought to attract customers from the opposite poles of the bourgeoisie by appealing to both the affluent and the penurious. Thus they enlarged their departments of luxury goods as well as those of ordinary articles, multiplied both the promotions of new fashions and the sales to liquidate them. Ideally, "The working girl would find there her good woolen Sunday dress, the middle-class woman, her simple but rich silks, and the great lady, the most original and sophisticated fabrics and designs that caprice might dictate."[33]

The department stores soon realized, however, that despite their broad range of goods, they could not really draw all customers into the same space. Each store targeted both its merchandise and its merchandising according to customers' income, social status, and age, categories that did not always overlap. Each store chose a style and adopted an attitude. A typology of department stores emerged. The Louvre, whose "ready-to-wear was generally expensive and intended for the affluent,"[34] was opulent, conservative, and conformist. Comparing it to the Bon Marché, Zola found the Louvre "more stylish and expensive," whereas "the Bon Marché smacked a bit of the provinces."[35] Le Printemps always saw itself as modern and daring, appealing to a young clientele from the petty and middle bourgeoisie. La Samaritaine had very low prices and attracted working-class customers, as did the Ville-de-Saint-Denis, which supplied "charity boards, parish vestiaries, police headquarters, the Imperial Insane Asylum at Charenton, and the General Linen Office of the Department of the Seine."[36]

Each store bought fairly specific products, hierarchically arranged according to their origin: fabrics and ready-to-wear articles from Paris or Lyon cost more but enjoyed a better reputation than those from Lille, Roubaix, or Rheims. Alongside these immense stores, smaller establishments, devoted exclusively to ready-to-wear clothing, also prospered. Located throughout Paris, they were ranked according to the luxury of their products and the elegance of their clientele. Although their psychological impact was less modest, the Bon Pasteur, the Galeries de Paris, the Palais de Cristal, the Quatre Nations, the house of Opigez-Gagelin (where Worth worked), and firms like Bouillet, Leleux, Dubus, and many others did a large volume of business that tripled in twenty years,[37] further stimulating the ready-to-wear industry that began to mechanize around 1860.

The sewing machine, perfected in 1829 by Barthélemy Thimonnier, created such a panic among the tailors that they rioted and destroyed the eighty machines at the Germain Petit uniform factory and forced Parissot, of La Belle Jardinière, to put his thirty machines away until 1850. Not until the middle of the Second Empire did Isaac M. Singer, drawing his inspiration largely from the inventions of Elias Howe and Walter Hunt, break into a still-hesitant French market with a machine that appreciably increased the productivity of workers.[38] These laborers still worked at home or in small production units using "sewing equipment" soon to be within the reach of bourgeois households. They were not gathered into factories until the 1880s,[39] with the only notable industrial concentration being the military workshops. The ultramodern Godillot firm, for example, founded in 1859, employed several thousand workers and as many machines. Later it gave its name, *godillots*, to army boots, of which it supplied over 1,100,000 each year.[40]

The conquests of the ready-to-wear industry were achieved at the expense of the small tailor who mainly worked to order. His working-class and petty-bourgeois customers deserted him day by day, and soon he virtually disappeared. Threatened by the same fate, the tailor-employers ignored the real danger of this new production, which they attacked with indignation or contempt. Their professional journals ritualistically forecast the imminent demise of ready-to-wear and the ineluctable return of custom-made clothing, deluding themselves about a future that they could not face.

> Our fathers were happier than we. They weren't faced with this constant competition from more or less grand factories, from clothing cut in "roughly" three sizes, produced "dirt-cheap" and sold at more than they're worth for the profit of a few manufacturers. Whatever the case may be, and despite everything, the real tailors will triumph because they alone can combine the two words that motivate both the artist and the man of the world: "elegance" and "comfort." . . . Let the fripperers, high- or low-class, assume responsibility for their twenty-five franc paletots. This obsession with cheapness no matter what will pass quickly enough, especially after people try it out. Let us occupy ourselves, seriously and conscientiously, with the normal proportions to be observed in all parts of a suit.[41]

But instead the fever for bargain prices caught on among other segments of the bourgeoisie, this time gradually dispossessing the middling tailors. The Coutard firm, for example, a pioneer in ready-to-wear, offered all the guarantees of superior, comme il faut clothing, if one can believe Charles Eck's 1866 description:

> The building has a simple, severe, and tasteful look, and its external appearance is not without interest: nothing flashy, garish, gilded. It is immediately apparent that this is a serious establishment: a single shop window with a few garments displayed, and a modest entrance opening onto immense rooms airy and well lit. In them, carefully arranged garments are ready to wear and ready to be shipped to customers. One warehouse holds ready-made dressing gowns; then come the departments of paletots, trousers, and vests, and a charming room for trying them on, with large mirrors that enable the buyer to spot the slightest defect. There is a measurement salon, also simply decorated, and through a large opening at the center, one can view an immense workshop in which forty cutters labor under expert supervision. . . .
> Senators, deputies, lawyers, physicians, ministerial officers, indeed all the better people get their clothes at the MAISON COUTARD, and, may we add, without intending a criticism of others, one will not find there eccentricities that not only deviate from good taste but are frankly bad form.[42]

Given the demographic growth and prestige of Paris, as well as a rise in the standard of living, the production of made-to-measure clothing did not suffer an absolute decline but was greatly outdistanced by the dynamic, many-sided ready-to-wear industry. In his *Report to the Internal Jury of the*

Exposition of 1867, the tailor Dusautoy exhorted his colleagues to acknowledge their methods as obsolete and their pride as suicidal:

> Two rival elements confront each other. . . . On one side, the tailors, steeped in their ancient prejudices, proud of their origins, and draped in the old reputation of their major craft guild, refuse any truck with improvements whose potential they fail to recognize.
>
> On the other, the makers of ready-to-wear, children of our times and only recently arrived on the scene, work and learn, adopt the best practices of tailors, and innovate, all the while expanding, intelligently and swiftly, their business activities. Newcomers, they mean to make whatever sacrifices are necessary to meet headlong the ancient tailoring establishment, so venerable that its members consider their craft a kind of aristocracy.
>
> The tailors of Paris had better rouse themselves from their torpor, learn from the ready-to-wear manufacturers, compete with their intelligent rivals, and remember that they are protected by no monopoly, no privilege; or else it's all over for their industry. For, sooner or later, it is certain that the ready-to-wear manufacturers will become the principal suppliers of clothing for Paris.[43]

Acknowledging the victory of ready-to-wear clothing as inevitable, Dusautoy pointed out (without real conviction) that because some manufacturers of ready-made also offered custom clothing, tailors should imitate them and sell both kinds of clothes:

> Will they listen to us? I doubt it. Today's tailors are as hidebound as their predecessors who warred with the fripperers. Frippery has become big business, ready-to-wear manufacturing, big industry, while tailoring has practically stood still, little different from what it was twenty years ago. A tailor would feel disgraced at the idea of selling ready-made.
>
> There, however, lies the salvation of their guild.[44]

For couturières the problem long remained different. For one thing, custom sewing was the general rule for women's dresses, which involved many parts that must fit the body closely. Moreover, their sewing techniques did not lend themselves to assembly-line procedures. For another, the dressmaking business was spurred on by the immense selection of reasonably priced fabrics that the department stores offered. Furthermore, the clothes they made were not in competition with the stores' ready-to-wear offerings,[45] which multiplied, but primarily for articles that did not require an exact fit.

The fripperers' trade, however, was not spared by the hegemonic expansion of the ready-to-wear industry, which quickly became a dangerous competitor. Alexis Monteil dubbed the age of the French Revolution the "decade of the fripperers," when pillage and confiscation enabled some members of the trade to amass considerable fortunes, when proscribed aristocratic vestiges like trimmed suits and braid sold for next to nothing and were profitably transformed. The latter half of the Second Empire marked, on the contrary, the historic decline of this millennial trade. "On the one hand," pointed out the Paris Chamber of Commerce, "since 1860 the rag-cutting industry has absorbed some of the trade in old cloth, and on the other, the fripperers have met a formidable rival in a ready-to-wear industry whose bargain-priced products are now preferred to mended clothes."[46] The trend intensified, as Kerckhoff noted in 1865, as textiles became less durable: "Today, general affluence and ready-to-wear clothing have largely deprived the fripperers of clients and wares. People prefer, and rightly so, to buy new garments that barely cost more than used clothes."[47]

Old-clothes merchants and wardrobe dealers grew rarer and eventually vanished from the urban landscape.[48] The Temple market still functioned, but a triumphant public health movement imposed a sanitary grid of new streets and exorcised the remnants of this disturbing world of dubious morality, shady dealings, and foul rags, carriers of moral and microbial infections. As early as the eighteenth century, the "contagious miasmas" produced and transmitted by used clothing had aroused concern and elicited a call for "charitable police regulations . . . to submit these old clothes to some kind of disinfection by fire, water, or aromatics."[49]

The nascent microbiology of the nineteenth century, however, created a real sense of urgency. Tracking down pathogenic germs in every nook and cranny of the body social, the 1860s' public health specialists were alarmed by the absence of controls over this vast exchange of contaminated rags. Dr. Michel Lévy observed that "no public health regulation subjects this merchandise to preliminary cleansing, even though it is a thousand times more suspect than the bales of raw cotton brought in by ship. . . . The frippery trade operates in filthy dens where needy workers bargain for articles of clothing that will infect their perspiration with the morbid contagion picked up from sick people."[50]

In 1863, the sheds of the Temple and the Rotonde were destroyed and replaced by a handsome iron building inspired by the central Halles. Six gleaming pavilions, each with four hundred stalls, were brilliantly lit by an ovoid glass cupola, but the effects sold there were not yet "beaten, aerated, fumigated,"[51] as the new prophylaxis would have liked. Nevertheless, the modernizing market became very middle-class. "Circulation is easy and the cleanliness remarkable," testified a Paris guide of 1870. It also noted, however, that "the new ready-to-wear stores where one finds reasonably priced clothes—poorly cut, it is true, but new—competes effectively with the frippery trade."[52] In fact, the taming and decline of frippery went hand in hand. "The police have almost completely eliminated abuses beneath the new sheds, but alas the trade has been radically altered; frippery is in decline. Only new articles are now sold there, along with shopworn items."[53] Some remnants of the former trade survived on the second story, where the *carreau* and its tumultuous dealings had moved. But because of the scarcity of supplies and customers, the volume of business steadily decreased, its problems further aggravated by increases in stall rental fees.[54] Frippery, as such, then became limited to exports,[55] especially to colonial Africa: "Even the most shopworn garments take on new life when they cross the ocean. In other climes they become fancy goods: the soldiers' red trousers and epaulettes are at a premium; the black kinglets grab the uniforms of generals and prefects, and even the gowns of academics and the livery of lackeys."[56]

THE TREND TOWARD UNIFORMITY

Getting the better of both fripperers and ordinary tailors, the ready-to-wear industry—especially for men—appealed to social strata whose way of life ranged from upper working-class to middle bourgeois. The purchasing power of those classes rose during most of the Second Empire,[57] so that the relatively low cost of ready-made provoked a veritable euphoria of clothes buying, all the more so since clothing was largely immune to a general rise in prices.[58] This trend toward "the well-being of the greatest number," to which commerce and industry contributed, was proudly displayed to provincials and foreigners visiting the 1855 and 1867 Universal Expositions.[59] Household linens, silks, furs, shawls, jackets, shirts, and paletots, all ready-made, were presented by the best firms at prices[60] that astounded a public not yet reached by either catalogs or branch stores.

Thanks to ready-to-wear clothing and inexpensive fabrics, the intermediate classes—the small, relatively independent businessmen, the low-level bureaucrats who fetched and carried for their superiors, the auxiliaries of the liberal professions, and the white-collar employees of industry and business, as well as the comfortable artisans and laborers—could now assume varying degrees of sophistication and entire wardrobes formerly reserved for their betters and protected by wealth.

Thus the proliferation of ready-to-wear foreshadowed the era of imitations, when authentic models, rare because they were old, original, and costly, would be copied and mass-produced as industrially manufactured, finished goods to be distributed by department stores. Just as such newly discovered chemical processes and products as pinchbeck, electroplating, paste jewelry, and imitation leather attempted to approximate the sign-values of gold, silver, diamonds, and genuine leather at a fraction of their cost, so too did the ready-to-wear industry enable those who could not afford custom-made clothing to acquire a copy, whose value was secondary and derivative but which gained them entry, by imitation and anticipation, into the purview of bourgeois appearances and their concomitant comportment, style, and ideology. As the social strata grasping at status symbols multiplied and elegant rarities further increased in price, industrially produced imitation chic became more widely available. Antiques well illustrate this development: when heavy demand pushed up their prices, ersatz replicas[61] replaced the originals, in the same way that an exotic object is worn out and then replaced by a mass-produced copy. In both cases, the imitation is not an exact copy of the original, which merely serves as a point of departure, with many other elements added. The fake chinoiseries produced in the Saint-Sulpice quarter and the Henri II buffets overladen with moldings and collerettes are typical examples of this syncretizing imitation, these bastardized fakes endlessly reproduced and distributed by the department stores. Although the ready-to-wear industry contributed to this industrialized false luxury, it remained closer to its original made-to-measure clothing. Having only the appearance of the reality it imitated, it compensated for this fundamental defect not by adding details but rather by improving its copying techniques. It thus became crucial in the spreading of bourgeois norms, for those ready-to-wear copies became pedagogical instruments of deportment and morality.

A century earlier, panniers had been reserved for noble ladies and wealthy bourgeoises, but crinolines were now worn both by working women who walked about hatless and by behatted ladies who rode in carriages. Crinolines did vary, however, depending on who wore them. An elegant, custom-made afternoon dress by a famous couturière could cost between 500 and 1,000 francs; its fullness, fabric, color, and the way it was worn all signaled upper class. Another one, purchased ready-made for 50 or 100 francs, of more modest dimensions,[62] with dull or garish tints, and less precisely fitted, betrayed its modest origin.

It is difficult to establish the social limits of crinoline wearing because the definition of *crinoline* remained fluid. In cities, dresses were generally, but diversely, bouffant, thanks to ready-to-wear and cheap fabrics. We need only leaf through nineteenth-century photographs taken along the grand boulevards during parades, where, amid the crowds acclaiming the soldiers, rows of crinolines lined the streets. The metallic "cages" that replaced layered petticoats were so cumbersome that they marked a distinct frontier separating the idle from the working-class populations. In France, the Thompson and the Peugeot[63] factories produced annually 2,400 metric tons[64] of these steel engines between 1858 and 1864 when they reached the height of their vogue. Averaging 500 grams apiece, this yielded some 4,800,000 units a year.

Excluded from real social mobility, the proletariat and the peasantry did not yet participate in this process of equalization, that is to say, in the apparent homogenization of vestimentary signs caused by the advent of standardized ready-to-wear. Here and there, traditional costumes adopted elements of the new styles, but no real cultural integration took place. Geographically varied, they were not affected by bourgeois models but existed outside the commercial and competitive rhythms of fashion. Their forms did change, but only over long periods. As Jules Michelet noted in 1846, an enormous improvement had been made when the lower classes adopted underwear and generally improved their textile comfort: "That was a revolution in France, little noted but a great revolution nonetheless. It was a revolution in cleanliness and embellishment of the homes of the poor; underwear, bedding, table linen, and window curtains were now used by whole classes who had not used them since the beginning of the world."

And indeed, a few years later, printed calicoes at last gave working women the right to wear colors: "Today her husband, a poor worker, covers her with a robe of flowers for the price of a day's labor. All these women of the people who now display an iris of a thousand colors on our promenades were formerly in mourning."[65]

Crinoline factory: installing the hoops (Bach, 1865)

Nevertheless, it was only during the Second Empire that some assimilation of bourgeois dress occurred in the working class, and this mainly among laborers in big cities, especially Paris. As the nineteenth-century *Larousse* encyclopedia testifies,

> In 1848 workers still wore smocks, not only in the shops during working hours and on weekdays, when it was a necessity, but on Sundays and holidays; when they walked about, some craftsmen wore costumes of cotton or velvet in a particular color that made it easy to spot their members. But these customs have disappeared in less than ten years and today are no more than an already-distant memory.[66]

This transition to wearing ready-made clothing and dressing up like a bourgeois on Sundays served more than a commercial purpose. Because the dominant social groups were forced to draw new class distinctions,[67] the adoption of bourgeois clothes was politically profitable. The thrifty worker was dissuaded from buying his clothes from the fripperer and directed toward department store displays to buy ready-made, fixed-price garments. He was thus drawn into a universe of consumption that imposed patterns of thought, acted as mental orthopedics, and moralized aesthetic perceptions as he internalized bourgeois norms of dress such as "propriety" or "respectability." The result benefited social control. Some workers hoped to be assimilated into the bourgeoisie by adopting its appearance, and there was even a tradition of workers' elegance among journeymen.[68] Others, on the contrary, displayed a provocative slovenliness, affected casualness, and flagrant dirtiness, which effectively challenged the "good behavior" preached by hygienists and philanthropists and thus threatened the social order.

Because the former was reassuring and the latter disturbing, a veritable civilizing mission was conferred on the ready-to-wear industry. Because of it, one observer noted that

> every worker can be appropriately dressed; during his leisure hours, the frock coat replaces the smock, and on solemn occasions he wears a black suit without financial sacrifice. The apparent vice of luxury is really a good. The worker will behave in accordance with what he wears; he goes to the cafe, reads, shuns the cabaret, and abandons the common dormitory for a room of his own as soon as he can. He dreams of furniture once he owns a wardrobe, and of a family once the furniture is placed in his garret. For him, cleanliness and comfort are the beginnings of morality; for society they are the guarantees of order.[69]

This view was supported by many other accounts:

The ready-to-wear industry must have contributed, it seems to me, to improving the morals of the masses. The worker who used to wear rough clothing or mended rags now puts on a suit: this kind of dress, which is now familiar to him, raises him to a higher station and gives him self-respect. Drunkenness has lost ground as the taste for clothing has gained. Orderly habits have followed the disappearance of intemperance, and family relations have consequently improved.[70]

Always conscious of material conditions and their symbolic representation, Michelet observed that these

> are not simple material improvements but progress for the people in those external appearances that men use to judge one another. . . . In this way the people rise to new ideas that they did not reach before; fashion and taste are an initiation into art for them. In addition, and more important, better dress changes a man; he wants to be worthy of it, and he tries to align his moral behavior with it.[71]

On the one hand, this acculturation functioned as social integration: the worker became integrated and acquired moral standing when he honored the socially accepted values of hygiene, sobriety, self-respect, order, family values, and thrift. On the other, the same acculturation made it necessary to create social distance within a hierarchy of sign-values and through a discrimination that relegated ready-to-wear clothing to the domain of the common or the vulgar.

Like the savage or the laborer, the poor or "ill-bred" child numbered among the new nineteenth-century barbarians. Like them, he scandalized people by dressing in a way that flouted the rules of "propriety" and "decency." Like them, he needed to have his moral standards raised, by being made to wear the external signs of a morality later internalized by the symbolic and social profit extracted from displaying these signs. The moralizing Louise Boyeldieu d'Auvigny comments self-righteously on the subject: "To make these unfortunate children, who run barefoot through the gutters where they learn vicious habits and laziness, understand that they have an immortal soul created to love the good and practice it, and to make them raise their heads and comprehend their human dignity as well as the necessity and joy of labor, first give them clogs and a jacket."[72]

In the countryside, urban ascendancy and the expansion of bourgeois clothing, which elsewhere resulted in the material and symbolic dispossession of the groups it contaminated, encountered passivity and strong resistance because people clung to old customs. One need only note the persistence of certain elements such as the fullness of the peasant smock, its "long-wearing" blue cloth, and the display of regional costumes on special occasions. The latter, however, did not go back much farther than the mid–eighteenth century. Before then, differences came from social roles rather than geography: on cathedral portals, the reaper could be distinguished from the wine grower by a costume found throughout Europe.

Then, inspired by local aristocratic models, the rich peasants' festive dress that would become characteristic of each region, indeed each village and valley, took forms that quickly became distinct since they evolved in relatively autonomous ways. However, when city fashions crystallized into types, they did sometimes influence the evolution of peasant costume: thus, during the reign of the crinoline, the "typical" rustic dresses grew wider. In fact, as with dialects and sociolects within a linguistic community, continuous exchanges and influences were established among various kinds of dress.

Oddly enough, French provincial costumes assumed their true identity after the French Revolution officially suppressed the provinces, and they became most splendid during the Second Empire, when they were threatened with commercial domination. Romanticism, which valued the particular and the picturesque, discovered and admired Alsatian headresses and Provençal embroideries; but the Romantics believed this finery to be the product of an ancestral popular culture, fixed from its beginnings. They did not understand that, in fact, it characterized a period of transition between the old and new vestimentary regime of the peasant world.[73]

Opening the mail at the Bon Marché

Was it a reaction against the centralizing state, a desire to assume the lavishness of vanished lords, or a product of mimetic rivalries between rival towns? What caused this splendid period of vernacular costume, between 1840 and 1860 especially, is still difficult to explain.

What is certain is that the unifying trend toward bourgeois dress, even in the countryside, continued inexorably, albeit more slowly, and along with it, the commercialization of economic life and the progressive disappearance of an earlier domestic or artisanal production system that included the spinstress, the shoemaker, and the itinerant tailor.[74] The department store, and the consumption it engendered, developed and prospered by seeking its clientele from beyond the socioeconomic limits of the middle classes and the topographical limits of the quarter or even the city. In Paris, Baron Haussmann's city planning, which encouraged mass transportation and thus drew shoppers out of their neighborhoods, enabled the new stores to attract and channel buyers. In the provinces and abroad, the extension of railroads[75] made it possible to order through catalogs, a practice that became widespread by 1860, and then to establish branches. In 1867, for example, La Belle Jardinière had branches in Lyon, Marseille, Nantes, and Angers, while the railroad tracks radiating from Paris focused on the capital 17,733 kilometers of track laid down by 1870. Accumulation of wealth and strengthening of power were impossible without an increase in speed. "Paris," noted Gustave Tarde at the end of the century, "lords it over the provinces, royally and orientally, more than the court ever did over the city. Every day, by telegraph or train, Paris dispatches its ready-made ideas, desires, conversations, and revolutions along with its ready-made clothing and furnishings."[76]

In the same way, the corrosive force of business practices alien to both usury and rural tradition penetrated the countryside, already crisscrossed and "worked" by the traveling salesman[77] who moved his stock and collected orders, using subprefectures and market towns as stopovers. The new attitude progressively eclipsed stout fabrics and changeless forms. The "heavy," "solid," and "durable" object was replaced by "light," "fragile," and "ephemeral"[78] merchandise; and the garment as symbol, organically tied to peasant life and activities, was replaced by the garment as sign, with its borrowed references.

Sunday, the day for seeing and being seen, had been the occasion to display regional costumes. Gradually it became the pretext for rich country folk to show off their black suits or crinolines, to mimic another constituency, and to exhibit the signs of another world, of the city and modernity.[79] Ly'onnel hardly exaggerated when he wrote in 1862: "The crinoline has invaded the remotest cottages, and scarcely a cowgirl can be found who doesn't get into her cage at least once a week."[80] Eugène Chapus was also astonished: "Who could have believed that the pannier, so inconvenient even for women of leisure and wealth, would become the indispensable accoutrement of the most humble stable girls or the overblown females who preside over kitchen stoves?"[81]

As white became the obligatory nuptial color, even wedding ceremonies ceased being an occasion for diverse vestimentary manifestations. This change was brought about by the spread of fashion journals and department store catalogs as well as by the 1854 proclamation of the dogma of the Immaculate Conception.[82] In short, "La Belle Jardinière invaded everything,"[83] even though up until the First World War and beyond, certain regions resisted the domination of bourgeois clothing, the symbol of the cities' ascendancy over the countryside. It is difficult, however, given the diversity of regions and the disparate nature of the documents, to establish a specific geographic chronology of this process.[84] During the same period, it took place[85] all over Europe, but differently according to industrial development, trading patterns, economic availability, and cultural influences. In 1855, on the occasion of Queen Victoria's visit to Paris, an event that attracted a considerable number of foreigners, the phenomenon was noted with surprise:

> One expected to see the most contrasting, disparate costumes, and a general sartorial confusion. It was pleasant to think of Turks in their dolmans with golden suns embroidered on the backs, Scots garbed in their indispensible garment, Tyrolians wearing hats trimmed with eagle feathers, and Spaniards solemnly dressed in cape and sombrero. But Turkey is becoming civilized, Scotland has abandoned the kilt for the common trouser, Tyrol has adopted the silk top hat, and Spain imitates our fashions with the most scrupulous exactness. Thus, everyone you see seems to have lived always on the rue de Rivoli or the Boulevard des Italiens.[86]

Export sales flourished for ready-to-wear, which already in the Second Empire gained some curious markets. Lemann wrote in 1857:

> All along the west coast of Africa the savages seek out our clothes. Who would have believed it? A firm in Marseilles, the Régis company, exchanges ready-to-wear clothes for the natural products of these countries. . . . The *Coniquet* or *Koniquay* is a small African country near the Congo whose black denizens always go about naked: the loincloth is the only advance that clothing has made among them since the Creation. Their king, doubtless seeking to increase his prestige in the eyes of his subjects by donning European garb, ordered from me a brocaded frock coat completely lined in red silk. His Negro Majesty, however, did not think it useful to order any pants. I have no doubt that the Negro chiefs will imitate their prince, and that soon, the masses having acquired a taste for luxury, I will be able to cover the traditional nudity of the Congo's inhabitants.[87]

Stimulated by the natives' penchant for European dress and by the religious, moral, and hygienic proselytism of the missionaries, a new market was thus opened for ready-made clothing. The explorer Henry Stanley, distressed by the nakedness of the blacks, declared to the Manchester Chamber of Commerce in 1877: "If we succeed in clothing the natives only on the Lord's day, this innovation in African mores would represent a new market for 320 million yards of English cottons."[88] The monetary profit derived from commercializing Christian modesty, whether among the Africans or among the working class, went hand in hand with symbolic and political profits, because the inner being was transformed through the metamorphosis of appearance. The injunction to clothe the naked became an apostolate participating in the domestication of savages whose Westernization was proved by their wearing of bourgeois clothing.

Guiding shoppers on a different itinerary, toward other forms of socialization and other aspirations, this new production—industrialized ready-to-wear clothing—and new system of distribution—the department store—established a dominant style and transformed vestimentary codes and comportments as they expanded geographically and socially.

New Pretensions, New Distinctions

Nothing is more poignant than to
be like everyone else.

—Balzac, *Physiologie gastronomique* (1830)

THE DEPARTMENT STORE exemplifies an expanding industrial society that produced for consumption and invented for production.[1] The department store created the material and psychological conditions for a new kind of consumption by new groups of consumers, who could finally acquire the vestimentary signs they had long been legally allowed to wear. Yet the spread of bourgeois clothing did not bring "vestimentary democratization." Intermediate classes were becoming integrated into bourgeois society, but unsure of their station, they coveted status symbols. It was for them especially that La Belle Jardinière or Le Printemps produced affordable copies of the unattainable forms, fabrics, and colors selected and combined by high society to create its own distinctive elegance. As Jean Baudriallard notes, however, "Classes did not all gain access to political power after the bourgeois revolution of 1789 any more than consumers acquired equality before the object after the Industrial Revolution."[2] And despite first impressions, the new consumption did not so much standardize appearances as create new expressions, which it integrated into a single code situated within a new hierarchy.

Men's clothing provides the most striking example. Increasingly less "distinctive" because produced in greater numbers, it elicited from the upper classes differentiating strategies—unknown during the ancien régime—to erect barriers against the lower classes now ascending and united at least in principle. Before the advent of ready-made and of democracy, social roles and status could be read instantly on one's clothes, which included details that formed part of a code in which every sign was laden with meaning. The end of legal restrictions and the standardization of manufacturing decisively disrupted the production and interpretation of vestimentary signs.

Sartorial Jacobins like Arnould Frémy were overjoyed by this prospect:

> The French Revolution has rendered us the signal service of dispatching
> the showy rags, the embroideries, the jewels and lace, the ceremonial swords,
> the taffeta suits, and all the smart and ruinous accessories of the aristocratic
> costume. Thanks to the Revolution, modern clothing has attained the simple,
> plain, and unpretentious form we see today.
>
> The fanatics of powdered hair and embroidered cuffs can fulminate as
> much as they wish against contemporary masculine dress and condemn it as
> "ugly," "gauche," "prosaic," and "inelegant." It has one great advantage: it is
> basically egalitarian.[3]

Others, however, inveighed against this surrender, and their royalist
nostalgia echoed the indignation of tailors. Eugène Chapus, for example,
exclaimed:

> Egalitarian ideas created our modern dress. This current of thought ex-
> presses itself in the trouser, which dissimulates graceful shapes so that bony
> and spindly shanks are not exposed; in boots that spare people with small
> incomes the extravagant luxury of silk stockings; in the dark colors of frock
> coats and tails which shroud the torso in shadows flattering to mediocre phy-
> siques; in white shirts whose puritanical simplicity, at odds with the laces and
> the rose point of the ancien régime, suits all classes alike.
>
> These ideas have been absorbed by the tailor, the coiffeur, the hatter, the
> bootmaker, and, for all we know, even the glover. The low income gloves
> itself for small sums, and we cannot be sure that today's courtiers do not
> sometimes acquire their gloves in dime stores, for as little as two francs, fifty
> centimes, or even twenty-nine sous. . . .
>
> If everyone destined by his prestigious origins and wealth to be distin-
> guished from the common herd adopted dress compatible with his luxurious
> and leisurely life, the inferiority of the lower orders would be immediately
> obvious. Undoubtedly, such a philosophy of dress and theory of elegance
> could spawn if not a social revolution, which would be too much to expect,
> then at least a new order of aristocratic distinction.[4]

In fact, subtle alternatives to this vestimentary ultraconservatism would
flourish. Whatever the satisfied Arnould Frémy or the vexed Eugène
Chapus might have thought, a quick look no longer took in the full meaning of dress. Now the social game would be played on the terrain of nuance
and detail, a terrain where secondary signs—the only ones that mattered
now—proliferated.

Bourgeois dress replaced the multiplicity of aristocratic costumes, but
beneath its superficial uniformity it created levels of meaning that bred
subtle differences and revealed novel qualities to be carefully cultivated. It
was between these levels that "distinction" developed, a new value in ves-

timentary discourse[5] and practice, which would become the cardinal element of a differentiating system that constantly improved as copies threatened its exclusive nature. Fundamentally bourgeois and quintessentially antidemocratic, "distinction" replaced the "grace" and *bel air* of the ancien régime, transformed elegance and etiquette, and complicated the science of style, signification, and appropriateness inherited from earlier days. "The result of all this," notes Veblen, "is a refinement of methods, a resort to subtler contrivances, and a spiritualization of the scheme of symbolism in dress. . . . As the community advances in wealth and culture, the ability to pay is put in evidence by means that require a progressively refined discrimination in the beholder."[6] Now it was no longer enough to be well born; it no longer sufficed to be rich, to be distinguished, or to distinguish oneself. One had to possess savoir-faire and social graces; one had to master the arcana of vestimentary propriety and its inexhaustible nuances.

As a result, relations between classes and signs became infinitely complex. During the first quarter of the century clothing functioned much as it had under the ancien régime, that is, like a lexicon. But afterward, especially after the Second Empire, social mobility was reflected in a fluidity of signs it no longer necessarily determined. Laden with differentiating connotations of status, prestige, and fashion, bourgeois clothing would reveal real social positions but also positions only imagined or anticipated. "Their dress," wrote Nietzsche, "must leave no one in doubt that they belong to one of the more reputable classes of society (to 'good' or 'high' or 'great' society), and on this score their pretensions are all the greater if they belong scarcely or not at all to that class."[7]

Tracking down signs that betrayed social positions that were either usurped or recently acquired, mercilessly flushing out, unmasking, and excluding the ignorant person who violated the new sumptuary laws of "proper comportment," became a compulsive preoccupation of the dominant classes. Industrial growth, the railroad revolution, commercial expansion, speculative fever—all aspects of Second Empire prosperity— changed social structures and relationships, bred overnight fortunes and dazzling ascensions, though inequalities remained and lent the social hierarchy an appearance of permanence.[8] The new conveniences, the vogue of seaside resorts, spas, casinos, Kursaals, and health resorts, and the rapid circulation of people and money all diluted the "reserve" that had distanced "high society," and thus helped produce the mixed cosmopolitan society that characterized the reign of Napoleon III.

Confronted with the dual onslaught of bargain-priced imitations on the one hand and pretensions based on new wealth on the other, the aristocracy and the older upper bourgeoisie joined forces to defend their position. The aristocratic families who lived in the Faubourg Saint-Germain, whose fortunes were collapsing or frittered away because the Civil Code had abolished primogeniture, crossed paths with the new capitalist elites who lived in townhouses along the Chausée d'Antin and whose banks and investment firms dealt in millions of francs. Their universes intersected, their interests overlapped and their ambitions merged. Linked by marriage and social intercourse, they shared the glamour of court festivities and the intimate luxury of the salon. Though irreducible differences between them remained, a common style—technical, ethical, and aesthetic—based on propriety bound them when it came to social distancing and, especially, vestimentary distinction.

Propriety is to ethics what fashion is to art. Both are forms, fragile and exemplary, of moral and aesthetic ideologies whose foundations and contradictions they illuminate. Like bourgeois morality, elaborated and systematized during the reign of Louis-Philippe, the rules of propriety that dictated practices and conduct in fashionable society reflected the odd ascendancy of an aristocracy that had been ruined and stripped of power. Though it had been forced to bow to the bourgeois order and accept the abrogation of hereditary inequalities, the aristocracy did not fade away through dissolution and assimilation. On the contrary, it retained the exclusive privilege of defining legitimacy in style, manners, and elegance and remained the reference point for fashionable society. The dominant bourgeoisie lacked the symbolic capital to justify its honor and merit its ascent. It had created an ethic based on energy, work, and thrift, which upheld its economic rationality. It had forged powerful signs such as magnificent restaurants,[9] comfortable villas,[10] prestigious uniforms, and respectable black suits. The aristocratic fantasy, however, which haunted the middle-class quest for legitimacy and self-affirmation in "society," revealed a fundamental difference: the bourgeois essence did not precede its existence.[11]

Without titles or aristocratic particles, without ancestral estates or natural superiority, its political, economic, and juridical power did not suffice: the middle class was what it *did*, and only what it did, while the aristocracy continued to be what it *was* and elevated the cultivation of aristocratic essence to a way of life.[12] In the great social game, the duty of the aristocrat was to show that his very being enabled him to uphold his exalted station; that of the grand bourgeois, to show that his possessions made him worthy of what he had conquered. In elegance, savoir-faire, and breeding, the aristocracy could not lose; the bourgeoisie was unable to challenge the rules of the game, just as it was incapable of creating values or pleasures without imitating, aping, or assimilating aristocratic models in an eclectic fashion.[13] One chronicler wrote:

> The Parisians are remarkable. They go everywhere: they call on commoners provided they're rich, and they call on nobles, even if they're poor. Names and money share the heart of the two thousand people known as "Parisian

society," but all are anxious not to stray from propriety, the quintessential coat of arms. This rule brooks no exception. It holds as true for great wealth as for those ruined by the Revolution, for the great names of the aristocracy as for the new names of the investment bankers. High society will accept one who is not wealthy, but not one who lacks in his dress, his speech, or his house the touch of elegance that is above reproach and in lock step with aristocratic exigencies.[14]

Aristocratic exigence lay at the heart of issues of acceptance, exclusion, association, and respect that obsessed the dominant social groups. In questions of clothing, it now assumed bourgeois forms, which had spread everywhere to everybody. But the distinctive value of a black suit, which was thought "egalitarian" and "democratic" and was the standardized symbol of the abolition of privilege, lay in virtually imperceptible refinements through which peeped, for those who knew how to look, aristocratic signs of prestige. This was why it did not suffice to master the rules of good manners. One's mastery had to be coupled with a discriminating buying sense. The cut and fabric of a suit, its up-to-dateness, and its position in the hierarchy of taste involved difficult decisions and pregnant choices for the person who wore it.

As ready-made clothing was ranked on a price and quality scale that corresponded to the gamut of the department stores and their clienteles, so, too, was custom-made clothing appraised according to the tailor's standing and ability. One's choice of a tailor was critical. Adviser, interpreter, and accomplice of the parvenus because he could hide the stigmata of lowly and shameful origins, he was the indispensable guide to elegance. Everything depended on him, from the silkiness of the fabric and the perfection of the cut to the finish of the tailoring. As one tailor noted,

> The modern suit should be made for the man who will wear it; it should harmonize with his looks, bring out the strong points and hide the defects that nature, education, or habits do not eliminate. There arises an intimate solidarity between a man of the world and his tailor, a bond that links the success of one to the success of the other. Hence anyone who does not want to dress merely comfortably must absolutely have a tailor to clothe him according to the arbitrary prescriptions of fashion, but above all so that he may be worthy of the society in which he moves and seeks success. He must dress elegantly, in a way befitting his disposition, character, person, age, and position as well as the laws of etiquette. These delicate nuances cannot be learned by social experience alone. Experience and professional knowledge are needed to acquire them.[15]

Beyond a certain income, a man's financial situation mattered less than his aptitude for making suitable acquisitions, which, incidentally, protected him from conspicuous consumption. For society women, however, sumptuary spending remained as imperious a duty as it had been during the ancien régime, despite the predictable traditional reprimands of the clergy or the tactical withdrawals intended to distance oneself from vulgar, loud display and the pretensions of social inferiors.[16] For other women, this part of the budget, within or beyond their husband's means, was just as essential. Through these expenses they refloated the precarious symbolic capital that, like beauty, manners, or the art of conversation, determined their social existence. "A woman whose husband is not rich derives her sense of worth from acquiring in any way she can a day dress of twelve hundred francs. Someone asked the owner of a fancy goods store if business was good. 'I am doing very well,' he replied; 'with a little more effort all the women will wear day dresses of two thousand francs.'"[17]

But the quickest way to expose one's poverty was to hide it by bluffing. "Women who rush into the race for clothing and frills do not realize that everyone sees through their phoney display. It does not take an acute observer to guess at the pain, privations, debts, and misery ill-concealed by satin and velvet."[18] For women, an elegant garment was more than tailored fabric, however beautiful; it was a technique, a comportment, and an appropriate education in the niceties, which permitted no false moves. Mme Amet d'Abrantès wrote:

> Even the way one carries a handkerchief has been systematized in the name of the je ne sais quoi that no one has seen or heard but that society obeys. Taste allows certain perfumes to be worn on one's handkerchief and forbids others. Musk and ambergris were once acceptable; now violet, iris, vanilla, and lemon are in. One can tell a society woman by the perfume she wears, and not merely by the perfume itself but by how much she wears. . . .
>
> Along those lines, some great ladies have added to their dressing rooms armoires lined with cedar or sandalwood, charming pieces designed by Tahan, in order to store linen, which retains the exquisite wood scent even when worn out of doors.
>
> All of this together makes the elegant woman; the practiced eye is never deceived, however alike the dresses.
>
> Two women may be dressed and outfitted alike, but they will betray differences in breeding. The way a hat is worn, to what degree tilted, or how close fitted, the way a mantelet is carried and a foot set on the pavement, the way a handkerchief is held; these are the indelible marks for which all women aim and only a few achieve with the elegance of great ladies. It is an indestructible coat of arms handed down to high-society women by their mothers and that they leave to their daughters, a challenge of one woman to another, the insidious vengeance of the true aristocrat over the parvenu in each new century.[19]

If vestimentary consumption distances through the difference that exists between a good tailor and ready-made, then vestimentary propriety becomes a determinant of social discrimination through the difference that exists between knowledge and ignorance. Both approaches spring from the same strategy, and both practices produce, and reproduce, systems of differences. Basically, they aim to defend the elite from two aspects of the same danger: imitation, which produces too many pretenders, such as grocers in their Sunday best, or excess, which produces loud, vulgar parvenus who strive, clumsily and vehemently, for the real thing. Simulation and excess—the cheap imitation of the poor, the overblown imitation of the rich—are the twin dangers that haunt society, fraught with confusing differences and laden with flaws such as *arrivisme*, greed, pedantry, vulgarity, and bad taste, which are the foils used in the legitimate definitions of what one must be and do.

VII

The Imperatives of Propriety

"Clothing is to the body what education is to the mind. Clothing consists of similar elements for everyone, yet it varies according to the taste, attitude, order, care, elegance, and distinction everyone brings to it."[1] In cases where appearances are concerned, as in many other domains, social characteristics matter only in their opposition to others, that is, when they are perceived as being different. This raises the question of the respective positions of these differences and their relationships within a common hierarchy, which is revealed through the dominant classes' sartorial discourse and practice, as seen from the top rung of the social ladder where these originate. Only in high society did decorum find its supreme expression; only there was the supreme model of propriety developed and defined, always negatively in relation to the rising classes for whom it served as a unique reference. It was, therefore, through comprehension, whether naive or subtle, vulgar or refined, of this model, all the more discriminatory because it was initiatory, that everyone's vestimentary behavior was distinguished and relentlessly classified.

The etiquette handbooks that proliferated in the nineteenth century provide an irreplaceable body of documentation on dress because they often devoted substantial chapters to the topic. The conformism of their prescriptions and the pains they took to preach the most acceptable and legitimate norms provide much better evidence of actual behavior than the fashion magazines. The latter thrived on the systematic discrepancy between their discourse and the way people actually dressed. They sought to break with previous canons by advancing propositions that were by no means generally adopted.

Both spoke in an authoritarian, threatening manner that transformed writing about clothing into an assertion of value, but the etiquette manuals referred to an already-accepted tradition, while the fashion magazines heralded and helped produce fresh controversies.

Like medieval courtesy books, like the manuals of courtly etiquette during the Renaissance and the age of Louis XIV, like the handbooks of "civility" that, from Erasmus to Jean-Baptiste de la Salle, taught children reading and "good manners" simultaneously, the nineteenth-century codes of savoir-faire reveal the realities beneath the appearances of a society, the relationships that function within it, and the evolution of its mores. There were numerous manuals published between 1840 and 1875—the *Catalogue général de la librairie française* listed more than sixty, not counting numerous reprints—which implies an enormous readership.[2] More accurately, they evidence an unprecedented demand from segments of the bourgeoisie still uninitiated (since they still needed to learn) but ascending (in reality or imagination) and in headlong pursuit of signs of belonging in order to complement their financial success (authentic or not) in order to legitimate their new status (real or fancied). Ponderously didactic, these treatises, which conscientiously marked off the boundaries of the "comme il faut," imposed new norms while removing certain sanctions. The aristocratic patronymics of these authors—a magical guarantee of their competence—did not, however, prevent the inevitable devaluation of revealed norms that had value essentially because they could be practiced properly only if they had not been consciously acquired. A supremely "cultural" domain in the ethnological sense, the "comme il faut," had to appear totally "natural" in the common meaning of the word.

Characteristic of this savoir-faire pedagogy was its function as a kind of footbridge between the aspiring, upwardly mobile segments of the bourgeoisie and the dominant portion by revealing the prerequisites of

Comme il faut salon

cultural access and social acceptance, without enabling the aspirants to cross over completely. Through this initiation—clearly expressed and thus basically limited—into handling the signs of "high society" the social function of vestimentary propriety took on special importance since it was immediately visible. Even before a person spoke or gestured, the laws of propriety enabled the initiated to spot him immediately as an ignorant offender and to put him in his place.

> "Good manners" were invented for the sole purpose of smoothly and confidently sorting people out, and thanks to etiquette, this sorting happens automatically. It is like the passwords and signals invented by freemasons to keep out the uninitiated. In fact, should an ill-bred churl blunder into a fashionable salon, he will feel so constrained, so embarrassed, so ashamed of his person that he will not wish to return; he will be content to malign it.[3]

Acting as cultural "barrier and standard,"[4] propriety in dress classified individuals very much the way language did.

> Just as a single word is enough to betray someone's origins or reveal a dubious past or present, so to the eyes of a discerning man or woman a clumsy piece of lace, a flounce, a feather, a bracelet, and especially an earring or any pretentious ornament can reveal social status or assign a particular level in the social scale. Affectations in dress are breaches of elegance, just as certain expressions are incompatible with cultivated language.[5]

The rules of good manners and of linguistic usage were equally arbitrary. As one manual declared:

> Let us agree, children, that you must never ask why such a usage persists, why a certain expression is considered in bad taste, and why the society that created these laws cannot justify them. The same is true for the languages spoken around the world. You cannot learn them unless you accept transpositions in syntax that at first strike you as strange and words that long seem untranslatable.[6]

Discourse on the "comme il faut" was all the more imperious because it sought to conceal the precariousness of the rules it wished to justify. Arguing by tautology—"it is not done because it is not done"—they threatened the offender with ridicule and apparent stupidity, in other words, with social ostracism.[7]

Like all know-how, vestimentary propriety implied an investment of time and energy, but its symbolic profitability stemmed from its financial unprofitability, reflecting the aristocratic ideology that considered idleness and conspicuous consumption as a vital necessity, as the very condition of social display and, consequently, all productive effort as disgraceful. Like social calls, invitations, promenades, charitable works, or table manners, clothing did not provide a pretext for manners and proprieties, it *constituted* proprieties and manners. Clothing was a science whose value resided in its very futility and fundamental superfluousness. It showed that the wearer had the time to devote to it and hence also possessed financial and cultural means. Contrasting the elegant with the active life, Balzac had theorized about this absolute rule of leisure: "To be *fashionable* one must enjoy leisure without having worked for it: or else hold four winning numbers in the lottery, be the son of a millionaire, a prince, a sinecurist, or a pluralist."[8]

Squandering time fashionably was not, however, a passive activity. Conditioned by wealth, and following the requirements of good manners, it was an exhausting exercise. It satisfied no economic necessity, but it did meet a social obligation, that of sacrificing one's "free time" to the ritualistic arrangement and continual care of one's appearance. This involved constant attention.

> Rest is not permitted the favored of this world; they owe themselves to their admirers and to their detractors. If they are not seen everywhere they lose their prestige. If they stop for a second, they're outclassed. Madame X did not attend this ball, or that race? She hasn't been seen in the Bois de Boulogne? Is she is perhaps ill? This question itself is evidence of forfeiture. Even as she utters it, the rival glances at the mirror in order to reassure herself that she is still youthful and healthy.[9]

And so, always in the breach, the

> great lady might have whims that even her chambermaid does not suspect, not because she is richer and more celebrated but because she has obligations to fulfill, because she must always struggle with her own weaknesses, and because, before any consideration of herself, she has obligations to her name, family, and rank, all of which prevent her from doing what she might want.[10]

The other's gaze—omnipresent—evaluates and approves, ceaselessly reminding her of the permanent, exhausting duty of self-control. If comportment, posture, temperament, and gestures constituted a sort of social heritage or a good hand dealt by birth,[11] other aspects of appearance required elaborate reconstruction daily, laboriously and tirelessly: toilette, body care, makeup, cosmetics, perfumes, epilation, coiffures, and clothing. Underlying the aesthetic rationalizations advanced, these techniques and practices, inspections and verifications, had but one aim: to show that useless labor had taken the place of utilitarian work.

The savoir-faire manuals were still far from the elegance that Balzac described and worlds away from dandyism, which, for that matter, they denounced. Resorting to them was tantamount to admitting one's deficiencies but at the same time to overcoming them, at least partially. This explains their importance: they formulated and clarified (but by so doing devalued) the grand norms that, beneath the surface changes of fashion,[12] governed clothing and the way to wear it. The first editions and reprints of this profuse literature during the Second Empire constituted a remarkably homogenous corpus in which the manuals differed little from one another or over time, except insofar as a few were more overtly Christian, and others spoke of forms with which some were not yet familiar.

A WOMAN'S WARDROBE

To bring her toilette into harmony, not only with herself, with her character, mood, age, face, complexion, and the color of her eyes and hair but also with her wealth and rank in society, with social events, hours of the day, and yearly seasonal changes, in other words with all the space she traversed, was the prime mystery of sartorial propriety, the laws of which minutely controlled the time and space of "society"—the ideal standard and absolute reference point of all manuals. The diurnal and nocturnal time of aristocratic and high-bourgeois society was divided into pretexts, marked by a relentless tempo for dressing and undressing; and doing so appropriately involved a veritable gnosis. While the manuals enable us to reconstruct these mysteries in a simplified version, the rich body of ethnographic material they assembled was a reference point of temporal and spatial oppositions (night/day, morning/evening, winter/summer, interior/exterior, town/country) that constituted basic dichotomies within which an impressive armory of vestimentary opportunites could unfurl: the wardrobe. Studying the "instructions" for the wardrobe requires not only describing the various components of dress but also breaking with traditional aesthetic histories of dress to consider, above all, clothing's daily social, moral, and semantic dimensions within the many polarizations of the dominant society where signs and behavior were organized according to a meticulous hierarchy.

Time Schedules

The fundamental requirement for social acceptance involved an enormous sartorial working capital.

> A society woman who wants to be well dressed for all occasions at all times needs at least seven or eight toilettes per day: a morning dressing gown, a riding outfit, an elegant simple gown for lunch, a day dress if walking, an afternoon dress for visiting by carriage, a smart outfit to drive through the

Bois de Boulogne, a gown for dinner, and a gala dress for evening or the
theater. There is nothing exaggerated about this, and it could be more complicated still at the beach, in summer, with bathing costumes, and in autumn
and winter, with hunting and skating costumes, if she shares these wholesome
activities with men.[13]

A woman's ability to keep up with this pace—with the demands it made
on her wealth, knowledge, and time—identified her as "comme il faut." In
fact, "for a woman, dress was a veritable science to which she devoted a
third of her day."[14]

After rising, secretly if possible or at least furtively, "so that her husband
did not catch her in unbecoming disarray, which might imprint itself on his
memory in a disagreeable way,"[15] after time spent in the dressing room
whose mysteries—ablution, epilation, and cosmetics—will be unveiled
later, she began the morning in a dressing gown or a peignoir. The first
was comfortable and warm, whereas the second strove for luxury, made of
muslin or nainsook, trimmed with bows, lace, and crimped ruffles. Beneath
peignoir or robe and over the day shift, a "half-corset should precede the
full corset, which is put on only when getting dressed, for no lady should
ever be completely unlaced."[16] No slovenliness in one's footwear either,
such as cloth slippers, and certainly never scuffs: "Fit only for concierges,
they are in the worst possible taste," stated Countess Dash, who prescribed

Morning peignoir, "after a design from the Grand Maison du Blanc"

"roomy slippers if you are fond of your comfort, provided they look like proper footwear."[17] We will have occasion to note how very weighty were matters of feet and waists in the nineteenth century.

Ordinarily on the head one wore a little batiste bonnet, but the problem of hair not naturally curly remained acute. "Curlpapers that cannot be removed upon rising, because the curls will not last until evening, should be hidden under a lace headband or a headband formed by the hair itself."[18] Nevertheless, they should be removed before noon, or at the very latest around two o'clock, along with all this morning costume, which could be worn in the bosom of the family, while tending to one's duties as mistress of the house, but should never be displayed to strangers. This dishabille not only would elicit embarrassment if seen by a chance visitor but of itself would present a serious moral danger.[19] Its very carelessness and comfort made one contract "harmful habits: one no longer laces oneself, decides that simple cleanliness suffices, neglects elegance, and avoids discomfort."[20] Therefore, in morning dress, one had to be groomed even more meticulously than at other times. Therefore, one had to discard it at the proper time without using the temperature, for example, as dispensation from the rule: "It is a mistake made by low-class, ill-bred women to assume that hot weather . . . allows wearing sloppy shoes, baring one's arms and legs, and assuming nonchalant, immodest poses. . . . It is likewise an error to assume that cold and damp excuse other liberties of this kind."[21]

A century later, functional and comfortable clothing would become prestigious. In the meantime, the richness and control of clothing over the body had to increase as the day progressed. "A woman, ravishingly elegant in her peignoir at ten in the morning, when she waters her flowers or leafs through a fashion magazine, is a changed person at two in the afternoon, laced in a stiff corset, the tyranny of which she has never tamed, or, in the evening, on the Champs-Elysées, buried beneath the emphatic folds of a skirt that spreads over three chairs."[22]

This minutely codified progression proscribed a woman from going out dressed in lace and feathers before noon. "Day dress should distinguish itself by simplicity and restraint."[23] Thus, day décolletage was in bad taste, as was wearing too-ample skirts or showy jewels before evening.

Within these general rules, however, important nuances appeared, depending on where the clothes were destined to appear. Visits called for luxury, but according to the degree of formality of the occasion: a short dress indicated an intimate visit, one with a train a ceremonious call, a distinction established since around 1865 by the popularity of the "Princess" ensemble, a shortened day dress. A colonel's wife would not call on the general's spouse in a short dress, unless she was an intimate friend; a major-general's lady would likewise wear a long dress to pay her respects to the wife of her husband's minister. "But when one is on an equal footing and knows the other person well, a short dress is acceptable and much more pleasant to wear."[24] In other circumstances one was to demonstrate a certain sartorial tact. "Are you going to console a friend in mourning and sorrow? Let your clothing be somber and plain so as not to contradict your expressions of sympathy, your assurances of affection and sincerity. . . . On the other hand, is it a sick friend who calls you to her bedside? Your clothes should not affect an appearance of mourning that could sadden or disturb her."[25]

Visiting one's charity cases, an obligatory item on a comme il faut woman's agenda, called for deploying a wily strategy whose political aims the manuals did not conceal. "A visit paid to someone who is unfortunate and living in retirement," said one of them, "requires . . . the greatest simplicity in attire . . . the absence of anything that might remind those you go visit of the advantages denied them."[26] Another manual recommended:

Indoor wear: gray taffeta dress

Do not visit your poor, as do many women who believe themselves charitable, in elegant dress and bright colors, in lace and jewels. Would you not fear that this display of luxury would cancel the good you try to do? Would it not elicit feelings of envy, or contradict the charitable expressions of consolation you will utter? . . . At the very least, would it not create, against the accoutrements of poverty, a sad and grievous contrast, one that would be obvious to human nature weighed down by misfortune and be painful for you as well?[27]

A third, more pragmatic manual decreed: "In clothes like these, you cannot speak effectively to those you visit about the advantages of poverty."[28]

Along with shopping and visiting tradesmen, riding in one's carriage occupied a major part of the afternoon, unless replaced by the opening of an exhibit, a charity sale, or a chamber music recital. The Bois de Boulogne, of course, was a central attraction where an unequaled fashion spectacle was played: the daily rivalry among the women of high society and the demimonde deemed elegant who came to outdo one another by the originality of their attire and the splendor of their carriages. Riding in a carriage, a woman was no longer restricted to the sober dress expected in the afternoon; in the Bois de Boulogne sobriety was banished. Clothes that no woman on foot could have worn without attracting a crowd of passers-by and being thought unseemly and provocative, she could flaunt in all dignity and glory leaning against the cushions of an emblazoned, luxuriously appointed carriage. "In a carriage," assured the Vicountess de Renneville, "one can risk any fashionable extravagance and novelty; it is the pedestal of eccentricity: pelisses in muslin, white embroidered dresses, rich silk dresses in soft colors, taffetas with impossible checks, bareges with Chantilly flounces, and pompadour or star-speckled tarlatans."[29] Let us, however, temper this advice, which was given—not by chance—in a fashion journal. Distinction maintained a certain reserve and an essential simplicity even in magnificence.

Society women hardly ever walked. Walking was made perilous by the fullness of their dress, a highly symbolic physical hindrance. As a corollary, the drama of a tear or a spot was understood as more than an involuntary offense against the aesthetic order: it was shameful evidence of "excessive" movement. Consequently, "while walking in the street a woman's primary concern is to take great care to protect her shoes and the hem of her dress from the mud,"[30] with certain manuals going so far as to advise her "not to go out on foot when it is raining, or even on days when the weather is unsettled."[31] In fact, a skillful walking technique was essential.

It is well known how remarkable Parisian women are in this regard: you can see them, laden with packages, crossing wide muddy streets, avoiding ill-bred passers-by and carriages that come from every direction, and returning home

without a single spot after shopping for several hours. To effect this prodigious achievement, which arouses admiration and chagrin in newly arrived
provincials, they must carefully step only on the center of the cobblestones
and never on the edges, because then they would inevitably slip into the
spaces between the stones; they have to put down the ball of the foot before
the heel; even when it is quite muddy, the heel should be lowered very
rarely. . . . While she "dances lightly over the cobblestones"—this is the customary expression—a lady should raise her dress nicely, slightly above her
ankles.[32]

Balzac had already observed that "from the way in which she lifts her
foot in the street, a discerning man can guess the secret of her mysterious
errand."[33] Whatever the case, evening dress simply ruled out any idea of
walking.[34]

La Revue des Deux-Mondes: "One walks, the other doesn't."

After she returned from the Bois or visits, the end of her afternoon was
consecrated to the new costume, and as always, circumstances, place, and
people she would meet determined its general aspect and its details. If she
stayed at home or attended a dinner of middling importance, the costume
would be reserved, with a moderate décolletage and in half-tones, a compromise between day and evening dress, although always dressy enough to
be worn in the drawing room after she left the table. Formal dinners,
which were often followed by receptions, called for more finery. Flowers,
diamonds, and lace adorned the chignon, while the majestic décolletages of
extraordinarily elaborate dresses framed the bare flesh of shoulders, arms,
and bosom.

Just as costumes became increasingly complicated and richer as the
hours passed, they also progressively revealed certain parts of the body.
Décolletage, rigorously banned from the peignoirs worn in the morning,
descended with day dress and in the evening attained impressive depth. At
night a woman could openly expose what would have violently offended

her modesty in the morning. On the other hand, below the waist and beneath the cupola of the crinoline, centuries of dark mystery lived on. This etiquette, which favored opulent busts, was pitiless toward both beauties who were a bit thin and elderly ladies. The latter were advised to "wear either a chemisette in tulle or a scarf to show that they were in protest against this dress that no longer suited their age."[35] For the former, adding pendeloques to their necklaces or increasing their strings of pearls remained their sole, and expensive, recourse. As hostess, the mistress of the house was the only exception to this overabundance of luxury and opulence: her appropriately modest dress left the honor of shining to her guests.[36]

Dresses with trains, complicated arrangements, and glittering jewels were all worn to the theater or the opera, but it was at the ball that they were gloriously resplendent, reached the height of opulence, and animated their owners.

> When her shoulders stunningly emerge from her bodice, when her trailing gown undulates behind her as she walks, when the brilliance of the silken folds enveloping her attracts everyone's gaze and displays her beauty, her only concern is the effect she is producing. This is the moment of her triumph. She is aware of it and has spared no expense to create it. Everything must contribute to the effect. Shimmering silvery fabrics, magnificent fabrics like those intended for queens, light gossamer fabrics, materials made of impalpable threads, like those worn by sylphs, golden brocaded cloth, twinkling like stars sown in the dark nocturnal heavens—these are the marvels that industry must create for her.[37]

Not all of the manuals, however, shared this lyrical enthusiasm about a kind of dress that was intended to metamorphose women by etherealizing them. On the contrary, some of them advised their readers to repress narcissistic exaltations of any kind in order to preserve a clear conscience and maintain an assiduous mastery of their deportment.

> It is especially at balls that you should resist the ridiculous temptation to be the belle. At home, because of the pains you take, you believe that you are ravishingly dressed. Your family's compliments reinforce the illusion. You arrive with the arrogant hope of eclipsing all the other toilettes, and as soon as you enter, you see your error and conclude that you are the least brilliant. You must guard against both this hope and this fear. First, it is unreasonable; and second, you run the risk of having to replace your triumphant mien with a disgruntled and fearful one, both of which are equally contrary to the modest and gracious appearance that characterizes a lady. In general, dress so that all of your clothes go together well and nothing clashes; otherwise, despite yourself, you will make a disagreeable impression offensive to courtesy.[38]

Young women had to realize that "dances have an enormous influence on the family's prospects and on social life,"[39] and that dress played—both as a sign of wealth and as a sexual value—a decisive role. A chaste but promising décolletage ranked high on the list of tactics deployed. A young woman's décolletage, very painstakingly arranged by her mother, who subtly calculated its erotic charge,[40] was not, however, displayed with impunity. "How many young women have paid with their life or their health for the charming audacity of their costumes, and on how many of those beautiful bare shoulders did death place his cold hand at the ballroom door!" lamented Dr. Lévy.[41] Brandishing their funereal lists on which consumption seemed to have mowed women down like a machine gun, the doctors vainly tried to alert those who left the ballroom without taking precautions.[42]

Presentations

On these solemn occasions, jewels—the quintessence of brilliance, dazzle, and wealth—always served a function that was both ornamental and
informative: as decoration they suggested the extent of a fortune, but how
they were worn was a far more reliable indicator of breeding. There were
many pitfalls: different stones went with different seasons, "so that those
who know how to dress well will never wear diamonds . . . during the summer, even at balls; they will substitute flowers, ribbons, and so forth."[43] On
the other hand, good taste required an ascetic luxury that induced women
to wear no more than one or two rings and only on the third finger. With
the exception the theater, concerts, and balls, moderation was imperative,
especially in the afternoon: "A woman who wears diamonds in the middle
of the day looks like a parvenu from a mile off," noted the Comtesse de
Bassanville.[44] In fact, only married women were supposed to wear diamonds; young girls were barely allowed to wear pearls and turquoise, while
widows were permitted only jade, black onyx, or black enamel jewelry.

The fan, which had a long history of gallantry, was another indispensable accessory in the ballroom. Along with the dance card and the little
bouquet of flowers wrapped in a lace handkerchief, it gave the finely gloved
hands of the young dancers something to do; but it was the more experienced women who made the most of this moveable curtain with its gleaming colors, delicate paintings, and extremely sumptuous mountings. Above
all, on the pretext of moving the air, the fan made graceful gestures possible; and the way it fluttered about, was folded or opened, raised or lowered,
revealed what seemed to be hidden and veiled what appeared exposed.
Continuing in movement what clothing could do only at rest, it made
other games, exchanges, maneuvers, and intrigues possible, thanks to the
furtive glances, whispered hints and the daring avowals it authorized precisely because it seemed to ban them.

When she returned home, a woman who was "comme il faut" at last put
on her final costume: the nightdress, which she would take off the next
morning when she got out of bed.

To make savoir-faire even more complicated, many other variables in-
tervened in the grand sequences that divided the day and regulated dress.
The seasons called for a range of specific colors and fabrics, and certain
recurring occasions required appropriate attire and behavior. At church,
for example, dress had to be very discreet; by so dressing, a woman could
demonstrate that she would not acknowledge there any kind of sumptuary
rivalry. Conspicuous underconsumption, which churchgoing endowed
with the new legitimacy of Christian humility, allowed one to distance
oneself from showy costumes, which were very numerous according to
fashionable sermon-writers, and which annoyed the manual-writers because of the behavior they encouraged. Comtess Drohojowska confided
the following to her imaginary young reader:

I was seated along one of the principal aisles; but as wide as it was, the *belles dames* found a way to brush against my chair with their vast skirts, causing their silken dresses and starched bouffante underskirts to cry out: it was a deafening froufrou made even louder by the incredible movements of their shoulders, their rapid, hurried gait, and the rough displacement of the chairs. I asked myself: "Are these the manners of a woman who is comme il faut, and should she appear to be so preoccupied with herself in the house of the Lord and disturb all the congregation with the rustling of her dress?

If the pretentious and noisy gait of certain women so sadly struck me, imagine my chagrin when, transforming myself into an observer for your benefit despite the holiness of the Lord's house, I noticed the arrogant, patronizing air with which far too many women took their places, disturbing, without even deigning to extend the courtesy of the apologetic smile called for by good manners, disturbing, I say, modestly dressed people, and paying no attention to the distraction and irritation they caused. But at least, I thought, once they have settled at their prie-dieux, these beautiful women will remember why they are paying a visit to the Lord and will put aside their arrogant manners. . . . My charitable hope was again doomed. After a very slight inclination of their heads, they took on their grand airs again, and, really, to see these adorned heads walk about the congregation or take their places without bowing toward the altar, one could easily forget where one was and believe one at a society gathering where the guests' only concern was to dominate and crush others beneath the weight of their own superiority.[45]

If a clergyman were invited to one's home for the evening, modesty required that "the female guests be forewarned to arrive in high-necked dresses," for "a man of the cloth would most certainly not remain at a gathering where women were in décolletage."[46]

Wedding dress constituted the sole exception to the rules of Christian reserve. It was to be chaste but luxurious. Indeed, "a young woman is permitted to display with pride many articles from her trousseau."[47] But on any other occasion, only after she married could a woman, thenceforth the manifestation of the socioeconomic position of her spouse, justify certain adornments and a level of expense that the single state still forbade and widowhood no longer authorized.[48]

Everyone knows that whatever dowry a young lady possesses, both the form and the ornamentation of her clothes should display less elegance and brilliance than those of married women. Cashmere shawls, very rich furs, and diamonds are not permitted, nor are various other brilliant adornments. Young ladies who defy these very sensible proprieties lead people to believe that they are possessed of an unbridled love of luxury and deprive themselves of the pleasure of receiving such finery from a husband.[49]

The extreme simplicity imposed on young women was primarily a matrimonial strategy that different authors clearly explained.

> The surest method for catching a husband is to appear "to have simple tastes."
> I know ten husbands ruined by their wives' appetite for luxuries, who had
> married them because they "had simple tastes." For a young lady to have
> "simple tastes" she must abhor cashmeres and luxurious furs and utterly disdain expensive jewels and diamonds . . . until she finds a good husband.[50]

These accessories, forbidden to young women who were to be "like angels and not reliquaries,"[51] could be acquired only through marriage. "A maiden, even if she has reached the half-century mark, has no right to wear them and would appear ridiculous if she did."[52]

Whatever the case, women of a certain age had to forego "bright colors, elegant designs, the latest fashions, and graceful ornaments such as feathers, flowers, and jewels. An elderly person who is bareheaded and wears necklaces, bracelets, and so on, or short-sleeved, décolleté dresses offends propriety as much as she harms her own interests and dignity."[53] A devalued aesthetic capital could not be refloated by finery that would only call attention to its erosion.

The handling of colors required an even more refined skill during the Second Empire as colors multiplied in number thanks to new processes that enlivened the assortment of fabrics wildly. Replacing traditional vegetable dyes, a myriad of synthetic colors such as "Solferino"(!) red, "Bismarck" brown, and "Empress" blue became particular favorites. Moreover, with the progress of organic chemistry, greens, violets, pinks, and yellows were combined.[54] All of them were harsh and raw, for this was the era when fashion inspired a riot of clashing colors and the loudest combinations. "Nowadays we are far removed from the middle classes of past centuries, who preferred to dress themselves in brown or gray on ordinary days and reserved white and black for important occasions," noted *Le Magasin des demoiselles*.[55] Nevertheless, good taste indulged in this chromatic euphoria and its solecisms only at a distance, and avoided the contrasts dear to provincials and parvenus. Instead, it skillfully harmonized gradations of secondary colors with the dominant color. Toward the end of the Second Empire, tones became more muted, but the dangers persisted. Thus, women were exhorted to avoid "combining colors that could attract epigrams, such as a straw-colored dress and a green hat, because if your complexion isn't perfectly white, . . . your spiteful rivals will certainly point out that your face looks like a lemon surrounded by leaves."[56] The whiteness of a woman's skin therefore affected the choice of colors. In his *Hygiène vestimentaire*, Auguste Debay expounded on the consequences of this at length.

All the shades of yellow, ranging from straw to the warmest ochre, suit a
brunette perfectly; yellow flowers placed in her hair lighten her complexion,
while the same flowers would make a blonde almost pallid. Soft pinks and
greens, lilac and azure, suit blondes perfectly; dark blue, violet, brown and
black are also good for bringing out the brilliance of their light complexions.
Tartan plaids, with their dominant greens and reds, are, on the contrary, very
bad for brunettes. Women with jet-black hair and very dark skin should not
wear red clothing, because this color darkens their complexions even more
and makes them look like mulatresses.[57]

To counter the dark pigmentation characteristic of the inferior dark
races and the sunburned skins of the lower classes (who worked outdoors),
an entire cosmetology of "electrifying baths" and "freckle-removing milk"
was developed during the nineteenth century.[58] This cosmetology would

Country attire

need only to retool itself when, during the 1920s, "tanning" in its turn took on the prestigious signification traditionally conferred on pale skin. This reversal of trends would correspond to a society that increasingly engaged hitherto inactive social groups in work, thus making "free" time more and more rare, and therefore precious. From then on tanning was integral to a new field of significative oppositions, so that in the twentieth century it symbolizes exactly what "milk-white skin" had signified in the nineteenth: idleness, or the economic ability to waste time "doing nothing" and to display this gratifying unproductiveness.

The colors of fabrics were also chosen for the way they looked in daylight, gaslight, and candlelight. A woman of taste knew that in the glow of candlelight violet lost its blue hues and appeared red, turquoise silk completely lost its brilliance, peacock-green yellowed, and all yellow shades in plush, silk, and satin became even richer. She knew that out-of-doors an umbrella lined with a mauve or violet fabric altered her complexion, and she was always looking for light colors to match her dress and remove the shadows from her face. She also knew exactly how the grain of cloth like wool could absorb the brightness of sunlight and how satin could reflect, muslin soften, and velvet dim it.[59]

This delicate education in textiles, which was subject to a multitude of moral and aesthetic imperatives, concerned the entire toilette. But rules and conditions of use also corresponded to each of the articles that constituted the wardrobe.

Hats

Excluded from balls, receptions, or the home, everywhere else the hat was always an indispensable element of appearance—a woman *en cheveu*, or hatless, was lower-class. It could affect physiognomy by shortening long or lowering turned-up noses, and it could affect the silhouette by making it seem taller. A favored object of fashion, its social value was tightly linked to the passage of time that ineluctably depreciated it, to the talent of the milliner who might be more or less inspired, and to the discernment of its wearer, who had to coordinate it with a series of variables. Birds, feathers, flowers, fruit, leaves, nosegays of wheat, tulle, lace, ruffled taffetas, garlands, ruches, ribbons, bows, or flounces—all of these provided the matériel for an infinite number of combinations. Care had to be taken with the position of the hat, for "if a hat is worn too high on the head its luxuriousness will not prevent it from making a sweet and dreamy physiognomy appear foolish or a woman of severe and reserved beauty seem spiteful."[60]

Despite its infinitely changing nature, headgear during the Second Empire did display several unvarying characteristics. Always modest in size, hats prolonged and terminated the slimming lines that rose from the ample crinoline to the shoulders and then redescended to the neckline. For day wear and social calls, bonnets, capelines, hoods, and all the hats with rounded front brims and side veils reigned without rivals over comme il faut heads. Embellishents were the only thing that varied in this basic form, which rounded into a helmet shape and fanned out at the nape.

Around 1866, however, along with the decline of the crinoline, these hats gave way to brimless caps that were even smaller and permitted, since they were worn forward, a considerable amount of hair—in a chignon, braided, or crimped—to be shown. In the country, for trips and visits to spas, on the other hand, round straw hats with narrow front brims or large floppy side brims decorated with rustic vegetation prevailed.

Shoes

At the opposite pole of the figure, forms of footwear evolved more slowly and varied less. The toe was sometimes tapered, sometimes rounded or squared, while heels were sometimes high, sometimes low, in cycles that lasted about five years. The diversification of footwear caused by technical developments in the shoe industry nevertheless increased the number of specific types. Jointed clogs, fur-lined slippers, pumps with French seams, flat or buttoned shoes, laced ankle boots, or seamless boots with embossed uppers—each was intended for a specific purpose. For outdoor wear a new trend asserted itself: "The ankle boot dethroned the shoe and reigned as conqueror. Nothing is as pretty as a light laced boot imprisoning and shortening a foot! It slims the lower leg and imparts elegance to a woman's walk."[61]

"The heart of all male fixations: . . . the foot."

Here we are at the heart of all male fixations, the spark that inflamed their desires, the anchor of all their fantasies: the foot. Ever since it was completely hidden by dresses, it became the object of a universal, ardent, and fanatical cult. "Oh! the foot!" exclaimed Ly'onell, the pseudonymous author of an extensive treatise, *The Art of Lifting One's Dress*. "Who wouldn't give his soul for a tiny foot, narrow and arched, proudly turned up at the instep, whose sole is so well formed that water can run under it without wetting it!"[62]

To speak of shoes is above all to evoke what they tightly enclose and also to recall what shoes prolong: ankles and calves, those hidden parts without which the *petits théâtres* would not have existed. Later on as feet became exposed, this fetishistic fascination would decline. Indeed, today, except for a few die-hard disciples,[63] it has even disappeared. But during the nineteenth century, the intensity of the reactions that feet aroused and the obsessiveness of the behaviors they induced constantly asserted themselves.

> If a clever coquette allows you to see only the tip of a dainty foot that attracts you . . . to the point of giving you an immoderate desire to see what is concealed, a damsel, on the other hand, innocent and naive, will find it quite natural to reveal her foot all the way to the ankle, without suspecting that the top of her boot may gape, that her stocking is creased, and above all, that very little need be shown in order to suggest even more.
>
> And that's not all: . . . How to show off her legs and knees is something that a sophisticated woman must not ignore, and which, moreover, very few of them do ignore. Show me the first woman to enter a drawing room, and only by observing how she places her feet and arranges her dress, I will tell you, first of all, if she is single, married, or a widow, if she has a lover, and finally, whether her lover is blond or brunette.[64]

It was in the privacy of her own home, when a woman was in a vulnerable dishabille, that the seductive power of a slippered foot seemed to reach its apogee. Henri Despaigne gave this advice: "Above all, madame, exercise all your taste in choosing those delicate slippers that are barely held on by the tips of your toes until, with a flirtatious movement that frees your foot from the folds of your dress, you walk, shivering, to the fireplace where the night fire is burning. A foot glimpsed in this way is so very seductive. Just ask your husband."[65]

Perhaps because it figured among the pleasures that could be talked about, the theme of the titillating slipper recurs frequently in sartorial literature.[66] This is why the pious and severe Countess Drohojowska condemned that accessory which was all too obviously sexually charged: "When you are well," she wrote, "wear slippers as seldom as possible."[67]

For dress wear during the winter, ankle boots were made of velvet or heavy cloth, and for the summer of lighter materials. Sometimes they matched dresses or skirts: "White for evening dress and black for the other times,"[68] whichever better suited the wearer. The erotic functions of heels that caused the back to arch and uppers that shortened the foot were inseparable from their social signification: because they hindered exertion and physical mobility, shoes also proclaimed the idleness of their owners, or at the very least the impossiblity of their doing any work that required them to really use their bodies. Their shoes forced them to stay within certain socially valorized spaces. It was, of course, "very difficult to show off a brazenly narrow and well-arched foot without pinching it, and to walk straight and steadily on diamond-shaped high heels,"[69] but this was one of the burdens of rank determined by social life.

Gloves

Glazed or matte depending on the time of day, cinnamon or amadou for day dress, light-colored and brilliant for evenings at concerts or balls, gloves, with their invariably muted colors, made what they covered look smaller. They refined the hand—another highly eroticized part of the body and another indication of social standing[70]—without, however, preventing the swelling of fingers from too tight a fit.

Covering the organs of touch and prehension, gloves, like shoes, emphasized sexual insinuations by simultaneously reining in and stimulating desire. Witness their influence in the amorous preludes recounted in novels, or the instructions on the proper gestures that called a delicate proxemics into play.

> When a woman of high rank pays a visit to your wife or daughter, you should accompany her to her carriage, and when her footman opens the door, you should present your forearm to the grand lady so that she can lean on it. If you are already somewhat intimate with her, you may give her your hand and even assist her by taking her arm.
>
> If you are leaving the theater, a concert, or the opera, you should take the same precautions, but above all avoid touching her bare skin. A woman's hand, and especially that of a young woman, may not be held in yours for more than a fleeting moment.[71]

These were perilous maneuvers that would disappear with the glove.

Dresses

Reigning elements of the feminine wardrobe and symbols of a society, the crinoline and later the bustle, in their textile exuberance and radical impracticality, reduced a woman to the role of dazzling idol, which distinguished her absolutely from men and distanced her physically from their universe.[72] Like the Napoleonic Code or the vogue of the cigar, crinolined dresses contributed to the sexual division of sociability that was physically expressed in apartments by the opposition of the boudoir and the smoking room.

As we have seen, the fullness of crinolines during the Second Empire was more the reassertion of a style than the sudden appearance of a new fashion. Moreover, the etymology of the word explains the beginnings of the thing. When dresses became fuller, for a long time petticoats that were starched or fitted with flounces were used. But stacking them layer upon layer had its limits, and in order to enable dresses to balloon, stiffened linen or woolen skirts were fabricated. Their warp and weft, made of horsehair, or *crin*, puffed up the layered petticoats even more. During the Second Empire "crinoline" still referred to this rigid underskirt, but by synecdoche, it soon came to mean the dress itself, especially when the latter became supported only by an immense underskirt made of steel bands. In fact, around 1854, the legs were liberated from that extraordinary prison of petticoats, which was both a burden and an oven, by a metallic armature made of concentric hoops.[73] One entered it by lowering the front part and then attached it to the corset by a system of hooks. Like the dress, it followed fashion changes, flattening out in the front around 1862 in order to spread out majestically at the rear, all the while remaining quite bouffant over the hips. At that time the hoops were oval and shifted the fullness of

Petticoats

the dress, whose great folds—now drawn back to the train—anticipated what was to become the bustle. From then on the volume of the crinoline decreased steadily, its trimmings became more discreet and its colors less violent. In the meantime, when the formal crinoline was in its most ample phase, it attained diameters of more than three yards and required thirty yards of cloth, thus forming a receptacle for a profusion of trimmings, lace flounces, loops of ribbon, pillow lace, gathered and pleated tulle, garlands, velvet ruches, decorated hems, tufts of bows, and clusters of gems, foliage, and flowers.

Moving about in these majestically rotund and magisterially decorated costumes required an extremely delicate skill because it was practiced in interiors cluttered with furniture and bibelots, in rooms and on seats that were only rarely suitable. Their excessive size barred access to certain spaces and led to innovations in furniture such as poufs, circular settees, s-shaped couches, and the tête-bêche armchair, which provided some comfort.[74] Nevertheless, sitting down remained a daily problem for Second Empire women. Because of the constant danger of the hoops coiling up, skilled contortions were required, not to mention "privies" that were inaccessible without the help of a domestic. For men, too, the crinoline was a great obstacle: "All courtesy and wit come to a halt before this iron citadel that settles itself down on your feet and scratches your legs, when it isn't rising up to skin your elbows."[75] Courting, dancing with, or offering one's arm to these recluses confined within the cage-dress required acrobatic moves made even more difficult by the corpulence or stiffness of the beaus. All their dexterity concentrated on orbiting around this cone of fabrics and maneuvering at its side without ever making a false step "on pain of hearing a disastrous and harrowing cracking noise."[76]

Walking out-of-doors also required a painstaking technique that did not always prevent unforeseen incidents, which were seized upon by vaudevillians and caricaturists.

Yet nothing could disturb the absolute reign of the crinoline. Neither the vituperations of the Church, the moralists' mockery, nor the jibes of street urchins who called it "street-sweeper" prevented it from being worn universally—on foot, in carriages, on trains, where narrow doors often gave rise to dramatic incidents, and even in the mountains by the first "hikers," alpenstock in hand.

Totally concealing the real shapes of female bodies, from pelvis to heels, this edifice exaggerated the unreal shape of an ideal body, whose miniscule and arched foot supported a well-fed calf, a rounded thigh under monumental hips and a grandiose rump. But among the fantasies that it inspired lurked also the fear of being deceived by appearances that were too flattering to be true. A thousand crinoline anecdotes made the rounds:

How many friends we know who thought they were marrying something! Alas!

Everyone in Bordeaux remembers how ridiculous a great lady was made to appear last year at the Bouscat racetrack. One of the cords holding her immense set of skirts broke, and she saw her sylphlike petticoat, which was fitted out with enormous flounces stuffed with straw and camlet, tumble onto the pavement. So that, finding herself in a state of utmost "platitude," she almost died of a stroke; yet only then did she appear a "natural" woman.

The wretched dehipped woman then left Bordeaux for good and retired to the coast at Floirac, where she is bringing a lawsuit against her dressmaker.[77]

"Unforeseen incidents . . . were seized upon by caricaturists."

Moreover, the cloth dome and its callipygian mirage could conceal all physical defects, and even a shameful world of infections and deformities. This was pointed out by a physician in an ironic *Defense of the Crinoline* that he addressed to a colleague:

Consider how admirably a case of dropsy some ten years old can be hidden! The crinoline . . . is a godsend for both doctor and patient because it not only removes from view the misfortunes that you know about but also constitutes a sturdy instrument under which we can place, at will, vesicatories large and small, drains of all sizes, and cauteries or moxas of any width. And also, note this: when you get a patient whose body does not exactly exude the scent of musk, . . . you can transform her into a perfumed odalisque by writing a prescription for an "iron-rimmed" crinoline, under which you can firmly fasten at the small of the back a little disinfecting instrument of my own invention, which, all false modesty aside, I daresay is as ingenious as it is effective.[78]

The crinoline did not invariably arouse such malevolent suspicions. Its mystery and majesty also attracted wholehearted partisans like Théophile Gautier:

They [women] are right to prefer these ample, full, richly displayed and powerful skirts to the narrow scabbards that sheathed their mothers and grandmothers. The waist now appears elegant and narrow amid this abundance of folds that spread out like a whirling dervish's fustanella. The upper body stands out advantageously, and the entire person becomes a graceful pyramid. The mass of rich fabrics serves as a pedestal for the bust and head, the only important parts of the body now that nudity is no longer permitted.[79]

But what was the purpose of the rows of eyelets, hooks, and buttons that fastened the garment in the back, fitting it to a cage that was itself attached to a patiently laced corset? What meaning can one assign to this piece of heavy machinery to which women were harnessed, to the interminable hours they wasted in preparation, and to their anxiety about obeying correctly the thousands of decrees issued in the name of elegance, unless it was their desire to appear seductive in their barricades and to distinguish themselves within the limits of comme il faut and its implications of leisure, wealth, spare time, and domestic servants?

Although an ideology of comfort imported from England began to influence intermittently the design of men's clothing, women's dress remained resolutely antifunctional and derived all its prestige from the constraints it imposed. But the bourgeoisie could not consciously accept the idea of waste or work at squandering time and money without moral ra-

A woman, crinolated (left) and real (right)

tionalizations. "Your toilette should be a duty, only rarely a pleasure and never a serious occupation,"[80] wrote the Countess Drohojwska. "To take pleasure in wasting time at your toilette would be to disregard your true duty. To neglect it because of indifference would be an even more blameful laziness."[81] Thus, "moderation" was ranged against coquettery and carelessness.

Shawls

The cashmere shawl, another typical constituent of tasteful finery, was a close ally of the crinoline because the latter allowed the shawl to be displayed at its full length. Shawls were folded down the middle or along the diagonal and draped on the neck or worn off the shoulder around the arms. In any case they particularly needed to display perfectly symmetrical and multicolored palm designs.

The 1855 Universal Exposition, which attracted a flood of exotic objects from all over the world, clinched the shawl's triumph by assigning it a place of honor. Shawls were very expensive—some cost as much as 10,000 francs—and for a long time they were the only truly durable item in a woman's wardrobe, long-wearing and almost immune to fashion changes. They were therefore often bequeathed, listed along with jewels or lace in wills, while all the rest of grandmother's accessories journeyed down the long, circuitous paths of the used-clothes trade. "The shawl witnesses the passing of every fashion, it outlasts all the new dresses; patient because eternal, it is the elegant woman's deity."[82] Nevertheless, the imperishable shawl was abandoned during the 1860s by the upper classes because mass-produced imitations, even if imperfect, spread widely and deprived the original of its signification and value. Moreover, the rapid growth of capitalism caused this durable heirloom to lose its attraction, while the financial and cultural ability to update one's wardrobe, continuously and judiciously according to fashion rather than wear and tear, assumed unprecedented prestige. Of course, because of its quality and its origins—generally Indian but sometimes North African[83]—and the way it draped, softly and sensuously, the cashmere shawl remained a brilliant sign of its owner's rank, even though it was no longer worn except on rare occasions.[84] Soon, even if it had vanished from the shoulders of rich bourgeoises, the precious shawl remained in their possession, in boxes, awaiting strange transformations. As Charles Blanc wrote in 1875, "We have seen and we will continue to see young women who, having discovered an exquisitely fine and delightfully colored cashmere in their trousseau, dare not wear it as a shawl but gather it around their waist to make it look like a tunic, fastened with a velvet rosette."[85]

On pedestals, tables, or pianos it was even transformed into a throw.

THE MASCULINE WARDROBE

After the Revolution male civilian clothing was significantly simplified, and its forms and possible combinations limited. Since the same costume was appropriate for several occasions, a man rarely changed his clothes more than three times a day.

Dressing gown

Dressing Gowns

At home when he was casually dressed, a man wore his dressing gown. Warm and quilted, made of velvet or brocade in bright and variegated colors, decorated with braid, embroidery, and designs usually based on oriental motifs, it had long symbolized an art of living, a quintessentially bourgeois comfort. Writers, notably Diderot and Balzac, warmly praised its charms, its comforting presence, and poetic uniqueness.[86] All the same, the dressing gown constituted a curious split between men and women, or rather a curious chassé-croisé in which men were dazzling and women drab. Constrasting sharply with both the modesty of the clothes women wore in private and the dullness of men's public dress, the dressing gown was like a fossilized remnant of the ancien régime's splendors. Auguste Debay observed that

> this costume is as sumptuous as outdoor or town wear is simple. . . . Formerly, when rich fabrics composed town dress and fashion sanctioned gold embroidery, braid, trimmings, and so on at home, négligé wear did not amount to much, but nowadays since fashion forces the black suit and top hat on dukes and bourgeois, financiers and shop clerks, our rich gents compensate for this insipid uniformity by wearing a magnificent indoor costume. Thus an elegant type makes his social calls in a simple black suit, but in his apartment he wraps himself in a superb dressing gown that cost ten times more than his suit. His velvet toque, embellished with embroidery and a massive gold tassel, could have cost him a five-hundred-franc note, and his admirable slippers, of morocco covered with velvet, gold, and silk, surpass the finest patent-leather boots. The apartment in which Monsieur receives is as luxurious as his dishabille. And, believe me, he is not the only Sardanapalus whose glory and honor depends on astonishing his visitors with this magnificent display.[87]

This departure from bourgeois sobriety, tolerated because of its implicit intimacy, ceased as soon as one went out. Then, black cloth was imperative and provided the material for two essential articles of clothing—the frock coat and the suit, which corresponded imperatively to the major sequences of the daily schedule, morning and evening (in the social sense). Bourgeois in origin, this demarcation in costume began in the eighteenth century and became more pronounced in the nineteenth.

The Frock Coat

"One knows that it would be as ridiculous to go out in the morning in tails as to enter a drawing room in the evening in a frock coat; likewise it would be strange for a woman to wear diamonds during the day, and a hat in the evening."[88] As town dress, simple and severe, the frock coat was proper for day visits, "subject to variations, of course, which the position one occupies and the capacity in which one is received should make obvious."[89] But we should note that a first visit or one to a person of a certain rank precluded informal dress: "To call on a superior . . . in a frock coat or a paletot would be grossly impolite."[90] Even during the day the black suit had to be worn on these occasions.

Frock coats: a gradation of ages and occupations

The frock coat did not change, on the whole, during the Second Empire. Nevertheless, through the differing lengths of its tails it served various purposes and acquired diverse significations and attributes. Thus, the age and the occupation of its wearer could be recognized easily within a gradation that ranged from the jacket (a kind of embryonic frock coat for adolescents) to the frock coat "à la landlord" (descending to cover the calves of old men), by way of the magistrate's frock coat (a veritable greatcoat) or the young man's coat (of middling dimensions).

A riding coat of English origin, the redingote was converted into travel and country wear when it was imported into France at the beginning of the eighteenth century.[91] Over the course of a long-term development, as in the case of many other articles of clothing, the frock coat, initially rustic, was refined little by little as it underwent urbanization to become the principal element of semiformal dress in the nineteenth century.

The Black Suit

With the exception of official and court dress, it was the black suit, or tails, that constituted formal dress, the other high point of the masculine sartorial program. De rigeur in the evening, at a formal dinner, ball, or reception, its cut was fixed—like the frock coat's—and varied only in details: collars rose or fell a bit, lapels grew or diminished, and waists were variously emphasized. Made of black cloth lined in black silk, without flaps, the pockets hidden in the seam, or under basques, and the back prolonged in tails, it was always accompanied by a vest in white piqué or black satin, a batiste tie, black trousers, and brilliant pumps. Like every other article of clothing, the black suit revealed nuances of wealth, occupation, or social origin through minute details of cut, quality, or wear that, by exaggerating these features, caricatures help reconstitute.

Caught between tails and frock coat, tailors redoubled their efforts in an attempt to impose more or less colorful and eccentric "seasonal" clothing for casual wear. But the weight of convention was not to be overthrown with a single undertaking. Except for some English imports associated with sporting activities, like knickerbockers[92] marketed under the name of *culotte de golfe*, the results were not very convincing. In travel clothing, and in clothes for the country or watering places, a relative originality and casualness of dress were tolerated. However, everywhere and anytime, vulgarity could ensnare the heedless: "In the country during the summer men have adopted white cotton damask or nankeen clothing. This may be in good taste at home, but it certainly is in the worst taste to present oneself in this way, either while promenading or in any other place where one might encounter women.

Even in the country, a man who goes out wearing a cap resembles a lackey and shows himself to be thoroughly vulgar."[93]

The Trouser

The abolition of knee breeches, rejected legacy of the ancien régime, meant of course the loss of elegantly shaped calves molded by stockings, but on the other hand, the trousers that replaced breeches concealed the unsightly legs of the majority. Henceforth it was only in the cut of the canons (which changed in width about every five years) and in material (black cloth for formal wear, pinstripes or fine checks for day wear) that trousers could still exhibit any distinctive charm.

The Paletot

During the Second Empire the paletot enjoyed an astonishing triumph. Edmond Texier, along with many others, underlined the paradox by recalling the paletot's origin: "Here is the last word in elegance for the *fashionables*, dandies, lions, and yellow gloves—they all wear this garment of the peasant and sailor."[94]

In fact, it became indispensable for more than one reason. Though its shape was not attractive, it was quite ample and enveloping, hiding from view other clothing and consequently any sign of status or occupation. Veritable zero degree of meaning, ideal product of democratic leveling, this garment prefigures that which would become neutral clothing because of its essential function of camouflage[95] and relative lack of differentiating connotations, though different degrees of wear, facings, or richness in the collar persisted.

Confronted with this dissolution of distinctions, the authors of manuals, such as Eugène Chapus, had to protest:

> Gradually all men were made to look alike, but general assimilation was not completely achieved because they were not blended into a single model. This general fusion needed to be achieved; we now have it. The tailors received the watch words: convenience, comfort, vulgarity, effacement; the paletot was created. They threw it at us, this perfection of the annihilation of dress, the ne plus ultra of egalitarian clothing, a uniform worthy of a Phalanstery. Try to find a form in this barrel of cloth. Guess if you can who is the gentleman in this rough, round shell. All your study and observation will be a dead loss. Is it a Hindu, a Chinese, a Tartar, an Eskimo who moves, walks, rolls before your eyes? You cannot tell.[96]

Yet the entire value of the paletot lay precisely in its invisibility, achieved through anonymity. With it "clothing had to be inferred, . . . which permitted a man of the world to dress simply, go out, walk around, make, if necessary, any sort of foray in the simple attire of an ordinary passer-by."[97] This offered respite in the war of appearances, such as was sought by even the great aristocrats of the eighteenth century who roamed the city incognito in their "chenille."[98]

The Vest

Paletots, tails, frock coats—these black, enveloping garments offered little room for ornamentation or imagination. These were concentrated on the vest, an article that acquired a signifying and aesthetic function, all the more exaggerated in that it was confined to an almost hidden region.

Avatar of a jacket that was all the rage under Louis XVI, vests "were magnificently embroidered with hunting scenes, cavalry battles, and even naval engagements. They were extraordinarily expensive," the Baronne d'Oberkirch reported.[99] In the next century, the vest was adopted by the bourgeoisie and quickly became an institution. Encasing and then supporting abdomens, which over the course of years and from dinner to dinner became increasingly portly, the vest often served as a corset. This functional aspect aside, it owed its prestige to its rich fabrics and, for a time, its ornaments and vivid colors, cherished vestiges of aristocratic glamour. Yet the red and green velvets with enormous motifs or delirious rosettes that covered the chests of the Romantics gave way, as early as the Second Empire, to more sober fabrics and colors, more discreet, less busy designs. Only white vests in kerseymere or piqué were permitted in formal dress, for example, and colored vests could appear only during social calls or at home. "In these circumstances," declared Emile Kerckhoff, "vests in the most varied weaves and colors can be worn, and they are adorned nowadays with carved buttons sometimes composed of enamels or stones."[100] Extravagant designs or loud colors were ruled out. After 1854, the manuals proclaimed: "We loathe . . . those vests with gigantic flowers that can be seen from one end of the street to the other."[101] The tendency was to harmonize the fabric of the vests with the rest of the outfit, so that soon vests, coats, and trousers were all cut from the same cloth—the three-piece suit.

Similarly, jewelry was driven out of the regions where it seemed to have taken refuge. "We loathe . . . those rings and charms that men load onto their fingers and vests like retired quack merchants," proclaimed the teachers of savoir-faire. "A snuff box, a watch, a lorgnon if one is near-sighted, all in gold, are the only jewelry that a reasonable man can allow himself."[102] An ascetic luxury, a chic simplicity—these were the surest ways to outdistance the nouveaux-riches.

Vests also varied in necklines and buttoning, according to the age, station, and gravity of the wearer. For example, the young dandy's vest had only three buttons at its base and opened widely on a skillfully starched shirtfront, while the honorable magistrate's vest had more than a dozen buttons that went all the way up to the cravat.

The Cravat

The cravat "is to clothes what truffles are to dinner," declared Balzac.[103] A critical and subtle detail of dress, dominating all the others, requiring a refined technique (knotting), and the only part of dress subject to somewhat rapid fashion change, the cravat completed one's appearance and imbued it with its own accent. Its history, rich in metamorphoses,[104] became more intense after the Revolution. Although the sans-culottes had momentarily replaced this shameful sign of aristocracy with a common foulard casually tied around the neck, the cravat nevertheless reappeared after the Terror in the dress of the foppish *muscadins*, and then during the Directory in that of the *incroyables* who flaunted enormous green cravats as the sign of their royalist sentiments.[105] An object of passionate attention among the dandies and "lions" who turned its daily construction into a ritualistic practice upon which they staked their honor, the cravat inspired a series of half-practical, half-humorous "physiologies" concerning its types and uses,[106] and this during a period—the Restoration and the July Monarchy—when its appearance and handling were unprecedentedly complicated.

Emerging from the laundry in the form of a starched band, the cravat was raw material to be transformed by a painstaking series of operations: its ends were folded; it was passed around the neck, and tied into a knot; then, the proper shape obtained, it was smoothed out again with the aid of a small iron, and so on. In short, so much time squandered, so many operations "lost," occupations still reserved for an idle elite.[107] Indeed, "the artisan hurries to arrive at his workshop at dawn, the clerk to be at his office on time; from daybreak the merchant thinks about what he will sell during the day, the lowly bureaucrat devotes himself totally to his thankless tasks and the businessman to his big deals. None of them has time to compete with the fashionable man who can devote two hours or more to dressing."[108]

The neck, to be sure, was no longer imprisoned all the way to the lower lip, but the silk, satin, or starched velvet cloth was wound around it several times, hugging it tightly with an even more refined knot. In addition, the newly invented detachable collar forced the cravat to imitate its stiffness by means of rather uncomfortable stiffening with slender whalebone, horsehair, or pig bristle. Of all the articles of clothing, the cravat was the only one that owed so little to its manufacturer and so much to its owner. Its construction, moreover, required too fine a skill to entrust it to anyone else.[109] Often surpassing the understanding of the master, handling the cravat always surpassed that of the servant.

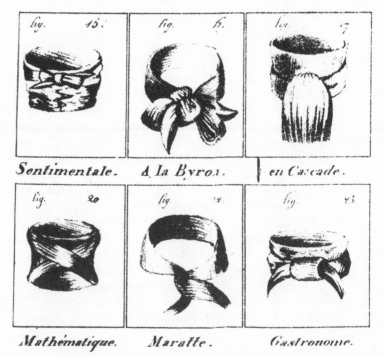

Pedestals for the head: the cravat "is to clothes what truffles are to dinner."
(Balzac)

The different manuals of cravat physiology were directed less at the dandies who, in essence, consulted vade mecums only to distance themselves from them,[110] than at the bourgeois in pursuit of elegance and anxious about mastering this sign, all the more complex and important in that it served as a pedestal for the head. "Thermometer by which was judged the degree of taste and intelligence of a *fahionable*,"[111] this accessory gave rise to a literature that revealed the cravat's power to confer distinction in a society that feared the lack of differentiation but had yet to experience the equalizing impact of ready-made clothing. "Amidst the general leveling that threatens society," noted the publisher of one of these works, "amidst the fusion of ranks and conditions, amidst the universal flood of petty, inferior pretensions directed at superior grand pretensions, we thought to render a signal service to the upper classes, to hold out so to speak, a veritable life buoy by proffering an *Art of Wearing One's Cravat*."[112]

In the second half of the century the inordinate role assigned to this piece of cloth diminished along with its volume. "If one compares," Emile Kerckhoff remarked in 1865, "the simple ribbon worn around the neck, more as finery than a garment, to the cravats in which the beaus of the Directory buried their chins as well as the lower part of their faces, one would easily be convinced that fashion has reached one of those extremities where a reaction begins to take place."[113] This statement, however, ignores the fact that the tendency toward greater comfort, no matter how relative,[114] can establish customs in which differentiating details still persist. Just as the tails of the frock coat lengthened according to the age, gravity, and position of its wearer, the cravat, along with the detachable collar, underwent a similar development: the cravat became fuller and the collar grew higher, hence the expression *se pousser du col*, or "to carry one's head high." Or, more precisely, propriety in dress forced each age group to respond differently to changes in fashion that shrank collars and cravats. Self-respect or age led men to diverge more and more from fashion up to the point of total resistance.

"Self-respect or age led men to diverge more and more
from fashion."

Although the cravat grew simpler it did not change color: white for formal dress, black for informal wear. Apart from these alternatives, however, the cravat, along with vests, was the only article of clothing "in which the brilliance of colors and embroidery found a refuge."[115] An elite of the cravat, model artisans of a task that was ephemeral and had to be begun anew ceaselessly, persisted into the Second Empire.

> Not everyone knows how to tie a knot as artistically as our Messieurs Dandizettes of the boulevards who spend two whole hours fashioning and destroying it. In elegant society, an irreproachable cravat knot is an essential part of dress. It does not matter whether the knot is "simple," "compound," "without ends," or "with floating tips": art is always involved. And there are certain apparently "casual" knots that require a long session before the mirror and more than one foot-stamping, more than one exclamation of impatience! A social lion swiftly appraises his rivals' strengths, weaknesses, and probabilities of success by their cravats; depending on whether he believes them superior or inferior to himself, envy or disdain slips into his heart and appears on his lips.[116]

It is easy to deride men with nothing to do who became skillful in tying the ends of a bit of percale because therein lay their entire genius. In fact they were conforming to a code of savoir-faire that decreed that "an ill-worn cravat is enough to create an unfavorable impression of the person being presented or recommended" and prescribed, "Wear your cravat properly, and never wear cravats of less than irreproachable freshness, the dual indication of orderliness and cleanliness."[117] They did not deny the logic of expenditure behind the rules of "comme il faut"; rather they openly embraced them and made an ethic of it.

The Glove

For the bourgeoisie, gloves were as imperative as hats.[118] They illustrate the dialectic of conformism and distinction inherent in clothing behavior in mobile societies. Casting an egalitarian veil over "chirographic" defects, over the original stigmata graven on the hands, gloves became also an indispensable accessory of social demarcation. "Gloves are worn for the same reason businessmen, financiers, and lawyers wear green or dark glasses—to conceal the cards they hold," noted Bertall.[119] Yet, as a physiology of the glove noted, "despite the confusion of ranks, the richness and simplicity of dress, despite the impenetrable veils which cover those driven by pleasure and their efforts to appear other than they are, the glove, this divine and powerful intermediary, exposes deceit and reveals truth. Order reigns, and everyone resumes his place in society depending on the degree of beauty and intelligence he received from nature."[120]

The glove hid the hand, but its form, material, color, and uses regulated by a meticulous code were revelatory. Shades (pale blue, pearl gray, peach, tobacco brown, fawn, pale yellow)[121] and materials (doeskin, beaver, kid, reindeer, dog) corresponded to the different phases of the quotidian cycle. Mornings called for dark colors, while medium shades were suitable for social calls. Yet "too light a shade was in bad taste, giving the appearance of having donned evening gloves early."[122] At balls gloves had to be brilliantly white; at the theater or in a drawing room, straw or buttercup yellow were preferred. These were the basic precepts, but color could also indicate social, moral, or political predispositions.

> After the death of Charles X, certain uncommitted, clumsy deputies attempted to use gloves for political ends. They appeared in the lobby of the Opéra and the Théâtre-Italien wearing a yellow glove on one hand and a black one on the other. The black hand opened drawing room doors in the faubourg Saint-Germain; the yellow hand was the one that dipped into the public till. Did they meet a legitimist? Quickly they withdrew from their pocket the hand in mourning and proffered it. But what if they found themselves before a member of the royal entourage? Then the yellow hand appeared.[123]

Whereas the cravat signified dexterity, the glove indicated a keen understanding of materials and their purposes.

> How many different meanings are in fact contained in the glove's material, from humble rabbit skin, cotton and lambskin, to white cannequin gloves embroidered in silk, by way of reindeer, chamois, beaver, kid in a thousand shades, and finally, the plain cannequin! What a host of significations in the various shades of kid! They are infinite. Without saying a word, a dandy tells you whether he is about to mount his horse, drive his tandem, make his calls, attend a wedding, visit an ambassador or a linen-draper, or go to the theater. You see his gloves, and you draw your conclusions.[124]

Between men and women, the glove helped mediate overly suggestive contacts and established the bodily distance required by modesty. Men, however, removed their gloves when they shook hands, at least when the handshake was meant to be felt, because the symbolic character of this ancestral form of greeting suggested confidence and a "straightforward" contractual agreement.

"A peasant" would feel "insulted if you touch his hand without removing your glove. In society, where gloves are now generally worn, it would be difficult to observe this precaution. Yet—though not with ladies for whom the glove has in a way become the hand's veil of modesty—we find that the grasp of two hands loses its character of cordial communication with the glove as cold intermediary."[125]

The Hat

The masculine hat also had to be removed for greetings. It did not evoke contractual agreements, but rather relationships of authority, allegiance, or deference.

In nineteenth-century streets the top hat covered every bourgeois head. To trace its history would entail a story of geographical displacement (because of its Quaker origins it emigrated from England to America), of amazing diffusion (the War of Independence made it prestigious, notably among the victorious French troops who brought it back to France and turned it into an emblem of liberty), and finally, of significant monopolization (it became the prerogative of the bourgeoisie).

After the July Monarchy the top hat was made no longer of felt but of black silk, and its crown was lower and narrower. Yet, it remained exceptionally uncomfortable, even after the spring system of a new, more practical model, the gibus, made it possible to open and collapse it. It fulfilled no useful purpose: its narrow brim provided little protection from rain or sun, and its height exposed it to every wind. It had no aesthetic alibis: everyone criticized "this unattractive and unfortunate form, known as the stovepipe,"[126] and excoriated those "responsible" for it, "the ignorant hatmakers who for fifty years have been stuck in the groove of routine."[127] This gleaming cylinder owed its long life to other virtues: notably, that of incorporating both bourgeois propriety, through its stiffness and funereal sobriety, and aristocratic bearing, because it made any physical activity completely impossible, and that of simultaneously integrating democratic equality, by abandoning feathers or embroidery, with hierarchical difference, through a new play of distinctive details, particularly luster and cleanliness.

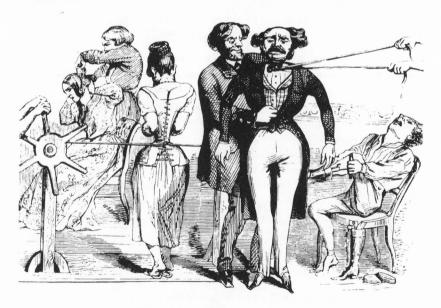

Obliterating, cleansing, concealing

Shoes

The morality of immaculate black and the aesthetic of brilliance also regulated shoes, especially after England introduced early in the century the fashion of glazing them: hence, a horror of mud and a terror of wear, both of which exposed walking and the lowly status of a pedestrian. But the other important function of boots and ankle boots was to hide unsightly bumps and to squeeze feet that were flat or too large into their leather shafts to make them appear slender and elegant.

This, too, was a task of obliteration, cleansing, or concealment, by means of an envelope that could relieve the body of its shameful stigmata even when it could not erase them.

Deviations from the Norm

Today dressing is more than a profession; it is
an arduous, difficult art; to its practice many are called
but few are chosen.

—MARC CONSTANTIN, *Almanach des belles manières
ou l'art du bon ton, de la politesse, etc.* (1854)

"NOTHING TAKES LONGER to acquire," Tocqueville noted, "than the surface polish that is called good manners."[1] What were the real applications of the model of good vestimentary behavior that we have so far observed in vitro?

By examining the values essential to any sense of propriety, such as cleanliness, simplicity, and correctness, as well as their technical, ethical, and aesthetic aspects, we can see that certain segments of the bourgeoisie distinguished themselves by their adequate mastery of these canonical ideals, while others were disqualified by their relatively naive or erroneous conformity to them. Although the former had completely acknowledged these ideals as legitimate and tried to follow them, they nevertheless failed to grasp all the nuances.

Between actual practice and the ideal definition of comme il faut, there appeared, therefore, a graduated series of increasingly stronger deviations and corresponding degrees of growing social distances that separated true initiates from aspirants of any kind.

Ideals of cleanliness, simplicity, and propriety, like those of distinction, stemmed from new social strategies that gave rise to new discourses and new kinds of behavior that were culturally and historically specific. Along with the rapid development of hygiene, cleanliness in clothes (though not as yet bodily cleanliness, which was still rudimentary) became much more prevalent in the nineteenth century, when for prophylactic and sumptuary reasons, laundering underwear played an unprecedented role. Simplicity in clothing, which was already a specific bourgeois trait during the ancien régime, was a virtue that could be contrasted not only to aristocratic splendor but also to nouveau-riche bluffing. Finally, because of the self-control it implied, propriety, very closely linked to cleanliness, indicated the emergence of a new figure in the history of vestimentary behavior: the gentleman and his radicalized version, the dandy.

CLEANLINESS

Clothing and body cleanliness are interdependent and endowed with meanings and aspects that unfailingly illuminate an entire society through successive representations, rituals, and practices concerned with odors or their masking, filth and its eradication, and the history of laundering and cosmetics.[2]

After the middle of the eighteenth century, discourses on hygiene (gymnastics, clothing, care of the body, etc.) proliferated, but washing injunctions and practices remained extraordinarily parsimonious[3] compared to our own times. The Revolution of course ended the particularly unhealthy wearing of wigs and the use of powder;[4] perhaps it encouraged the use of public baths[5] a bit, but throughout the reign of Napoleon III, a bathroom fixture such as a shower was exceptional in secondary schools, hospitals, or barracks and rarely used.[6] The most bourgeois of dressing rooms sometimes had a bathtub, but this was never a mandatory accessory.[7] People preferred to have a tub delivered to their domiciles now and then, but the emollient powers of its hot water were not without danger for the proprieties. "Never take more than one bath a month," recommended the Countess Drohojowska. "There is in the taste for sitting down in a bathtub a certain indolence and softness that ill suits a woman."[8]

So far as washing hair was concerned, the precept of the school of Salerno, championed by Dr. Goulin, seems to have been widely followed: *saepe manus, raro pedes, nunquam caput*, or, "hands often, the feet rarely, the head never."[9] A fine lead comb repeatedly passed through the hair generally served as shampooing.[10]

Other parts of the body, however, seem to have been more regularly visited by soap, at least among the upper bourgeoisie. And even though negligence led "some women to . . . put off cleaning their teeth, ears, and nails[11] until holidays," the manuals indicated that this should be done daily.

Such regularity, on the other hand, was not without its risks, especially for a man who paid too much attention to himself and ran the risk of slipping imperceptibly into an unwholesome affectation. Instead, "it is good to accustom yourself to spending the least time possible on these cares: this is a wholesome measure, required by social decency."[12] In his *Relaxations Permitted Pious Persons Obliged to Live in the World*, the Rev. Father Huguet reaffirmed the subordinate roles to which these practices should be restricted: "Cleanliness becomes pettiness as soon as it is exaggerated," he wrote. "You reveal a better disposition when you neglect yourself in unimportant things than when you are too delicate about them."[13]

But thanks to the behavior it encouraged and the attitudes it inspired, cleanliness always had consequences that made it a virtue, which in the case of those naturally dirty and rebellious creatures—children and workers—were also a comforting indication that they had been tamed.

Moreover, as our ecclesiastic explained, it was both edifying and gratifying:

> When the parts of the body are maintained in a state of purity they function more efficiently: orderly habits and ideas of decency become more familiar to young persons; vigilance, moderation and restraint are necessarily practiced; the mind is better disposed toward work, and the business of life is made more agreeable. This quality gains one goodwill and, as a visible sign of inner purity, is regarded as a mark of respect and judged worthy of consideration.[14]

Thus, because of the correspondence commonly established between the "physical" and the "moral," the signs of bodily cleanliness were associated in a sort of spontaneous physiognomony with psychological and moral appropriateness characterized in social terms: the "proper" bourgeois, the "good" worker,[15] and so on. "A neat and well-groomed woman," wrote the Countess Bassanville, "is almost always a decent and virtuous woman, and a neat and well-groomed man displays a considerable integrity of spirit, often also of conduct."[16] In the epigraph to his *Medical Dissertation on Garments in Direct Contact with the Skin*, Dr. Deglaude similarly noted that "cleanliness is to the body what decency is to morals."[17]

Thanks to Pasteur's revolution, which justified cleanliness, this moral reinterpretation of cleanliness (for which many other examples could easily be cited) was at the very foundations of the hygienic policies that obsessed the nineteenth century. The fantasy of a total annihilation of pathogenic agents, of an absolute sanitary and moral order, called for flushing out and radically extirpating this polymorphous filth from the body social. "Frankville," the model city of health and well-being depicted by Jules Verne in *The Begum's Fortune*, glorified the enterprise: "They [the children] are . . . accustomed to such strict cleanliness that they consider a spot on their simple clothes quite a disgrace. Individual and collective cleanliness is the great idea of the founders of Frankville. To clean, clean unceasingly, so as to destroy the miasmas emanating constantly from a large community, such is the principal work of the central government."[18]

But if this formidable social utopia of a single, universal hygienic compulsion based on physical and moral health haunted the imagination of legislators, doctors, and educators, cleanliness nevertheless remained a scarce, inequitably distributed economic and cultural commodity. As such, it was always an indication of class, a status symbol imposed by one's education in a society that on the whole washed very little compared to the Middle Ages and our time. Yet within this society, the bourgeois, especially the wealthy ones, dirtied themselves less than the workers[19] and the peasants,[20] whose filth provided a foil for the cleanliness of the others.[21] As Nietzsche wrote, "That which separates two men most profoundly is a different sense and grade of purity."[22]

In the domain of clothing this distinguishing function therefore required tireless attention. "You would be pardoned for a threadbare suit if you were a man of letters or an artist, but not for a grease spot on your vest."[23]

Questionable linen, a rumpled suit, a spattered overcoat were so many signs of a needy and laborious life compared to the clean and neat appearance that suggested, even if it did not prove, affluence and leisure. Why did "well-groomed men adopt the praiseworthy habit of carrying a small pocket brush in the winter, which they used outside the vestibule to lift the few mud spots on their trousers" if not to remove from view the telltale signs of useful work that required the use of the body, or simply to hide the fact that their economic status required them to walk? "Others in fact, when they make social calls are careful not to carry an umbrella, the witness and informant of their voyage on foot, something that can . . . appear ridiculous to very distinguished persons."[24]

With the development of underwear and its spread in new strata of the population, the eighteenth century had already witnessed the progress of laundering in domestic life and of the linen merchant in social life.[25] But during the next century, with the increase in the number of women's undergarments and the abundance of white cloth in men's wardrobes, these became very much more important. In country washhouses the tradition of washing linen once or twice a year still weighed very heavily. Linen's transient whiteness did not seem to serve a social function but was the consequence of a ritualized preservative treatment (with the possible exception of solemn feast days, family celebrations or Sunday observances).[26] In cities, on the other hand, the economic aspect of clean clothes was an essential feature of its appeal. The immaculate whiteness of starched shirtfronts, collars, cravats, and shirt cuffs enjoyed the prestige conferred on it by its brief existence (threatened by a thousand accidents), the gestural constraints implied, and especially the costs entailed in laundering and replacement. Fresh linen, because of its cost, promoted one to an elevated social position.[27] The result of exhausting[28] work that laundresses devoted to sorting, soaking, draining, washing, soaping, rinsing, blueing, wringing, then drying, ironing, starching, crimping, folding, this freshness indicated first of all, behind the usual aesthetic alibi, that one had the means to consume without really producing or even saving. (Thus, one never wore in the morning gloves used the previous evening.) Of course, this waste only aped aristocratic luxury, for although it theoretically espoused the values of squandering, it did not in fact accept its financial consequences. As far as laundering was concerned, thrifty calculations were never absent from bourgeois preoccupations, as is indicated by practices such as the keeping of household accounts and the handing down of a trousseau from mother to daughter.

SIMPLICITY

"Too much is not comme il faut"[29]—there, laconically formulated, is one of the major principles of propriety. As we have seen, relationships to cleanliness effected an initial classification that summarily separated wealth and poverty. Among the wealthy or the pseudowealthy, simplicity revealed and separated good and bad social lineage. Forced upon the Third Estate during the ancien régime, simplicity became a coveted sign of belonging and a protest against aristocratic excess. After the Revolution it helped to

—"Funny people! What are those bejeweled
    reliquaries over there?"
—"It's my comb merchant's family. He's made it."
—"I was thinking: those people are too rich to be
    comme il faut."

establish the dominant moral clothing code. To be sure, while men's clothing became blacker and more austere every year, the luxury and magnificence of women's dress increased, perpetuating after the revolutionary interlude the aristocratic tradition of lavish display. But the cultivation of simplicity should not be viewed only diachronically; its modalities must be studied synchronically within a single society. Simplicity opposed pretensions, fads, and affectations, thus acquiring its value. In so doing, it assumed different forms and content but remained, whatever its form, the main "barrier and standard" that revealed class distinctions. Of all distinguishing strategies, elegant simplicity (which is defined in relation to excess, itself perceived negatively in relation to simplicity) was formidably efficient. For example, Valéry Giscard d'Estaing's pullover is a case of conspicuous but chic underconsumption, of perfectly mastered manifest hypopropriety. J. Plumyène and R. Lassiera gave a penetrating exegesis:

> For him, everything began with a sweater worn in the metro. This sweater was historic. It was an insolent sweater, a sartorial challenge for all fashion systems. A manifesto of independence and dandyism. No sloppiness at all in this sweater. Quite the contrary: it had something ascetic about it. Monkish-colbertist work clothes. In short, a right-wing sweater.[30]

During the Second Empire, properly understood simplicity remained the prerogative of aristocratic families who reconverted their distinctive markers by relinquishing ovbious display.

> Accustomed to their chateaux, their townhouses, to the crowd of lackeys that surrounded them, they [duchesses] are generally very simple and completely devoid of vanity. . . . In the morning they wear beautifully a little hat, a plain dress, and a faded shawl: one could recognize them in a nun's coif. They alone can go out at any time in the simplest of dress without being mistaken for anyone else. Even the most obtuse boor could not fail to recognize them, because they are never taken for what they are not.[31]

This singular domination, this charisma, resided less in the object acquired (the clothing) than in the mode of acquisition, the manner of owning and using it. Thus, the eloquence of aristocratic simplicity lay in its distance from acquisition, its casual attitude toward possessions—itself the supreme possession—this distance radically separated them from the parvenus for whom triumphant ownership compensated previous deprivations but also revealed them.

> To understand the charms of simple elegance one must [observed Baron de Mortemart-Boisse] live in close contact with a great lady who owns a hundred

thousand *écus* worth of diamonds that she wears two or three times a year, who
owns antique laces and new silks but "dresses up" only on special occasions.

Accompanying this grand lady during the summer, you would see her wear
in the country simple "linen dresses" that look ravishing on her!

This confounds the marquises of the rue du Helder, the Lady Lauras, . . .
and others of the rue Taitbout, and the lorettes of the Breda neighborhood.[32]

The serene condescension of Mme de Girardin deserves to be quoted at
length. No one has better expressed the effects of this spectacular understatement:

There are bonnets full of pride that you have never understood and humble
plumes whose delicacy and dignity you have never appreciated. . . . This bonnet is haughty by dint of simplicity because only the wife of a millionaire
could wear such modest headgear—the bonnet of a nursing-home resident—
at a brilliant soirée. That prodigious panache, on the other hand, is full of
humility; for only the wife of an employee who makes a salary of a thousand
écus could have the noble courage to visit the wife of her husband's superior
decked out in an enormous toque of fantastically wide, yellowed plumage that
has endured many a winter. Its age, its very absurdity reveal the most generous
abnegation, the purest conduct, the most tender sentiments. The bonnet tells
you nothing, but it speaks to us; to us it says: "I have an income of a million
francs, the loveliest townhouse, and the handsomest horses in Paris. My diamonds have attracted attention, my emerald necklace is renowned, my opals
are classic; the other day I wore a lace dress that was the only thing women
talked about for three days. I want to prove to them that I can make an impression in a drawing room without these marvels and that I do not need any of
them to be more beautiful than they." The old, humble, but decent toque that
tells you absolutely nothing says to us: "I am well aware that this headgear is
ugly and was never in fashion during any reign; but who is looking at me?
And, anyway, does it matter if people look at me? I am a good mother and I
would rather buy a new bonnet for my little girl than a pretty new hat for
myself. Society is so boring and sad! Courtesy calls are such a chore! I long to
go home to put the little one to sleep myself. The dear little love is so delicate!
A mere nothing gives her a cold." Aren't we right to say: haughty bonnet,
modest panache. Isn't the simplicity of the former insolence? On the other
hand, isn't the latter's showiness really deference and respect? Poor women
have to put on all their finery for grand soirees. Only immensely wealthy
women can be excessively simple.[33]

In this case the ridiculous luxury displayed by the employee's wife posed
no danger to the identifying arsenal of rich, comme il faut women. But as
upward mobility and social mixing accelerated, they aroused vindictive

pretensions, which hardened strategies. The Countess de Ségur was an exemplary representative of an aristocracy that reflected the bourgeois rejection of waste, excess, and affectation. She readily stigmatized figures of sartorial exaggeration and excess. In *Les Petites filles modèles*, her description of Mme Fichini testifies to the behavior of parvenus as well as that of refined people:

> A few moments before dinnertime Mme Fichini arrived in a costume that was ridiculously elegant for the country. Her pale lavender silk dress was decorated with three large flounces trimmed with ruffs, lace, and velvet; her bodice was also trimmed with a thousand ornaments that made it as ridiculous as her skirt; the fullness of that skirt was such that Sophie had been relegated to the front of the carriage, while Mme Fichini and her dress spread out majestically in the rear. Only Sophie's head could be seen amid this heap of flounces that covered her. The barouche opened; the company stood on the steps. Mme Fichini descended triumphantly—fat, red, pimply faced. Her eyes gleamed with a satisfied pride; she thought that she was the object of general admiration with her Mère Gigogne dress, her big, bare arms, her little hat with feathers in a thousand colors covering her red hair, and her string of diamonds on her pimply brow. With concealed satisfaction she observed the simple dress of all the ladies; Mmes de Fleurville and de Rosbourg wore plain black taffeta dresses; no coiffures decorated their hair, which was raised in simple coils and braided at the back; some of the ladies of the neighborhood wore mousseline, and the others light silk; none wore flounces, jewels, or extraordinary coiffures. Mme Fichini was not wrong to believe that her clothing would produce an effect; she was wrong about what effect—instead of admiration, mocking pity. "Here I am, dear ladies," she said, as she stepped down from the carriage, displaying big feet shod in lace-trimmed lavender satin shoes that matched her dress; "Here I am, with Sophie. Just like Saint Roch and his dog."[34]

This was where excess led! Mme Fichini was so eager to accumulate signs she thought prestigious—though their very redundancy produced the opposite effect—that she amassed errors in sartorial propriety and collected on a single person most of the examples of incongruity. Topographical-circumstantial errors: the pertinence of the town/country opposition was not grasped; esthetico-moral errors in the choice and combination of forms (excessive fullness), materials (accumulation of flounces, ruffs, and lace) and colors (pale lavender shoes matching the dress, red hair and multicolored feathers); errors in the choice and the suitability of accessories (string of diamonds, feathered hat in broad daylight); and finally, errors of judgment about herself and others in her triumphalism. She saw her dress just as her fellow parvenus would: an admirable object, in the latest fashion and more, assured of approval by its very excessiveness. Viewing the simple clothes of Mmes de Fleurville and de Rosbourg she expected to produce an even greater sensation. She believed her integration into high society more likely the more she accumulated the signs of what she believed to be "comme il faut." The parvenu's logic was naively arithmetical: the more one displays wealth, the more one is rich and worthy of esteem. On the one hand, she had internalized the norms establishing the hierarchy of signs; on the other, for lack of social pedigree and the resulting ignorance of how to handle these signs, she, a neophyte user, irredeemably discredited herself.[35]

Mme Fichini's overloading herself revealed a troubled awareness of her shortcomings, the kind that led parvenus to reassure themselves of their "proper" conformity to the rules by compounding the surplus of signs. They thus implicitly recognized their own limits and indirectly acknowledged an inadmissible status. Parvenus were pretentious because, in ways that were more or less effective, such as affectation in manners or the display of luxury, they had to hide the fragility of their social legitimacy while they constructed it. Their triumph was fierce because it was compensatory. Mmes de Fleurville and de Rosbourg enjoyed the height of luxury; they did not need to display their wealth because their own legitimacy was beyond question. Strategically, their understatement signified absolute superiority, one that permitted a "mocking pity."

"Here I am, dear ladies, . . . with Sophie—just like Saint Roch
and his dog."

Among the arrivistes and the nouveaux riches, the inflation of signs led less to their devaluation than to a kind of semantic twisting ("Mme Fichini was not wrong to believe her clothing would produce an effect; she was wrong about what effect"). Moreover, this inflation did not conceal flaws of body and face ("fat, red, pimply"), which revealed origins, positions, or trajectories through telltale details:

> Displaying recently acquired aristocratic particles on the forehead is not yet the fashion. But parvenus compensate for this by giving themselves airs and sometimes wearing on their index finger monstrous rings emblazoned out of a d'Hozier armorial, for fear that people might doubt their noble origins. They are fooling themselves, because behind their airs and haughty pretentions, which their glossy kid gloves and plump, well-kept hands reveal, you can quickly recognize these vain men. They have more pretentions than quarterings of nobility. They are never mistaken for a great lord who is remarkable for the perfection of his hand, who seeks to shine only through that elegant simplicity that has always been and always will be the touchstone of the comme il faut man.[36]

Sometimes even the fashion magazines assumed the mission of revealing, describing, and explaining how the body betrayed classes that were rising or trying to, and of recommending resignation to less able plagiarists.

> A would-be lady of fashion sees a real lady wearing a dress and likes it; she admires the details, the whole, the style, and finds it beautifully becoming on the woman wearing it. But that is all she has seen, and vanity blinds her to the rest. She orders one just like it, and this dress, which is identical to the model, makes her look frightful! . . . The bodice fits well, the sleeves are of the right length and well cut; the skirt is properly fitted to the bodice; its hem is even, and it puffs up as it should for a well-dressed woman. But the dress does not suit her. . . . It simply does not! The woman is ugly, frightfully ugly! If only the dressmaker, instead of looking for defects in her work, had told her, "Madame, if this dress does not fit you as well as it fits Mme X., . . . it is because you have a shorter waist and a longer neck. You are lively and vivacious. She is sedate and sweet. In addition, you are petite and she is tall. My talent and skill can do nothing at all about that, and all my good will cannot change that certain something that does not combine harmoniously with the dispositions of this fabric and the design of this dress."[37]

Another kind of excess, not very distant from that of pretender, was embodied during the Second Empire by the demimondaines (tarts, cocottes, *cocodettes*, lorettes, etc.). They did not always borrow the complicated, oblique tactics of distinction—of which they were for the most part ignorant—but rather they hypertrophied the sexual function of their clothing and raised the value of their shares on the amorous stock exchange. This is Taine's detailed description of them at the opera:

> In the circle, in full view, three or four boxes of lorettes make quite a show. Their skirts puff up to the very edge of the box: their hair, built up in crimps and curls, attracts the eye like the fleece of some exotic animal; Roman earrings rattle above the overwhitened shoulders; they lean forward purposefully: they must be either wanton or majestic; they put on little airs, they smile to excess; such as you see them, with their seven-franc gloves, their new carriage, their two lackeys, their hundred-franc box, their boyish manners; they think themselves ladies, and in misanthropic moments we ask if they are not right.[38]

These "boyish manners," that is, the absence of the grace and reserve "natural" to a society woman, can also be found in other places and other forms. Sketching the portrait of the courtesan riding in a carriage, E. Feydeau enumerates the loud and eccentric marks that served as shop signs:

> With that one, everything is outré and exaggerated. The horse that pulls her carriage walks too fast, her servants' livery is in bad taste. Seated at the back, with the hems of her skirt dragging on one of the wheels of her carriage, badly coiffed, her face plastered, she looks insolent, laughs very loudly in bursts, or, when she tries to appear distinguished, only succeeds in looking surly, which makes people laugh. If wearing flowers on one's hat is fashionable, she is not content with two or three rosebuds but will have a basketful, for fear of seeming to have too few. With her everything is pushed to excess: the fullness or tightness of her clothes, the color of fabrics and the shape of the most insignificant object. Her perfumes are violent, her shoes too narrow, her gloves so exceedingly tight that they deform her hands.[39]

For people of limited means, on the other hand, the attempt at excess or overloading revealed their absurdity in the meagerness of the resources employed. Imitation goods were one of the important techniques against which the manuals attempted to warn the nouveaux riches. Imitations only emphasized the imbalance between their social pretensions and economic means.

Financial sacrifice was another illusory method of climbing higher on the scale of appearances, but it, too, did not deceive for long, even if some shabby or dated item did not show beneath a brilliant new outfit. "In society, money knows money: people have a pretty exact idea of the worth of what you own, and more than one woman, happy in clothes fit for a queen, does not suspect that, with the exception of a few simpleminded admirers, the luxury she displays makes people smile and invites comments that injure her own reputation, touch upon her husbands's in passing, and harm the future of her family."[40] Thus, in the name of a domestic and familial morality that deemed deprivation honorable, "the clothing of these [women] of modest means must not exceed the limits of elegant simplicity. Considerations of a higher order, of good spiritual order, the dignity of the married state, a mother's duties, all come to the aid of this law of propriety."[41]

For those better off, abandoning simplicity was not an option; rather, as we have said, they quietly enriched it, fashioning and refining it with veiled, delicate, and ascetic luxury: "If you want to compete with someone in elegance, the only way to win is with exquisite simplicity, that kind of skillful simplicity that would vanquish two million francs' worth of diamonds with a mere rag. The great merit of an outfit is to seem natural and improvised when it has cost hours of study and preparation for those who wear it and those who made it."[42] Savoir-faire therefore enjoined an unending cleansing operation that did not bring a woman back to the natural state from which culture would tear her but rather would lead her to a degree of cultivation increasingly distant from nature, in which a "natural" appearance was the acme of "culture." This asceticism was to obliterate the traces of a petty-bourgeois culture too insistent and explicit about signs of possession and sexuality, in order to replace them with discretion, restraint, and reserve wherever the body, its movements, and its coverings played a signifying role.

For men, whose clothing was more simple, degrees of cleanliness and propriety served as signs of belonging. Nevertheless, the wearing of more or less abundant or precious accessories was revealing. Excessively heavy chains across the chest, large rings and jewels that caught the eye belonged to the arsenal from which Balzac's Gaudissart borrowed his notorious red cravat. Even when these were authentic, a well-bred person banished them "because they can be mistaken for imitations."[43] Pinchbeck was to gold what ready-to-wear was to made-to-measure: an inferior, derivative value that cheapened what it imitated.

Shunning excess in men's clothing did not, however, require much individual perspicacity, for the model of the sober and neutral gentleman was an invitation to an easy effacement limited to a few axioms:

"Your hat is not odd."
"Your trousers are not eccentric."
"You avoid badly matched and garish colors."
"For, above all, you do not want to draw attention to yourself."[44]

Although one might become comme il faut in this way, elegance, on the other hand, demanded other assets and a different, more elaborate knowledge that proceeded from propriety. We will see that even slightly overdone, studied elegance, affectation, and dandyism, because of the excess they implied, were not understood in the bourgeois meaning of propriety.

PROPRIETY

Acting on each other, sartorial and bodily propriety could not be separated. In the nineteenth century, what was known as "bearing" became the subject of discourses, practices, representations, techniques, and behavior that marked a singular and capital moment in this history.

From the corseted curvatures of the classical age to the overencoded casualness of today's blue jeans, the forms and norms of the body's modeling and of the framework of clothing evolved from physical coercion—external and spectacular—into an abstract, internalized, and insidious manipulation.[45] In the nineteenth century the bourgeois conception of bearing raised to their highest pitch the ideals of self-control, self-possession, and the constant mastery of affect, which Norbert Elias has analyzed throughout "the civilizing process."[46] Victorian England, embodying these in the highest degree, served the various European bourgeoisies as a supreme reference for middle-class sociability and as an instruction sheet for their men's clothing.

The canonical ideal of this posture—fashion plates show it well—was first a silhouette, a profile, and a posture. The body was straight and no longer slightly curved as it had been during the eighteenth century; the chest was broad and thrown out, the stomach drawn in, while the belt, which henceforth strangled the waist, took on a new importance: "Is it not at the place occupied by the belt, near the center of the body, that the gaze of one who observes severely the good behavior and bearing of civilized men almost always comes to rest? Nowadays the belt has replaced suspenders, which tend to disappear."[47]

All this inspired feelings of solemnity and gravity that made the fine manners of court society impossible. The soldier's stiffness was added to puritanical austerity: "Your clothes should call to mind the military bearing that suits men so well," one manual pointed out.[48]

For women the rigidity of this posture took forms that changed more rapidly because it was tied to more labile fashions. The post-Revolutionary period briefly liberated them from the enormous "corps" that had constricted the body primarily to prevent malformations. But it reappeared around 1810 under the name of "corset," in a relatively lighter, more supple version that had an aesthetic purpose. At the same time, it shaped a woman's sides, squeezed her waist, and flattened her stomach during all the hours she did not spend in bed; but it did so to enhance her "natural" forms by emphasizing her hips and pushing up her breasts. The torso was long and the back always straight. But the fashion of bustles bent the spine at the hips into a sort of generalized lordosis—the S-shape—which gradually disappeared around 1910 with the advent of the tubular dress and the slip-on girdle.

Bearing, however, is more than a matter of morphology and posture; it also involves gestures and behavior appropriate for particular occasions, and among other things, a technique of bodily and sartorial cleanliness, domestication of skin and hair, an art of pleating and starching, in short, the entire organization, upkeep, and surveillance of one's physical person and the result this achieves. Like modesty, which is part of it, bearing calls for continuous control, a perpetual effort to avoid infringing on the morality of respect that underlies it, and confers on it legitimacy and influence: "A woman should always be 'well groomed' at home: her hair, hands, and clothes should be clean, her boots laced, just as if she were going to appear before strangers, and this habit will augment the respect that everyone around her, including her children, owes her."[49]

Because of its manifold aspects and the social and symbolic stake it represented, the imperative of bodily and sartorial propriety went much beyond simple decency. Everywhere—in school, in the army, on the street, in drawing rooms, at home even in the most intimate spaces—it was a matter of incorporating and living this second "nature." For to be proper and well groomed was an aspect of appearance, but at the same time it became an aspect of being. Propriety in appearance implied a moral guarantee of successful socialization. This semantic equivalence between the concrete and the abstract, the literal and the figurative, made propriety (exactly like hygiene) an ethic as well as a technique. In the nineteenth century it legitimized and encouraged a pedagogy increasingly obsessed by the educative and edifying values of good grooming, while the thunderbolts of social anathemas were hurled against the symptoms of dereliction, negligence, dissoluteness, or indolence:

A lazy young woman looks, converses, and wears clothes in characteristic ways; she betrays herself in a thousand ways: by her deplorable ignorance, the triviality of her conversation, the carelessness with which she listens, the listlessness of her gaze. Finally—dare I say it?—you can also recognize her by her messy hair and dirty clothes. Thus, laziness not only leaves its indelible mark on the soul, but also an incurable boredom; it even breaks out into the open; it is, so to speak, a public shame. And thus does God surely punish the being who fails to observe the first law, the law of duty and work.[50]

Propriety had to contribute to the child's moral development, social education, and cultural capitalization.[51] The iconography and over abundant literature devoted to it show this: by stigmatizing failings in orderliness, cleanliness, attentiveness, or comportment, and by describing their frightful consequences (physical deformities, pain, humiliation, etc.), the authors hoped to convince readers of the moral and corrective benefits of good manners, the gratifications they brought, the affection they engendered, and, later, the social acceptance they guaranteed by the respect they inspired.[52] Louise Boyeldieu d'Auvigny, the author of *Happiness in Duty*, summarized the role that bourgeois ideology intended this pedagogy of sartorial propriety to play, especially among the "working classes." This ideology, like ready-to-wear (which supported it physically), had to suppress the unbearable symbolic violence of slovenliness and filth by contributing to the moral regeneration and political domestication of the worker:

> A child who has been taught self-respect from the earliest years, if I may make so bold, will never do anything that might cause him to lose his place in society. He knows that he must present himself respectably and with attire suitable for meriting esteem and consideration. Do we not every day see people who know how, even amid the most frightful poverty, to maintain an appearance of cleanliness that is good to see; they have only shabby clothes, but these are so clean, so well kept that immediately one feels moved to love those who wear them, to respect, venerate such poverty so nobly borne, to come to their aid, for one feels that where there is so fierce a resignation, there could be nothing but dignified and elevated sentiments; while others to the contrary abandon themselves to a deplorable slovenliness, and judging from the disorder of their clothes and the carelessness of their toilette . . . seem delighted to parade their destitution. . . . On all of these unkempt, ill-worn, and dirty clothes one reads sloth, indifference, physical and moral degradation.[53]

In its desire to universalize its moral and political order, the bourgeoisie dreamed of a social control exercised over everyone, and consequently of "good manners" shared by all. They were not, however, to assume the same forms for everyone. Certainly "persons of all incomes and social positions can acquire good manners and ought to follow their dictates,"[54] but with manifestations and procedures appropriate to different incomes and positions.

Establishing the typology of these comportments amounts to an inventory of the specifics that define social origin and trajectory, economic level, socioprofessional habitus, or political affiliation: the humble, deferential propriety of the worker in his Sunday best; the satisfied and avaricious propriety of the petty rentier; the sober and superior propriety of the wealthy bourgeois; hypopropriety, provocative in the artist, tolerated in the elderly scholar, and ridiculous in the provincial; and hyperpropriety, insecure or overconfident in the petty bourgeois, but outrageous and eccentric in the dandy. A main characteristic of affluent bourgeois or aristocratic propriety was the banning of any trace of useful work. The hierarchy of proprieties and their taxonomy were derived from more or less satisfactory interpretations of this model, which depended on the economic and cultural means invested hiding the signs of labor. Profoundly revealing, sartorial wear and tear, and deformation, for example, did not escape Balzac's observation. He sketched a complete identifying system based on them:

Set up a coat rack and hang a few suits on it. . . . Good! If you haven't walked about like a fool who can't see a thing, you will recognize a bureaucrat from the shiny sleeves, the broad horizontal crease imprinted on the back by the chair on which he so often leans to take his pinch of snuff or to rest from the strain of doing nothing. You will note the businessman by a bulging breast pocket, the flaneur by the stretched-out fobs where he often puts his hands; the shopkeeper by the extraordinarily wide mouths of his pockets, which gape as if to complain about being deprived of their usual bundles. Finally, a more or less clean, powdered, pomaded, or frayed collar, buttonholes more or less worn, a drooping flap, the tightness of a new lining—these are infallible indicators of professions, mores, and habits.[55]

The active life, because it requires doing things and assuming postures that wear out clothing slowly or suddenly degrade it ("A tear is a misfortune, a spot is a vice," wrote Balzac),[56] thus precludes any hope of superior propriety, any possibility of real elegance. Idleness—authentic or not, it does not matter—was the necessary if not sufficient condition. Vestimentary "doing as," whether in dignified poverty or ridiculous pretention, could not disguise the imprint of work visible in faded, worn, or shapeless clothing. On the other hand, "doing too much," because of the very way it laboriously removed this mark, revealed recent affluence, imperfect education, and a false note that real savoir-faire abhorred. "Overpomaded hair, pretentious coiffures, overcurly mustaches and sideburns . . . make one look like a hairdresser's dummy." And "women dressed to the nines, to use the common expression, show that they are emptyheaded persons occupied only with themselves."[57]

The greater the effort, the less distinction was "natural" and taken for granted. Balzac excoriates these attempts burdened with fake elegance:

> Have you not often seen that these demifashionable men who exhaust themselves chasing elegance blush to have one pleat less in their shirt, and sweat blood to attain a false propriety, like those poor Englishmen who are always pulling out their pocket watches? Keep in mind, you poor cretins of the elegant life, that other principle which results from aphorism XXXIII, and entails your eternal condemnation: self-conscious elegance is to true elegance what wigs are to hair.[58]

The implied corrolary of this aphorism was, in the end, a sentence without appeal: "Dandyism is a heresy of the elegant life.[59] Eugène Chapus, another clothing theoretician, agreed with Balzac on this point. "We have noted . . . that the word 'elegant' is almost always used improperly today. A man whose clothing is studied is not for that reason an elegant; he is rather a dandy, a fop, a *petit-maître*, a beau, *incroyable*, *fashionable*, *merveilleux*, *fat*, *faro*, *bozor*, or swaggerer, depending on the period and the regime."[60]

Like upwardly mobile arrivistes or already established parvenus, dandies made too much of the sartorial esthetic and ethic when compared to the bourgeois ideal, but in different ways and for completely different reasons. Arrivistes and parvenus, failed mannequins, naively accumulated the signs of the groups with which they believed they could identify themselves and from which they hoped to acquire prestige. Dandies, accomplished mannequins, manipulated these signs meticulously and rigorously, thus radically setting themselves off from the rest of humanity which they despised. But the result of these two totally opposed practices in their respective excesses—one in comformism, the other in eccentricity—remained contained within the outer limits, if not of "comme il faut," at least of elementary proprieties.

The desperate stoicism of distinction, ultimate revolt of individualism, asceticism striving for rarity and nuance, the historic dandyism of Brummel or Byron, like the later mythic dandyism of Barbey or Baudelaire, recreated in a hardened form the aristocratic ethos which they opposed to the rising, egalitarian tide of democracy. A dandy was the

> Black Prince of Elegance, the demigod of boredom who looked at the world with an eye as glassy as his pince-nez, suffering because his disarranged cravat had a crease, like the ancient Sybarite who suffered because his rose was crushed. He is indifferent about the horse he rides, the woman he greets, and the man he encounters and at whom he gazes a while before recognizing him. He bears, written on his forehead—in English—this insolent inscription: What do you and I have in common?[61]

He sought to be absolutely singular: he did not attempt to respond to any legitimate definition of elegance that the dominant society could approve or share. On the contrary, by the ceaseless invention and the constant updating of distinctive features, he turned his clothing into a personal creation. Th. Bourgeau, in his *Usages du monde*, expressed the judgments the dandy provoked: "The person known in society as a dandy, a *fashionable*, is a well-groomed man. Therefore, study him. You see, he exaggerates the rules, makes them ridiculous. What he seeks is the triumph of the bizarre and the singular over the natural."[62]

Above all, this quest mobilized a technique that was essential to the virtually metaphysical spiritual value of a dandy's clothes. His clothing arrived in a raw state, and he had to individualize, treat, shape, and force it to express his own individuality, but without making it vulgarly eccentric[63] and thus dangerously imitable. Waxing the soles of his boots, constructing a cravat knot that only scissors could undo, sporting pink gloves, making a suit threadbare with a piece of glass or having his servant wear it thin— these practices and crucial details established his identity. While dandyism cannot be reduced to sartorial behavior, this practice did at least monopolize the dandy's demanding consciousness: he "must aspire to be sublime without interruption," noted Baudelaire; "he must live and sleep before the mirror."[64] Ideally, he wore nothing that might fall into the collective domain and be adopted by a public that sought out but feared the dandy, a public that was both a player excluded from the game and the fascinated spectator of the dandy's oeuvre. The dandy assaulted the public in order to exist, but without it he could not exist. Thus he engendered fads and mimicry in spite of himself and never followed them. For him, fashion—which he never followed—was only foil, a follow-the-leader phenomenon that he had to shun. "To define distinction while discrediting the admirers of distinction"[65] was his perpetually renewed goal.

Along with the ostentatiously slovenly "unruly worker" (and a few artists and writers),[66] the ostentatiously proper dandy opposed and rejected bourgeois appearances. Like the worker, he could (if successful) avoid the bad taste, vulgarity and pretention that were the forms of a sartorial morality based not on values opposed to the dominant ones but on secondary, derivative values. This was noted by observant columnists. For example, the *gandin* of the Second Empire saw himself as the dandy's successor. But he was only his puny bastard, who displayed the self-satisfaction of one decked out in his Sunday best and achieved all the originality of a small-town swell.

> The part in the middle of his hair should really continue down his back; he yaps a cynical argot gussied up with *petit-théâtre* jibes; he gives the impression that he's been everywhere, but he hasn't gone any farther than the Mabille Garden on the Champs-Elysées. His clothing embodies the ideal of elegance that a tailor's apprentice left to his own devices might dream up. . . . In fact, the *gandin* is not a Parisian. He was born to bedazzle a small, provincial city. From here I imagine that I can see him traveling to Brives or Pezenas in a triumphal tilbury. His cravat blazes, his waistcoat greens, his varnished boots shine in the Parisian fashion; from daybreak onward he wears white gloves. His "groom" shouts "Out of the way!" in a terrifying voice, and people in the deserted street pretend to step deferentially aside.[67]

In the *gandin*'s case, excess was a value derived from the dandy's asceticism, just as dandified asceticism derived from bourgeois simplicity. There was, however, this difference: the *gandin* tried but failed to imitate a model, whereas the dandy radicalized the model the more to distance himself, overdoing refinement, propriety, and even cleanliness.

Because comme il faut society could differentiate itself only through the interplay of these differences, it set itself apart with a kind of ostentation opposed to these pretentious or hostile parodies. The strategy was complex: ascetic luxury and rich sobriety, elegant plainness, cleanliness both relative and obsessive. In this chemistry the most precise doses were needed to indicate true propriety, respectable wealth, the right social connections, in short, measured distinction. Determined negatively, therefore, by its appearance and its opposite, distinction was the residual zone between these dual exclusions, a zone that made it possible for distinction to exist somewhere between being simple to distance oneself from the parvenus and being rich to distance oneself from the common herd; being discreet to distance oneself from the presumptious and being brilliant to distance onself from the colorless; keeping up with fashion to distance oneself from provincials while not following the latest fashion to distance oneself from the demimonde; being well groomed to distance oneself from the slovenly and being "natural" to distance oneself from the stuffy; being active to distance onself from the idle and being at leisure to distance oneself from those who had to work.

Invisible Clothing

Many maladies are caused by . . . corsets. Thin bodies,
narrow shoulders. Out of four two are bones of some promise;
one, bones which promise nothing; a fourth go to Nice
with the consumption; another fourth will at twenty-six drag
out six days of the seven in an invalid's chair.
—Taine, *Notes on Paris* (1875)

A woman in a corset is a lie, a fiction, but for us
this fiction is better than reality.
—Eugène Chapus, *Manuel de l'homme et de la
femme comme il faut* (1862)

Two crucial topics have been deliberately omitted from the chapters
devoted to propriety in clothing; one concerns dressing, or, more properly
speaking, undressing, unveiling underwear and its arrangement along the
body; the other relates to sleepwear, bringing the nightgown on stage.

A code does regulate these underlying secrets; but, hidden from public
view, they function in a dimension moral and sexual rather than social.
Intimate in essence, they cannot be apprehended apart from the naked
body—which they package and shape, simulate and dissimulate—or apart
from visible clothing—with which they maintain underground relationships of reciprocal dependency—or from the spaces—extraordinarily private—where they are worn. Subjected to quips too consistently "racy" not
to reveal the welter of feelings that it aroused, underwear was accompanied
by a ribald mythology with recurring themes that reflect a period's favored
representations of the body and its erotic postures. Underwear is therefore
a precious indicator of morals and sensibilities. Yet its study, even at the
level of forms and practices, is generally overlooked in the history of dress,

which tends to belittle it as "trivial" or "coarse."[1] In fact, while the moral aspect of visible clothing meant that it could be discussed, that of hidden clothing required silence. Unseen, unknown, unmentioned (women's pantaloons were often called "unmentionables"), underwear was closely related to erotic desire and to the body's indignities—as were the bidet or the water-closet, other unspeakable objects associated with equally unspeakable practices.

THE UNDERSIDE OF THE PANNIER

During the period stretching from the 1830s to World War I, women's underwear was the object of a frenetic cult[2] and corresponded psychologically to a time during which underwear was abundant and hidden to an unprecedented degree.

It was too suggestive for the moral order to allow its display in fashion magazines or department store catalogs, and its iconography became even rarer during the Second Empire, surviving only timidly in certain paintings (those of Constantin Guys, among others) or more boldly in caricatures.[3] Yet we do not lack surreptitious or oblique accounts of the remarkable development of lingerie corresponding to the widening of skirts. In fact, because of the number of articles piled one on top of the other, because of the wealth of embroidery and lace, and also because of their extraordinary diffusion throughout society, the Second Empire marked a crucial period in the development of women's clothes as well as in the history of the behaviors they induced.

But this development took place within a more general movement. An obsession haunted the bourgeoisie as it took its place in the world, which was manifested in the spaces occupied and possessions acquired: the obsession of covering, enveloping, carpeting, padding, or burying at any cost a nudity that seemed, like emptiness, threatening.[4] Never before were so many wall-hangings, window curtains, and table coverings unfurled, so many globes placed over clocks, covers on arm chairs and tea pots, mats under bibelots, and even, as we have seen, muffs around piano legs that might have aroused too many guilty thoughts.[5] And never before had bourgeois women worked so hard at crocheting, knitting, embroidering, weaving, and at making garlands and festoons in this gigantic and frenetic project aimed at covering everyday objects constantly and flagrantly guilty of impudicity, malfeasance, and decadence. And the bourgeois woman who withdrew from the world that she mediatized, withdrew even more through her clothing: not only did the enormous cone of fabric make contacts perilous, but the abundant, labyrinthine, and armored underwear prodigiously complicated any advanced incursion. Screens against desire,

Dressing

which frustrated and exacerbated it simultaneously, they sustained the image of an absolute, inaccessible, unreal woman and of an erotic experience in which the duration of a glance or a gesture acquires extraordinary significance.

Should the moral obstacle give way, the technical obstacles in undressing had yet to be feverishly overcome. "The exasperating delays convinced the fortunate mortal of the supreme favor he was about to receive. It was the dismantling of the fortress, the amorous stations of the cross."[6] A result of bourgeois underwear, and a perverse effect of the modesty it embodied, was to raise before the irresistible advance of pleasure tactical delays, thus increasing the tension by delaying its release.

What composed the essential supporting structure of dress? Let us leave the daily, visible changes in the dress of a "comme il faut" woman and proceed to that machinery of fabrics, buttons, and hooks that together conspired against impatience and readiness. Let us slip furtively into her dressing room, where those clandestine and therefore all-important operations were plotted. For, whereas ablutions were perfunctory, dressing was complex.

Pantaloons

First, she slipped into chemise and pantaloons. The latter, with legs that ended at the ankle in a finely embroidered flounce, were among the most recent additions to her wardrobe. "As for the unmentionable," wrote Violette in 1855, "bear in mind, my lovely reader, that it is absolutely modern, even contemporary: it is an English fashion unknown to our grandmothers."[7] They appeared at the beginning of the century and came into widespread use in the last years of the July Monarchy. "Before 1854 . . . there was little or no trace of pantaloons in account books," noted G. Bienaymé in his article on the cost of laundering in Paris, "and it would be futile to look for them earlier, especially when narrow skirts provided protection from the misdeeds of high winds."[8]

In the sixteenth century Brantôme noted that drawers were fashionable among the ribald noble ladies he described; Marguerite de Valois wore them, certainly more for reasons of coquettery than modesty.[9] But the seventeenth and eighteenth centuries did quite well without this tubular underwear, the direct ancestor of today's panties and briefs.[10] Painting and literature sporadically provide evidence through pictures like Fragonard's *The Swing*,[11] or accounts of falls from horseback,[12] tumbles,[13] and patriotic spankings.[14]

At first glance one would think that the bourgeois concept of modesty would logically have led to the adoption of pantaloons. Instead, that very concept generated resistance to pantaloons. Originating in England, where they were intended primarily for young girls and had assumed a moral function because of the "jumping exercises practiced in schools,"[15] they were introduced in France as a sign of youth. For grown women, however, this kind of undergarment, even if it had not resembled men's underwear, called to mind the underwear of dancers and actresses who had long worn it.[16] Moreover, as these women exemplified, pantaloons allowed postures that were much too free and encouraged far too casual movements. Henri de Saint-Simon had even seen the general use of pantaloons as a stage in women's emancipation.[17]

Finally, this novelty established contact with regions so serious and crucial that they were bound to disturb people, at least in the beginning. Despite Doctors Desessartz and de Saint-Ursin, who recommended their use for hygienic reasons,[18] pantaloons were only occasionally mentioned and rarely seen during the Empire.[19] "This semimasculine garment has something strange about it, and the few women who appear in pantaloons on the boulevards and at the Tuileries have been the object of such a disturbing curiosity that only tarts have dared to adopt it."[20]

Pantaloons

Under the Restoration, however, skating, gymnastics, riding, and travel sometimes served as pretexts for pantaloons: they began to be worn by the better people, but only on those occasions. One might think that the period's short ballooned dresses would have favored pantaloons; but only with the advent of the crinoline were they definitively adopted, first for day-wear and then for balls, to protect legs from the indiscretions of waltzes and polkas. The iron cages, which kept petticoats and skirts away from the body, made the pantaloon "indispensable," so that this term came to designate it, along with "inexpressible" or "modesty hose." This rampart of fine calico percale, or lawn, tubular at the bottom, tight at the waist, completely closed except for a slit that allowed the tail of the chemise to pass through, would slowly ascend toward the knee and perhaps acquire adornments of scallops and lace. Above all it would crystallize a fashion, establish a practice, and inaugurate a custom that long outlived the crinoline: even today, although corsets, petticoats, and garters have disappeared, abbreviated versions of the pantaloon—panties or briefs—persist.

The spread of women's pantaloons within the bourgeoisie—and eventually among workers and peasants—did not occur without resistance. Medical opinion was itself mixed. According to Casimir Daumas, "In our temperate climate there are women who habitually wear underpants as their first garment. This is a superfluity that is usually unrelated to the harshness of the climate. . . . However, beneath a vast, open, cold crinoline, underpants might be necessary."[21] Moralists did not necessarily approve: "I always distrust women who wear drawers—this is modesty displaying a shop sign," asserted one of them.[22] But that invisible shop sign was closely watched in amorous circles[23] and became, when it was toned down, a social marker multiplied by the ready-to-wear industry. Appearing in trousseaux, the "indispensable" was soon unknown only to the lower classes.[24] Small or youthful bourgeois girls could display their pantaloons below their dress or short crinoline without giving rise to misunderstanding—at the knees for girls between four and twelve, at midcalf for those between about twelve and seventeen. It signaled that they were young, not yet nubile. Thus, like all women's underwear, pantaloons adopted forms and appearances that mirrored short-term life stages and the long-term history of repression, still simple and visible. Contemporary with and familiar to the hysteria-generating world explored by Charcot and Freud, these physical obstacles to instincts would disappear with (among other

Lingerie counter

factors) the insiduous internalization of a self-control effective enough to render external, concrete armor unnecessary. In 1896, when Vacher de Lapouge analyzed and condemned the pervasive textile obsession, his sanitarian concern presaged the reverse movement, which the moral order[25] that would inform the next century directed and transmitted:

> The clothing invasion proceeds, and the horror of nudity is firmly fixed in our minds. During the last century clothing still allowed a bit of nudity because it did not cling to the body. Today we are so completely packaged that no skin shows. Early in the century women's necks and arms were still bare, and their bosoms partly so. They did not wear pantaloons, and air circulated beneath their bell—shaped skirts. Contemporary modesty rejects that and abets anemia and neurosis. In the last thirty years pantaloons have generally been adopted by little girls under the influence of nuns, pious murderesses who prepare their students for heaven, anemia, and tuberculosis. As soon as they can walk they are put in long dresses. Air circulation is reduced to a minimum at the age they need oxygen the most.[26]

The Chemise

Let us return to our *cabinet de toilette* where Madame, helped by her chambermaid, slips into a chemise, a much older garment.[27] In batiste, nainsook, lawn, cotton, linen, or duck depending on social status, it falls straight to the bottom of the pantaloons. Like the nightgown, it is viewed by too few to warrant significant variations in cut, elaborate decorations, or luxurious material. These changes would come when it became more visible,[28]

"The chemise" (Daniel Casey)

but at midcentury and for twenty more years modesty was its principal mission, its primary quality. "A woman's chemise is something to respect, not to criticize. White symbol of her modesty, it must not be touched or observed too closely," wrote Dr. Daumas, who was nevertheless preoccupied by hygienic-functional considerations. "The sleeveless chemise held up only by shoulder straps ordinarily covers only half the chest. The system is good, or at least convenient, for nursing women." But "chemisettes of tulle or batiste that must be worn to cover the shoulders . . . never overlap hermetically enough. . . . In that region of the body cold winds are keener and more penetrating than a man's gaze. They slip through the cutwork, through imperceptible fissures; they worm their way in, spread, and wreak havoc, causing coughs, hoarseness, and throat infections."[29]

While the rest of the body was enveloped, harnessed, trussed up, and buttoned, the bosom remained exposed to view, cold, and illness, the sacrificical portion offered to men, just like waists strangled by corsets.

The Corset

Drawing in the waist, supporting the breasts, rounding out the rump, and arching the figure according to the erotic-aesthetic canons of the moment constituted its principal purposes[30]—"to have it both ways," as the English laconically put it.

In the nineteenth century, the corset no longer corrected and straightened the body, at least not in the same way or to the same extent as formerly. The strange, protean, and extraordinarily persistent career of constrictive devices—from the Roman fasciae to the contemporary girdle by way of the medieval "bliaut," the Renaissance "basquine," the seventeenth-century "quilted body," and the eighteenth-century "stiffened body"[31]—raises significant questions about the body and reveals images, beliefs, conceptions, and techniques concerning it.[32] Thus, the pre-Revolutionary corset, the "body with stays," was viewed mainly as a continuation of swaddling clothes, as a protective mold, the preventative or sometimes corrective tutor for soft, passive bodies, especially in the case of children whose bones were "tender" and figures "fragile." In the nineteenth century, on the other hand, binding had disappeared, at the very least in cities,[33] and the corset was no longer its logical successor. Children no longer wore it, and young girls adopted it only at puberty. Less bulky[34] and less constraining, it corresponded to new representations of the body.

Around 1750, a medical-pedagogical crusade had been launched by Drs. Winslow,[35] Desessartz,[36] and Vandermonde.[37] It was clamorously pursued by Rousseau[38] and Buffon[39] and eventually by Drs. Tissot,[40] Leroy,[41] and several others who defined its content. It blamed stiffened corsets and swaddling clothes for anatomical degeneration, weakness, and deformation and advocated freedom and exercise, which alone would permit, they argued, the body to grow strong and appropriately shapely.[42]

This new radical criticism[43] ran counter to the period's established practices[44] but nevertheless made its way. If during the Revolution it did not play a decisive role in the disappearance of the "stiffened body," which was proscribed because it was an aristocratic symbol like swords and wigs, the discourse would nevertheless serve as a reference when the corset reappeared in a shortened form near the end of the Empire and throughout the century. It either condemned the new version or assigned it a function—principally aesthetic, social, moral, or hygienic—that promoted, along with physical education, the designing, manufacturing, and marketing of specifically orthopedic corsets. The corset was no longer a preventive mold,[45] and though the ordinary corset still corrected, it did so less by reshaping the body itself than by changing its appearance, through concealment, subterfuge, and enhancement. Nonetheless, the corset participated in strangling the waist, and consequently in reshaping the rib cage.

In contrast to earlier *corps*, or "bodies," the "Ninon" corset that appeared around 1810 was only slightly stiffened and considerably shortened; its purpose was to separate the breasts, as fashion then required. With the Restoration, the "Ninon" became larger and once again reduced the waist, until then placed beneath the bust, while skirts, which had hung straight during the Empire, began the swelling that would lead to the extravagant fullness we have already discussed. Until roughly 1830, stiffening grew heavier and became harder, the busk longer and thicker, gussets supported the breasts and fully enveloped the hips. But this new armor, supplied with shoulder pads, corresponded to an image of the female body as a softness to be supported and a waist to be compressed. The intent was hygienic and aesthetic: to strengthen a basically weak anatomy and enhance its privileged aspects.

By preserving the aristocratic principle of ostentatious hinderance of the performance of useful labor or any suggestion of it, nineteenth-century bourgeois canons of feminine beauty perpetuated the prestige of strangled waists, dainty extremities, delicate wrists and ankles, and alabaster skin. But it entailed a cost. "Useless and expensive," in Veblen's phrase,[46] women were kept in exchange for the force of nonproduction, of pure consumption, which they represented notably because of the brutally constricting device that flayed and mutilated them.[47] Like the contemporary fascination with trim figures, the small waist mystique tormented bourgeois women from the Restoration to the Great War. The sacrifice was somewhat alleviated when fabrics became more elastic and light steel wire replaced heavy whalebone, but the corset never stopped making women erotic, prestigious objects, kept from the sphere of action and bereft of power outside their small domestic world. Around 1840, however, an invention marked an important stage in the technical and social history of the corset: a new method known as "the lazy woman's lacing" was perfected, enabling a woman to dress and undress without the help of a servant, husband, or lover. Until then, obligatory dependence provided caricaturists a thousand opportunities, and novelists sometimes described an expert or clumsy lacer, such as Wenceslas, Valérie's sculptor in Balzac's *Cousine Bette*.[48] Now, unless she wanted to be very tightly laced, a woman did not have to seek outside help.[49] This self-sufficiency democratized the accessory and brought it into more general use. Before 1828 there were only two corset patent applications, whereas from 1828 to 1848 there were sixty-four.[50] And in 1832 the Swiss Jean Werly built at Bar-le-Duc the first factory to weave seamless corsets that left the loom stayed, busked, sized, and ready for sale.

"Oh! My word! This is odd! . . . This
morning I tied a knot on that lace,
and this evening there's a bow."

During the Second Empire the corset became shorter, and its neckline was lowered. This was the period of sloping shoulders and majestic breasts that were no longer pushed upward in eighteenth-century fashion, but carried low, like pears collected in two hemispheric bowls, allowing deep décolletage. The waist, still pinched, had to contrast pleasingly with the crinoline's width, which exaggerated the hips.

Because the corset served this representation of the body, abetting its luxuriousness, it became the object of innumerable discussions—moralistic or ribald, hygienic or aesthetic, reformist or traditionalist—in which the most contradictory arguments intertwined. The equally discordant voices of physicians—or references to them—dominated the discussions. Although the device provided vital support to the body, at least symbolically, it also threatened it, some asserted, with sickness and death. In order to make his point, Dr. Debay cited appalling statistics:

> May the following table open the eyes of those blind mothers who, in the hope of giving their daughters an elegant waist, imprison them from an early age in an inflexible corset. This table averages forty years of observation.
>
> Of 100 young girls wearing a corset:
> 25 succumbed to diseases of the chest;
> 15 died after their first delivery;
> 15 remained infirm after delivery;
> 15 became deformed;
> 30 alone resisted, but sooner or later were afflicted with serious indispositions.[51]

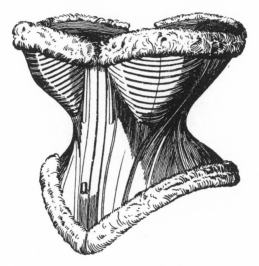

"The corset is the framework of a woman's body. It is the foundation of the edifice."
(Dr. Casimir Daumas)

Tight lacing was the principal danger. Verardi gave other sinister numbers: "Four-fifths of the young women of Paris who die from tuberculosis murder themselves because they want the slim waist achieved by a corset."[52] The fateful consequence of constriction was reiterated by Countess Drohojowska in her handbook of manners:

How many cases of gastritis, liver complaints, migraines, and anxious or de-
pressed moods would have been easy to cure at the onset by loosening a corset. But, having reached a certain stage, they become incurable and dig a
premature grave before the eyes of a weeping family, who often, by admiring
bodies deformed by deliberate distortions, have encouraged this aberration.[53]

Deploring the misuse of the corset did not inevitably lead to proscribing
its principle. One thing was agreed upon: children should no longer wear
it unless absolutely required to do so for orthopedic reasons. For young
girls at puberty, the development of breasts and hips demanded the wearing of corsets. But even at this stage, opinions diverged. On one hand,
there were those who, following Winslow and Desessartz, increasingly
criticized premature use of these appliances, charging them with debilitat-
ing and deforming effects; on the other, there persisted indications inherited from the eighteenth century that attributed to the corset preventative,
indeed corrective functions. The great abolitionist Dr. Debay argued that

a very grave misconception held by mothers sees the corset as an excellent
means of correcting defects in the figure and posture of their daughters. They
eagerly apply this straitjacket to these frail creatures whose torso soon devi-
ates from its normal erectness, leaning forward, backward, to the right or left.
This error greatly augments the very defect or deformity mothers are trying
to correct.[54]

In his *Hygiene and Physiology of Marriage*, which went through 171 print-
ings, he condemned the corset, which was as "dangerous for young girls as
swaddling clothes were for infants" and repeated Rousseau's argument
against the "stiffened body":

If you see so many chests squeezed and deformed at the base, if the bosoms of
young city women of eighteen have neither the volume nor the firm shape of
those of country girls, if the city girls in general have soft, prematurely flabby,
undeveloped breasts, without adequate nipples, blame the corset. If so many
city women are puny, deformed, and, once they become mothers, do not have
enough of a breast to nurse their infant, they owe this sad result partly to the
corset. If so many of them die consumptive, it is again the corset that is to
blame.[55]

On the other hand, Dr. Bouvier was totally opposed to this interpretation:

As for today's corsets, . . . people still believe that this garment causes spinal
deformations because they are worn much more by city than country women,
by rich than poor families, by the peoples of old Europe than those in many
European colonies, as though the individuals under consideration differed

only in one aspect, namely, the greater or lesser use of corsets, as if differences of constitution, physical strength, way of life, heredity, illness, race, and so on did not provide as many other causes capable of accounting for their differences in spinal development. Today, moreover, when young girls are not given corsets until they approach puberty, it is impossible to attribute to their influence deformations that almost always begin before then. I have sometimes seen lateral curvatures of the spine develop more rapidly because corsets were not used in due time; on the other hand, I have never observed that their use contributed to this deformity.[56]

Preventing weakness and correcting physical deformations in young girls by constriction was thus encouraged. Other physicians, such as Michel Lévy, urged "the development of the girls' physique by exercise, gymnastics, and cold baths." He denounced the aesthetic justification of corsets for that age. "Does it conserve the bosom's freshness and firmness? No: it softens, creases, and stretches it, sometimes preventing the development of the nipples and causing the mammary glands to harden."[57] Dr. Daumas agreed:

No one received in a house where young girls are brought up under high pressure has failed to hear this order repeated a hundred times by the mother: "Mademoiselle, sit up straight!" To obey, the poor little one would need to go outdoors to run and play, a rope or hoop in her hand. Instead she is given a busk to wear. She is imprisoned in a stiffened, steeled corset that bruises the body and smothers her. Now, here is what happens: by the time she is sixteen the young girl is a hunchback. If she is not hunchbacked she is chlorotic, her stomach no longer functions, her breathing is shallow rather than deep, her arms are like spindles, her legs like drumsticks, and she eats plaster or charcoal: it's time to get her married![58]

One of the missions of this anatomical modeling was to obtain a slim waist and an attractive carriage, which were erotic stocks on the matrimonial market, social assets, and symbolic guarantees. "The corsets, the steel stays, the horsehair pads, all of the secrets of orthopedics are employed to compose an irreproachable maiden from bits and pieces."[59] Dr. Debay bemoaned this: "In the evening [young girls] are removed from their cases and put back in them the next morning. Poor children! And it is to make you attractive that your blind mothers torture you this way. . . . Oh! Enlightened Hygiene! You have proscribed swaddling clothes; when will you discredit the corset?"[60]

The corseted adolescent body remained the object of controversy, not only among doctors but also among moralists, some seeing it as a guarantee of good behavior and virtue, others as the opposite. Women's bodies, on the other hand, attracted a broader consensus: their opulence, softness, and fullness required wearing a corset, essentially for support. "The corset is the framework of a woman's body. It is the foundation of the edifice."[61] Housebound, idle, submerged by cascades of fabric, girdled and whaleboned, she was trapped in concentric circles that were in effect vicious circles, preventing muscular development and decreasing muscle tone. Thus, in a kind of endless dialectic, the corset contained a softened body that it both caused and cured.

> Their social condition condemns women to a sedentary life and weakens their muscular system for want of exercise. This is the cause of the fatigue they immediately feel in a seated or standing position. They overcome this by wearing a corset, not so much to straighten the spinal column, as to provide a fulcrum for the trunk when it leans forward. The state of forward half-flexion is usual during their sedentary occupations, and, without the resistance provided by the corset, it would be exaggerated by the weight of the head, breasts, and all of the abdominal and thoracic internal organs.[62]

For Dr. Bouvier as well, "aesthetics and the social role of women ought to encourage the physician to permit corsets. . . . In addition, there are other considerations, such as the volume of the breasts, the weakening of the abdominal muscular wall, habitual arching of the trunk, or lateral deviation of the spine, which positively indicate the use of this kind of bandage."[63]

For his part, Dr. Donné wrote in a *Hygiene for Fashionable People* (1870) that "the kinds of corsets worn today are beneficial because they brace and support the body and internal organs that tend to be dragged down by their weight or that are badly contained in their cavities."[64] And even Dr. Debay allowed the corset for "fat persons," when its "sole purpose is to hold in overabundant forms and contain abdominal development."[65]

Discord reappeared, however, as soon as the question of the habitual use of corsets arose. In this regard, Drs. Bouvier and Debay are the exemplary figures of two radically opposed views.[66] For the first, not a moment's hesitation: "Not long ago we heard our venerable teacher, Professor Roux, exclaim with profound conviction that 'all' men should wear a supporter. Could it not be said with equal justice that all adult women should wear a corset, a true supporter of the mammary glands, which are no less sensitive than the spermatic glands, no less exposed to dangerous shocks and tugging."[67] The second argued, however, that "the corset is suitable only for women afflicted with imperfections of the bust or deformities of the figure, in order to disguise these beneath the garment. For well-shaped women the corset is an insult to nature and beauty; far from contributing to the attractions of a supple figure, it on the contrary stiffens it and deprives it of grace."[68]

Consumption, palpitations, aneurisms, cephalgia, stomach pains, hysteria, leucorrhea, amenorrhea, and miscarriages—none of these dire consequences deterred the tenacious general use of corsets, any more than moral exhortations, religious pamphlets, or reform proposals.[69] In fact, its use ended only during World War I and for functional rather than medical reasons, namely the entrance of many women into the work force. Until then, more important than health itself, the corset signified status, socialized the body, repaired imperfections, and modeled shapes according to the dominant canons. In the erotic geography of the female body certain rotundities were allowed as generously given by nature—even when they were deceptive—while other modifications were judged artificial and forbidden as offensive to bourgeois decency. For example, a slim waist emphasizing a steatopygous figure and sharpening desire was scandalous; yet here, too, contradictions abounded. A "comme il faut" woman had to have a trim waist;[70] but the very same might arouse a deplorable lubricity. "Put your corset on early, accustom yourself to not being able to do without it, for it will be equally useful to your health and good posture,"[71] declared a guide to comportment, which nevertheless noted that "if decent women knew that a slim waist and a crinoline please men only because they arouse secret images of shameful debauchery, they would give them up."[72]

"A slim waist emphasizing a
steatopygous figure and sharpening
desire was scandalous."

In fact, these features represented a considerable economic and symbolic interest. Especially as an aesthetic dowry, they invited maternal attentions that often bordered on torture. Speaking of deaths caused by excessive compression, Verardi wrote that "many parents, and especially mothers, are accomplices in this kind of murder for the mere vanity of having a daughter built like a spider or a wasp."[73] To read Charles Dubois's *Considerations on Five Plagues: The Abuse of the Corset, the Use of Tobacco, the Passion for Gambling, the Abuse of Strong Drink, and Speculation*, published in 1857, it was mothers, certainly, with their hopes for a good marriage in mind, but it was also prospective husbands, seduced and debauched, who were responsible for this disastrous practice:

> Madame V. had a daughter of eighteen, perfectly reared, noted for her grace and attractions, with a charming personality. She told her: "You will never make a good marriage if you don't pinch your waist! Look at your cousins. To what do they owe their fortunes . . . ?" And the poor child squeezed her figure, not for the mercenary reasons her mother evoked but out of obedience.
>
> Madame V. married her daughter to a Monsieur, thirty-six years old and ugly enough to make her think him much richer than he was; but he adored wasp waists. The poor young woman continued to lace herself tightly to please her husband. This ugly character, whom I knew, was not only egotistical but also vain, crochety, and curt.
>
> After eighteen months of marriage and torture, his unfortunate wife died of an intestinal inflammation. The doctors ascertained that her corset was from eight to ten centimeters too tight.[74]

When not criminals, the worshipers of strangled waists were adulterers. "Any woman," wrote Dubois, "who has conquered her husband by the slimness of her waist has married . . . a fool or a rake and shortly will see her captive break his chains of artificial flowers to run after waists not as well dressed perhaps, but 'trimmer' than his wife's."[75] A rule of this deadly struggle with oneself and others, to squeeze the trunk between the ribs and the hips, was not to admit one's pain: "Tell that pale woman about to faint that her corset is hurting her: she will promptly deny it."[76] Her waist could not appear other than naturally trim even though, upon fainting, cutting her laces would bring recovery. In fact, excessive constriction of the body led to consequences akin to those of infamous masturbation: they slowed demographic growth, weakened the race, and in short endangered the fatherland as well as the practitioners:[77]

> If in twenty years we are engaged in a serious struggle that we must sustain for a while, army recruitment in France will become more and more difficult, assuming that the corset continues its ravages.

And no one should forget this: despite our keen desire for a general peace, for a long time to come extremely powerful interests will demand war. . . . To fight and win, to attain glory, it is not enough for a soldier to have courage, he also needs a body and strong limbs; is it not the same for a nation?[78]

Achille Tola-Poix, in a short work that appeared in 1861, entitled *Belts That Talk*, proposed that women be judged precisely on the basis of this accessory, "for her waist is the first to display the incriminating proof of her weakness or the evidence of her fulfilled duty." If too tight she "must not, cannot be other than a bad mother,"[79] he observed; and in a hymn to procreation, he exhorted women's wombs to recover—along with embonpoint—their fertility: "O, young women! O, young mothers! Undo your girdles! Do not be afraid to admit that from birth heaven created you to become mothers; that this sentiment, this duty, the first and most sacred of all on earth, is for you an aegis against false shame and against the frivolous disappointment of being no longer able to tighten your girdles. Leave to fallen women the reprehensible fear of becoming fertile: they are speculating on their fall."[80]

Some women, however, seeking to combine the signs of virtuous maternity with a desirable body, laced their corsets even tighter during their pregnancy. "I have known," wrote Boitard, "a very vain woman who delivered only crippled infants because she crippled them in her womb to keep a slim waist."[81]

But distress and alarm weighed little compared with desire and prestige. The production of corsets grew apace: the 6,500 workers who produced them in Paris grew to 10,000 in 1855, and the volume of business increased from 7 to 10 or 12 million francs.[82] In 1861 Jules Simon estimated the number of corsets sold annually in the capital at 1,200,000.[83] Choice proliferated: lightly stiffened morning corsets, very tight corsets to wear under ball gowns, short-waisted corsets for resting, undershirts for little girls, nuptial corsets for the young girl, maternity corsets with elastic ties, nursing corsets with drawbridge gussets, long, stout, riding corsets, very elastic traveler's corsets; in heavy red drill costing from 3 to 20 francs each for the peasant or worker; in batiste moiré, brocaded satin, or silk damask from 25 to 60 francs[84] for great ladies and the actresses of the *petit-théâtres*; some embroidered with grey braid at 20 centimes the meter, others ruched with Alençon lace at 200 francs.

Skirts and Petticoats

After the corset, and over it, one donned petticoats, as many as a dozen, or, after 1854, a cage covered with only one or two. In each case, the first petticoat was soft and plain, often of wool in the winter and percale in the summer, whereas the others became richer as they came nearer the dress and ran the risk of being glimpsed during a pirouette or a gust of wind.

Under evening clothes, petticoats of lawn, silk, or nainsook were flounced and heavily starched in order to support full skirts with trains.

"After the corset . . .
one donned petticoats,
as many as a dozen."

Finally, the skirt circumscribed and contained this cascading tangle of layered petticoats. Although white, and occasionally black, still largely predominated in this intimate lingerie, it was enhanced by marvelous laces. Skillful combinations of color, monochrome mauve for blondes, crimson or orange for brunettes, appeared shortly after the Second Empire. "Color in women's secret clothing," wrote Pierre de Lano in 1896, "is a completely modern notion, born of the nervous torments of our imagination, the dulling of our sensations, and the insatiable desire that makes us suffer, almost, and that drives us in all the manifestations of our fevered life."[85]

Stockings and Garters

Stockings were subject to the rule of white or light colors. Greens and reds sometimes worn at the beach or in the country were never seen elsewhere. Black was reserved for widows and elderly women. In open lisle or fine guipure, tightly hugging the curve of the calf, suggesting its milky skin while still veiling it modestly, stockings often ignited strong eroticism.

The garter, that little elastic band, often finely decorated, which was succeeded at the end of the century by the garter belt, made it possible, as did its successor, to catch and pull the stocking above the knee to mold the calf, that sacred domain where every detail aroused desire. On this point, the scrupulous aesthete E. Feydeau was inflexible: "A woman who commits the crime of wearing her stockings below the knee does not deserve to live."[86] On the other hand, because of its accidental character, the loss of a garter did not seem irremissible, although "prejudice attaches a serious significance to this accident."[87] In short, the liturgy of the stocking was so serious that deviations quickly became blasphemous.

MEN'S INTIMACIES

Like the black suit, nineteenth-century men's underwear displayed no suggestive elegance and was worn without the least erotic intent. It testified to the bourgeoisie's wish to deny the presence of the body that lust or a glance would reaffirm. Subjects of an extraordinarily discreet hygienic discourse, underpants, shirts, undershirts, stockings, and socks evoked an embarrassed silence or general derision.

The time when Rabelais could celebrate the padding of "beautiful and magnificent codpieces," decorated with ribbons and gems, had long passed.[88] Male underpants, which appeared with trousers,[89] were a prosaic sheath of linen, cotton, or flannel covering the lower trunk and the legs to the calves, and supported from the shoulders by suspenders. Elegance was excluded from them.

Some refinements were displayed on the shirt but only in its visibile regions, such as the collar, faux-col, shirtfront, or cuffs, which thenceforth no longer belonged to *under*wear. Today the entire shirt is considered outerwear. Its long history, therefore, consists of secular alternations between concealment and visibility.

Finally, the flannel vest covered the torso like a camisole, either over or under the shirt. At midcentury its usage was still recent, as were the socks that gradually replaced stockings.

Little documentation exists of these pieces of men's apparel, their slow modifications, their degree of cleanliness, and the frequency with which they were changed. On the subject of underpants, for example, account books themselves remain obscure and confused. In his study of the cost of laundering in Paris, G. Bienaymé noted that "information on underpants which have been worn for a long time is too vague to be used."[90] The shirt, thanks to the parts that emerged from the shameful subterranean world of underwear, avoided general opprobrium—as though it had been ennobled by the open air and unambiguous exposure.

In fact, only medical and hygienic discourse enabled one legitimately to approach an intimate subject considered both ridiculous and indecent. Although such a monumental *Encyclopedic Dictionary of the Medical Sciences* as Dechambre's[91] did not devote the briefest entry to underpants or shirts, it nevertheless treated subjects as diverse as camels, tobacco, California, fog, and the Cagots! The relation of underwear fabric to the skin it covered was seriously debated by some physicians. In particular, the problem of flannel and its effects on the skin seemed important to those who studied it, even though their conclusions differed. As early as 1841, Descuret discussed it in relation to the "treatment of the passions": "Tunics made of coarse wool applied directly to the skin cause a constant friction that finally dulls sensitivity and thus contributes to lowering the heat of passion. This is the principal reason its use has been prescribed in some religious communities."[92]

In his *Study of the Action of Flannel in Direct Contact with the Skin*, published in 1855, Fulgence Fiévée de Jeumont, citing numerous cases ranging from dental neuralgia to priapism, by way of insomnia, established on the contrary the persistence of its "electrogalvanic" effect on the organism.[93] Nevertheless, for others who recommended it for the benefit of sick, convalescing, or elderly persons whose calorification needed to be supplemented, this material was not always harmful: "A shirt, underpants, and undershirt of wool are the equivalent of a soft, continuous friction over the entire skin; at the same time they circumscribe an atmosphere around the body and, if one can put it this way, an individual climate, the only resource of those who cannot afford to emigrate to warm regions."[94]

But for young people, wearing flannel for too long or without medical reasons could make them vulnerable to pulmonary afflictions and engender an irreversible dependency: "We have the right to say, and quite correctly, that once the habit of wearing flannel is contracted, it is difficult and often imprudent to abandon it; you must endure the yoke you have imposed on yourself, or at least you must abandon it with the greatest caution and during the time of the year when warm temperatures are known to be stable."[95]

These medical discussions of the various influences of wool cast some light on the organization and practices of men's underclothes. Corsets, for example, are rarely mentioned, for their use—still frequent between 1820 and 1840 among men of fashion—declined considerably afterward. The reason for this was the decided clash between honor and returns on investments in a bourgeois male's appearance. Honor had been garnered from an aristocratic ethic of spending and idleness that the profit motive increasingly denigrated, while wealth was produced by an ethic of thrift and work. More precisely, a bourgeois's prestige resided in his wife's idleness and consumption, which were underwritten by the returns on his investments. Thus, from the middle of the century on, men's corsets were ridiculed as effeminate and pretentious, like brilliant colors or wigs, in short, like everything that recalled the ancien régime too blatantly. "If compressing the body is cruel and harmful for women," noted Charles Dubois, "it is singularly ridiculous for men, which does not make it any less dangerous. This failing in our sex ordinarily indicates excessive self-conceit."[96]

The fact that this practice was criticized even in the savoir-faire manuals indicates that it nevertheless persisted here and there. They were often worn by soldiers, principally cavalry officers, heirs to a period when men had displayed themselves as much as women and in the same way, and also by men struggling against potbellies, who used the corset's constrictions to reject that emblem of bourgeois success. Hygienists and moralists were sometimes disturbed and angered by "this ridiculous and pernicious custom,"[97] without understanding its symbolic function, often more vital than life itself:

> Is there not already enough steel, lead, and exhaustion to cut warriors down? Do we need to allow the addition of voluntary strangulation? . . .
>
> How many times have I seen these Sons of Mars pass by pinched like dolls, and the public turn around to look at them and hurl, at their backs, energetic rebukes and comments as biting as they were mocking, which met with nothing but approbation!
>
> One can understand that women and young girls, who have lost their common sense because of excessive coquettery, kill themselves by squeezing their bodies to the limit; but that warriors who excel by their courage, training, and martial physiques should fall into this absurdity, now that is something well designed to cause stupefaction![98]

"If compressing the body is cruel and harmful for women,
it is singularly ridiculous for men." (Charles Dubois)

Nevertheless, the military model of posture, indeed even the practice of girthing, which produced a compressed waist and puffed-out chest, considerably influenced the civilian model of bearing. But aside from the fossilized, restricted use of the corset, men's underwear was not assigned, as we have said, any true seductive function. Its forms changed very slowly, white fabrics remained the rule, and it took nearly a century for it to become involved in the short cycles of commercial fashion, to take on colors, and by means of a suddenly triumphant advertising image, acquire a new legitimacy[99] that corresponded not to an unleashing of the life of the passions but rather to its mastery. Nothing is farther removed from Second

Empire bourgeois sensibilities and representations than our own dedramatization of nudity and banalization of underwear. In this sense, by their
very mundaneness, shapeless white underpants mirrored a significant stage
in the process of self-control, which as yet contained these impulses only
by repressing them, expelling them from the social sphere, and restricting
them to the narrowest intimacy. The introduction in the late 1960s of
attractive, "presentable," colored briefs indicated another stage in this
process, the fulfillment of which would, perhaps, result in so thorough
an internalization of the standards of modesty that covering nakedness
even partially would become unnecessary, inflation having so devalued
nudity.[100]

NOCTURNAL CLOTHING

After the Middle Ages, day wear was a socially sexed object assigned to
biologically sexed bodies. Cultural attributes were added to natural ones,
as though to emphasize sexual identity and ward off any ambiguity. Yet,
the nightdress—when it was worn—distinguished the sexes much less
clearly because both men and women were indiscriminately covered by the
full nightgown, which hung like a dress.

The history of the nightdress embraces extensive conjunctures and involves vast domains such as intimacy, sleeping, beds, heating, and sexuality.
It spans a thousand years—Isidore of Seville spoke of it at the beginning of
the seventh century—but its career was discontinuous. However, even the
interruptions cast light on periods or societies and their representations

Amoroso, allegretto

and practices regarding the body in sleep. Thus from the eleventh to the sixteenth century, people in the West either kept their clothes on or slept "naked to naked," as the fabliaux put it.[101] This ingenuous nakedness and absent modesty, accompanied by a very strong sociability in and around the bed,[102] disappeared during the sixteenth century, allowing the "nightshirt" to reappear during the seventeenth[103] and to last for more than three hundred years. This nighttime garment reflected a new sensibility about what touched the body; precisely like the fork and the handkerchief, which appeared at the same moment, it indicated a change in the boundaries of modesty that mediated certain acts such as eating, hid certain functions like blowing the nose, and privatized activities such as sleep. Still prestigious and theatrically displayed to courtiers at a great lord's ceremonious levee or couchee, the nightshirt was confined within an increasingly narrow and private space as the bourgeoisie ascended.

Undressing

In the nineteenth century the nightshirt no longer left the bedroom, which was itself completely set apart from social life; it was taboo in conversation and invisible to strangers. A cause of shame and agony when glimpsed, even by the closest family members, because, like the bed, it every day lived in greatest intimacy with the body, the bourgeois nightshirt was consequently devoid of any elegance in cut or ornamentation. At least such was the case among "comme il faut" people, because, conversely, excessive affectation in this domain, as in skirts, immediately indicated indecency and depravity. Yet the rule of simplicity was not the same for every period of life. Although a young girl's nightgown had to express innocence, a married woman's was allowed a few more suggestive decorations, but within the bounds of a becoming modesty, and only during her childbearing years. This subject was more eloquently and less prudishly discussed after the Second Empire. The following description, which dates from 1883, both emphasizes the traditional difference between the nightdress of a young girl and that of a young wife and shows how the latter's decorative and erotic role accentuates the difference:

> It would be regrettable to pass over in silence the most winning of all [the chemises]: the conjugal chemise. Do not describe it to young girls—one must respect the exquisite and somewhat excessive modesty of the seraphim—but it must be placed in their bridal trousseau. They will not wear it immediately; but after a while they will understand the value of this oriental silk or batiste, with large lace inserts, all aquiver with valenciennes flounces that embellish it at the hem. They will become accustomed to this transparent network, which in front—from the beginning of the bosom to the belt—reveals the charming graces of a young and supple bust.[104]

Fashion, however, acted slowly on the forms of the chemise, which changed hardly at all during the century, in silk, batiste, or lawn for women and calico for men. Nor did the nightcap change, though it tended to disappear in well-off, urban milieus,[105] especially among the young.

Pajamas began to compete with this open, full, and unisex system only at the beginning of the twentieth century. First made for male customers, their success soon turned the nightdress into an exclusively feminine attribute until pajamas were also adopted by women.

The Circulation of Fashions

Fashion dominates provincial women, but the Parisiennes
govern fashion, and know how to turn it to their own advantage.
The first are like ignorant and servile plagiarists who copy
even spelling errors; the latter are like authors who
are master copiers and know how to correct
mistakes in the original.

—JEAN-JACQUES ROUSSEAU, *La Nouvelle Héloïse* (1761)

FASHION WAS LINKED to sartorial propriety in many ways. On the one hand,
it was subordinated to propriety: "manners" set limits to fashion's domain,
limits that could be overstepped with impunity only when new "manners"
were established. On the other hand, fashion complemented and complicated the mechanism that defended the space of dominant social groups
against incursions by would-be imitators. Propriety was the venerable, recognized science of appropriately handling possibilities in clothing according to place and circumstance, while fashion was the unstable, ever-changing science of optimum management of the possible within an interplay of
innovation and obsolescence. Depending on the groups and places it traversed, fashion was in effect geared down, just as variations became apparent even amid the seemingly uniform products it distributed.

FASHION VECTORS, FASHION PLACES

To understand the social and geographic circuit traveled by fashion we
need to consider its driving force. Serving fashion were artisans whose task
was to shape, prolong, or shorten novelty. But as we have seen, the phenomenon often appeared to fluctuate independently of any outside
influences. No one "invented" the crinoline, the bustle, or the spindle-

shaped dress, the three constituent moments of an often-repeated cycle. They allowed the great houses, such as Worth, Paul Poiret, or Redfern, to display their respective talents, without making them by any means ingegious demiurges. To know, however, where a certain fashion originated, how it spread, and when it expired pertains to the historian's domain.

A new fashion, always deemed extreme at first, would emerge from the shops of the great masters of made-to-measure who stamped it with their style, and travel through the population for whom it was first and essentially intended: the "demimonde," so called after the expression popularized by the play of Alexandre Dumas, fils.[1] This was a specifically Parisian fauna, situated, as its name indicates, between the *monde* or "social world" of virtuous and well-born wives and the "nothing" of people with petty pretensions. It was at once complex, because of the social origin of its recruits, and homogenous, because these women played a common role. In the matter of dress, the demimondaine's social and material existence required her to risk ridicule, to flaunt excess and to dare impose the latest extravagance, in short, to introduce fashion. Modern hetaerae, also called *cocottes*, and *biches*, ("does," because of the "animality" they evoked), they, like Zola's Nana, came from the working-class faubourgs and the *petits-théâtres*. Their function was to exalt the prestige of their lovers by displaying spectacular finery, the emblems of their own success and the wages received for their keep.[2] Henri Despaigne, in reproving the men they enthralled for what he believed to be contradictory attitudes, actually indicated the importance of the function *cocottes* fulfilled, a function both sexual and social that complemented that of wives:

> Why do you bestow admiration, time, and wealth on what fashion calls high doedom when you do not want your wives and sisters—from whom you often lack the decency and skill to hide your separate establishments—to attempt pleasing you by displaying the same unwholesome extravagance that seduces you? You are attracted by artfully flashy clothes, against which your austere economy protests. You are seduced by the brilliance surrounding them. Your eyes and imagination are captivated by the audacious coquettery of glances and finery, the artifices of makeup, the easy, shameless manners, and the strange but real radiance. You cast your gold and duty to the wind and enter that banal boudoir whose pungent perfumes inebriate you. You return home still reeking of its scents, drained by its voluptuous exhaustion, and yet to defend the love, happiness, and sometimes the wealth of the family, you want your own women to forego the seductions they know so effective![3]

Another contemporary figure, the *cocodette*, also a member of the guild, sported a more modest splendor. She was a declassé society woman, excluded from her class because of a scandal, divorce, or open liaison, who had espoused the immoral life of pleasures and excesses typical of the *cocottes*, but preserved more tasteful habits, manners, and speech. Unfettered by prejudices but less threatening, she blurred the demarcations between these zones of the social hierarchy.

The demimondaines ritually inaugurated fashions according to a calendar and in places that were progressively institutionalized. They thus maintained with the women of the real *monde* subterranean complicities marked by reciprocal fascination and complex rivalries in which both parties watched their appearance and reinterpreted what seemed the exclusive prerogative of the other: for one, distinction and discretion, for the other, audacity and novelty. The resulting confusion in elegance alarmed moralists who observed "this singular disarray: the peaks aspire to descend, the top envies the bottom, and great ladies strive to become *cocottes*. The emulation of evil has shifted the battleground."[4] "Despite their use of bold colors and styles, . . . [they] often successfully affect . . . simplicity and an opulent, tasteful sobriety that deceives the most practiced eye."[5] No longer

Demimondaine (Constantin Guys)

distinguished by the "comme il faut" it once monopolized, the *monde* had to borrow new distinctions from the everyday arsenal of the demimondaine, thereby, at least tacitly, reinforcing the demimonde's legitimacy, a legitimacy sustained by the fascination it aroused at balls, the races, or the promenade. Reported by rumor and newspapers, the spectacular comportment of madly adulated and madly extravagant women such as Paiva, Alice Ozy, Esther Guimoud, Mogador, or Cora Pearl rapidly became legendary. Fashion and finery, of course, figured prominently in the spectacle. Whether they paraded along the Champs-Elysées, in the Bois de Boulogne or at Longchamp, on the stage or in theater boxes, on travels or at watering places, everywhere they attracted notice so as to be recognized. They were the testing grounds for new fashions, creating the event, posting scores, sizing up looks, evaluating astonishment or irony, envious admiration or open contempt.

The public's choice of certain places at certain times of the year can often be explained by the "latest fashions" launched there. During the winter the leading actresses of the *petits-théâtres* introduced or reactivated fashions. They resorted to renowned milliners and tailors who executed creations for the occasion, and the success of the outfit could contribute to that of the show. Because of the actresses, a costume—like the vaudeville or the operetta that introduced it to the stage—could fail at the Variétés but triumph at the Bouffes-Parisiens. All the fashion journals published a theater rubric since they were expected to criticize the clothes. Costumes received as much attention as the performance, especially at premieres, because the immoral beauties also displayed their toilettes at the event.

> There [said the Larousse Encyclopedia], from the boxes and the dress circle they occupied, these women fought their battles with the diamonds and opulent clothes provided by the obliging cavaliers who were seated next to them or by the men who had preceded them in their good graces. It must be admitted that the show these hussies put on with faces daubed with powder and rouge, borrowed hair strewn with jewels, and eccentric dresses in gleaming colors is no less interesting than what takes place on stage.[6]

Excluded from salons, official receptions, and society fetes, confined to the theater and certain balls, the demimonde reserved its ammunition for the spring, the season for new fashions, its season par excellence, which traditionally began during Holy Week at the first races. This event mattered more "from the point of view of improving fashion than the horses' bloodlines."[7] On this occasion an endless flood of carriages, signed by celebrated Parisian carriage-makers, went wheel by wheel and in step up the Champs-Elysées, down the avenue de l'Impératrice (now the avenue Foch), and headed for Longchamp. Aboard were women dressed in the most sumptuous costumes, already watching their competitors for the coming battle. This spectacle had its rites and a long history.[8] It began at the racetrack entrance when the women, attired with various degrees of refinement, extravagance, and shocking contrast, stepped down, mingled, and looked about before leisurely spreading around the track according to a topography that assigned a particular spot to each part of the public. The weighing enclosure, the stands occupied by Jockey Club members, stud officials, and the prefect of the Seine received "fashionable society," while the other, less distinguished spectators took their places on the green and in the open stands. One could not cross over from the terrain of the innumerable "impures," to that of the "proud elects";[9] the barriers were insurmountable. "This was definitely the only place in Paris where high society's appalled sense of decency retained this rigor," noted Amédée Achard in *Paris-Guide*.[10] Ocular exchanges were nonetheless intense:

> This was the battleground of dresses . . . of which there were a hundred, a thousand, ten thousand. The most extravagant were worn most elegantly, some too long, some too short, some hiding everything, others uncovering all. . . . The elegant multitude came, went, walked up, walked down; it was a whirlwind of lively colors, a chaos of brilliant shades: cherry and purple, sea green and emerald green, azure blue and Sèvres blue. Ribbons fluttered, jet beads streamed, taffeta shimmered. It was like a living meadow on which Diaz would have spilled his palette. Ordinary bourgeois women, excluded by their modest income from the reserved enclosure, drew up along the barriers protecting the boundaries, and gazed at the crowd and bustle. Sitting on top of their barouches and breaks, the social outcasts gazed also, but in so insolent a fashion that one had to take notice. What glances! What smiles! If looks could kill, death would have decimated the ranks of the lovely strollers.[11]

Zola described this venomous climate when he sent Nana to Longchamp for the Grand Prix: "As courtesans were absolutely forbidden to enter the enclosure, she began making exceptionally bitter remarks about all the fashionable women therein assembled. She thought them fearfully dressed up, and such a funny looking lot!"[12] Her revenge, therefore, was sartorial:

> When she had made her appearance at the entrance to the field, with two postilions jogging blithely on the near horses, and two footmen perching motionless behind the carriage, the people had rushed to look as though a queen were passing. She sported the blue and white colours of the Vandeuvres stable, and her dress was remarkable. It consisted of a little blue silk bodice and tunic, which fitted closely to the body and bulged out enormously behind her waist, thereby bringing her lower limbs into bold relief in such a manner as to be extremely noticeable in that epoch of voluminous skirts. Then there was a white satin dress with white satin sleeves, and a sash worn crosswise over

the shoulder, the whole ornamented with silver guipure which shone in the sun. In addition to this, in order to be still more like a jockey, she had stuck a blue toque with a white feather jauntily upon her chignon, the fair tresses from which flowed down beyond her shoulders and resembled an enormous russet pig tail.[13]

Zola here gives a full description of the great demimonde at the races: superb equipage that impressed the crowd, daring fashions (introducing the bustle when other women still wore crinolines), vivid color contrasts, pursuit of the chic, and the cultivation of personal detail: Nana's dog, Bijou, for example, accompanied her in the carriage.

At departure time, "good taste required that one not wait for the last race to sound the retreat";[14] the fragmented mass reformed as it returned to its carriages. And again "people gathered around her [the courtesan], not only to look at her but also to copy her dress or hat, to study the way she draped her shawl, and absorb, perhaps, her stylish way of driving a panier drawn by one or more horses that millionaires would have fought over. This desire to ape fashionable *cocottes* . . . is so pronounced that their suppliers become the most sought after."[15] This taste angered the anonymous author of a pious work entitled *High Society Ladies* [*Ces dames du grand monde*]:

> On those days Madame sports a ridiculous hint of a hat, a little blouse . . . cynically pretending to be modest, a very short skirt sixty-five centimeters in length, quite close fitting, almost more like a swimming costume than a dress. In this way the legs are visible to the passer-by . . . like the daily special presented to a diner.
>
> With such casualness, such abandon in their attitudes, they seem to belong not to themselves but to everyone. . . . What kind of madness drives a decent woman to array herself in the livery of vice, a livery that often misleads about the social position of the person who wears it?[16]

The demimonde's season of splendor lasted until the Grand Prix. Surrounded and scrutinized by the stares of countless people, among them agents from abroad, couturiers, illustrators, and fashion journalists, all trying to discern beneath sumptuous excess the trends of the season, the demimondaine triumphed.

The Bois de Boulogne was also dedicated to and consecrated by fashion. There, where innovations were worn in a more casual, more normal way, confrontations of clothing and equipages displayed in a permanent potlatch took place daily. Here, too, the great *cocottes* boosted rivalries by an extravagant elegance that had to be reinterpreted tastefully rather than slavishly imitated. The ceremony traveled a route, followed a schedule, and performed an immutable ritual that began with the Avenue of the Champs-Elysées, "vestibule of that marvelous and verdant summer drawing room called the Bois."[17] At three o'clock began the parade of "the great lady in her coupe, the bourgeois in his barouche, the loose woman in her *colimaçon*, the dandy in his brougham. . . . This avenue where everything happens and everything changes, where people greet, envy, hate, and admire each other, witnesses the birth of the newest fashions and bouquets. On the avenue baubles were first seen, and many extravagant outfits bloomed in broad daylight only in order to be seen there."[18] When present, the sun haughtily participated in the first stage of the journey: "Beaming on the sea of humanity, [it] shines like an electric beacon on the steel and copper of the harnesses. Under its warm rays, lantern crystals gleam like diamonds, the horses' rumps glisten most brilliantly, gold-braided liveries and silky dresses shine, dazzling even the most indifferent onlookers."[19]

It was in the shade, however, beyond the Étoile, in the lanes of the Bois and along the Grand Lake that the competition took on its official character. This costly obsolescent investment that yielded nothing but symbolic returns was the principal stake in a game, the legitimacy of which was constantly reaffirmed by the number of competitors, the pack of escorts, and the astonished gawking of spectators who jostled one another in the side paths. In the ebb and flow of eight-spring barouches, pony carts, tilburys, phaetons, dukes, and mail coaches that passed one another,

> A mantelet, a new hat, a remarkable fabric are noted down the line. A novel display, a new carriage, liveries, and even the faces of those wearing them— everything is noted. People know which women walked alone. The genealogies of the children who "adorned" the others are recited. People keep notes on unfamiliar faces. If these appear a second time their story becomes known and circulated. The slightest adventure, look, conversation is noted and entered in a balance sheet that gets larger and larger until it is totted up.[20]

Fame and fashion tyrannized the demimondaines most of all. For them, no respite: "Migraines are unmentioned, neuralgia ignored. One had to be seen or die."[21] Relaxing with a somewhat cheap grace on the cushions of their carriages,

> these creatures who appear, shine, and go into eclipse in an atmosphere of rice powder, truffles, and absinthe, . . . these escapees from cheap cafés who've become fashionable beauties, . . . bayadères of the Chateau des Fleurs who pluck the goose that lays golden eggs by lifting their legs to eye level, . . . princesses who are daughters of porters and wanton dance-hall girls, courtesans, can-can dancers, bearded women, and girls of marble, plaster, or mud; virtues bartered for twenty francs and those sold for a hundred thousand; . . . made-up, musky emeralds, . . . butterflies and moths whom champagne inebriates, rags terrify, gold attracts, gas burns, the poorhouse claims, the gutters await,[22]

are ignored by "comme il faut" women who scornfully measure them up and down, all the while devouring and pillaging them with their eyes.

People inquired about stock prices set from day to day, rising or declining according to the sumptuousness of jewels, dresses, and carriages. They noted profitable or unfortunate speculations. In short, "the Bois is a Stock Exchange and exposition, as well as a battlefield with its victors and vanquished, its wounded and dead."[23]

Sundays brought a truce of sorts to these ruinous and fearsome tourneys. On that day, in a vast exodus from east to west, every Paris neighborhood furnished the Champs-Elysées and the Bois de Boulogne with its contingent of modest strollers and curious onlookers, working people who deserted their counters or workshops for these magnetic spaces. Driving away much of fashionable society, this mob, seated or strolling, of workers, shopkeepers, clerks, or small investors gathered along the avenues or relaxed beneath the trees. Edouard Gourdon describes them as

> a motley crowd . . . upright, but not trained in fine manners; decently, but modestly dressed; respectable, but pipe-smoking; endowed with all of the family virtues, but wearing impossible hats and hobnailed boots. It mingles with fashionable society but does not become one with it. Servants in brilliant livery regard it contemptuously, the horses are astonished by it, and dogs bark at it. . . . Poor, it admires wealth without hoping ever to acquire it, just as it admires prime beef without hoping ever to eat any. The only thing it does not admire is itself, so deep and intimate is its love of beauty.[24]

But let us return to the magnificent demimonde adventuresses who glorified the dress designs of an ephemeral luxury. Wherever they appeared, an avid curiosity seized high society, which, behind its reserve and offended airs, sought to imitate them,[25] though processing, toning down, and muting new fashions too singular or provocative. The passage from excess to distinction was accomplished either by the passage of time, which made new forms and colors familiar and domesticated them by assimilation into the daily scene,[26] or by rearrangements that softened details, clashing contrasts or outré trimmings. Both processes endowed costume with milder signification, as if it had been softened.

A woman of refinement did not seek to outstrip current fashions or to prescribe them: "Exaggeration in fashion suits only parvenus or women of questionable lives," propriety recalled.[27] Once established, a fashion had to be followed closely enough to avoid any appearance of protesting against the times but not so closely as to suggest one was their slave. Neither could a fashion be abandoned too tardily, because ridicule lay in wait for the out-of-fashion outfit, another, opposite form of excess.

The death of a fashion, like its extension to the dominant social group, happened differently depending on age groups or social class, and the constituent parts of a given group. Thus, a new fashion did not get adopted in the same way among the rich bourgeoisie of the Chaussée-d'Antin and the old aristocracy of the faubourg Saint-Germain. Among the first, where salons received a large and animated company and where the decor—often modern—indicated recent opulence and the enlightened taste of the masters of the house (generally bankers or financiers), new fashions were stripped only of the most outlandish aspects sported by the demimonde or suggested by fashion plates. In short, although a certain sartorial bluffing was tolerated there as the "result of money," one remained wary of falling

Chausée-d'Antin fashions (left); Faubourg Saint-Germain fashions (right)
(*La Mode 1830*)

into the extravagance characteristic of the parvenus from the faubourg Saint-Honoré.

Among the old aristocracy, on the other hand, where "the sacred flame of the former good taste was kept burning religiously,"[28] where the ceremonial and the solemn was still cultivated in seclusion, fashion was received only in a euphemized version, bereft of any extreme aspect. Sobriety and austerity functioned as a "foil." As opposed to the Chaussé-d'Antin, in the faubourg Saint-Germain the experience of ownership went too far for wealth to be displayed arrogantly, the acme of possession being to avoid conspicuous display, or rather, displaying conspicuously one's lack of display,[29] conspicuous underconsumption distancing itself from compensatory overconsumption, a position of supremacy assumed by opposition.

> Should a beauty from the Chaussée-d'Antin go to a banker's ball, in a gown trimmed with [eight flounces], . . . she will be thought charming. The eight flounces will be appreciated and envied by rival dresses with only four, five, or six flounces. To have eight declares: I do things more lavishly than you; I am elegant to the eighth degree; I have more than your two quarterings of nobility. I value myself, and I am worth two flounces more than you. . . . But suppose that the same beauty, before going to the ball, calls on the true-blue residents of the faubourg Saint-Germain, the people who do not cross to the Right Bank, never attend plays, and devote themselves to atoning in a profound retreat for the pleasures other Paris neighborhoods enjoy. Can you imagine the effect of those eight flounces on that nobly simple and charitably reasonable world? Those eight flounces are scandalous; that "cachucha" finery appalls everyone's good taste.[30]

On the other hand, at court, which Napoleon III revived with the splendor of balls and receptions held at the Tuileries, Saint-Cloud, or Compiègne, this sober nuance disappeared from clothes that had to dazzle. Exclusivity of luxury and innovation had vanished with the old regime, but these events were duly reported in the press. Thus, a trip to Compiègne, where "batches" of guests followed one another, gave rise to competitions in elegance, resulting in prestigious designs. As *Le Coquet*, a journal for dressmakers, noted,

> Orders have already been placed with our celebrated houses by these wealthy, privileged women. Because each series has only a limited number of guests, a triumph is difficult to achieve, each costume being studied and criticized at leisure. And the competition is keen because every elegant woman must have a complete arsenal of costumes—for morning wear, promenades, hunts, dinner, concerts, plays, balls—and she cannot, without risking her position as a leader of fashion, wear an outfit or a dress that resembles the one in which Madame de——caused a sensation in an earlier group.

Consequently—and this is why the visits to Compiègne are, I believe, an "important event for fashion"—the great artists must increase their production tenfold and simultaneously create complete series of new designs from which the winter fashions will be chosen.[31]

But these lavish mimetic confrontations served to prove wealth rather than inventiveness. "A creation that . . . has appeared at the theater . . . will easily make its entree at court if it is worn by an aristocratic godmother."[32] She would endow it with a special glamour quite distinct from demimondaine extravagance: tasteful extreme luxury became the path to follow, especially because it had become a kind of political imperative and social duty after the parsimony of Louis-Philippe's reign. As in social gatherings organized for a charitable pretext, splendor was justified by the work it provided. "Every fete at court means millions for industry. A worker who walks by a rich man's splendidly illuminated townhouse and hears its distant orchestral harmonies should say to himself: a share of all this joy will come down to me. When they spend on high, no layoffs below."[33] No longer a divine-right prerogative, luxury exculpated itself as an economic responsibility. At Compiègne sumptuary exigence took on the aspect of tyranny, and the guests—the emperor and empress frowned on wearing the same attire more than three times—had to bring a nearly complete wardrobe. The Princess Metternich recounted the almost epic beginnings of these sojourns:

> About twenty minutes after the arrival of the masters the luggage vans were unloaded! This was a unique, extraordinary spectacle, for it seemed that all of Paris had moved. The number of cases we saw unloaded was incredible! One day we counted almost nine hundred! Every evening gown was packed separately in a pine box like the ones used by seamstresses for their deliveries so that, expertly packed by Parisian packers, they could arrive unwrinkled at their destination. Thus I gloried in eighteen boxes for myself alone, while others more elegant than I had twenty-four. And as we were in all—men and women—some sixty guests, that figure of nine hundred will not seem implausible. You had to see the swarm of panic-stricken valets and chambermaids shouting and yelling in the courtyard to sort out their baggage! . . . This was a priceless spectacle, and we doubled up with laughter behind the windows while those poor wretches fought below.[34]

The court may have been excessive in its luxury, but it was only one of the relays in a circuit that it no longer controlled.[35] Of course, the empress did have a certain charisma as far as fashion was concerned. Had she not stimulated the textile production slowed by the Crimean War and the depression of 1857 when she successfully launched the heavy Lyon silks she called her "political attire"? But her influence was limited, restricted to the court, and many famous *cocottes* had more legitimate claims to initiating fashions.

Every summer, the sartorial jousts of high life continued in the provinces owing to the vogue of thermal baths and seaside resorts, and were made possible by the extension of the railroads and supported by a flourishing hydrotherapeutic discourse[36] and a rapidly expanding infrastructure of hotels.[37] Fashions introduced in Paris were confirmed in Kursaals, in English gardens, or on the beaches. In fact, "attire for bathing beaches and spas is every bit as, if not even more elegant than, clothes for walking along the Champs-Elysées or in the Bois de Boulogne."[38] The contests threatened reputations. As Countess Drohojowska warned, landmarks were uncertain and pitfalls multiple:

> There people outdo one another other in luxury, coquettery, slander, and caustic wit. There one acquires dangerous flatterers and irreconcilable enemies. There one is exposed to curiosity, envy, all the passions that pride unleashes and excites. There intimacy with people whom one has not seen before, whom one will perhaps never see again, makes thoughtless and careless mistakes easy and irreparable. It is an arena to which combatants rush in droves but from which few victors leave in triumph.[39]

But not all of these resorts were equally renowned for stylishness or morality. German watering stations enjoyed great prestige.[40] At Baden, for

Beach wear

example, "the regal avenue lined with orange trees along the portico is a veritable Longchamp, but a Longchamp for pedestrians where one can contemplate carefully the beautiful clothes and the elegant women who enhance them. . . . It is a delectable sight for those who do not pay for the war. In this struggle, feminine and hence relentless and merciless, the demimonde's elite confronts the highest aristocracy with opulence and extravagance, and one encounters "princesses" whose wardrobes cost the equivalent of the budget of a small principality."[41]

At Baden, the *biches* could easily find or accompany a keeper. Society there was brilliant but mixed. Ems, on the other hand,

> is particularly interesting. It is one of the most accepted emporia of true fashion. Fashion here foregoes the adventurousness it dares in second-rate spas. At Ems, fashion bears the cachet, the stamp of truly distinguished people. There are famous Paris practitioners whose clothes have never been noticed in the Ems Kursaal and even dressmakers celebrated in Paris whose gowns never attract a laudatory inspection. At Ems, only a design by Véronique or the cut of a Humann of Paris or London merit being singled out.[42]

The demimonde did not belong there. Spa, Vichy, Plombières, Bagnières-de-Luchon, Divonne, Aix, and Evian each adopted a distinctive style that drew a certain kind of clientele and fostered its own kind of sociability.

As for the seashore, the luxury, balls, fetes, and fireworks, the deployment of mousselines, flowers, diamonds, silver lamé faille skirts, laces with golden torsades, embroidery-laden tops, silk brocade dresses were concentrated particularly at Boulogne and Dieppe where "the *merveilleuses* changed as much as five times a day."[43] But in the fever of speculative investment in casinos and seaside resorts, Fécamp, le Havre, Trouville, Étretat, Cabour, Saint-Malo, Le Tréport, Royan, and Arcachon also attracted the "fashionable set" of the *Almanach de Gotha*, or its margins, with its subtle distinctions and furious extravagance.

Fashion spread variously through high social circles, but it also flowed into the lower strata by means of a well-known mimetic mechanism, though in ever slower cascades and increasingly altered forms.

Shopkeepers, petty civil servants, or modest rentiers of the Marais accepted styles circumspectly, when they had become "outmoded," and with a delay characteristic of a neighborhood savoir-faire that manuals advised readers to avoid: "There you will become common, heavy, skimpy, a fussy dresser; you will become a gossip, a great reader of classified ads. But a polished man, a man who knows how to live, a man of taste? Never."[44]

Taine, as he moved from aristocratic salon to bourgeois ball, emphasized the contrast: in one everyone "is on the same level; every man, every woman almost stands at the summit of this civilization and this society by their toilette and their taste, or by their rank and culture." At the other "the women are not women; their hands are not hands, but paws; a peevish, vulgar air, a demitoilette, ribbons that clash in color. It is hard to say why, but the eye is shocked, and, as it were, sullied. Their gestures are angular, wanting in grace. They are working machines, and nothing more."[45]

In aristocratic circles new fashions—even bowdlerized—aroused such distrust that it could be said that "the Chaussée-d'Antin proposes, the faubourg Saint-Honoré adopts, the faubourg Saint-Germain legitimates, the Marais executes and buries."[46] With the growth of the ready-to-wear industry, however, this diffusion of fashion through time and social classes no longer stumbled at the boundary of the petty-bourgeoisie. Reaching this level of the social ladder, it no longer rebounded but rolled down until it reached rich peasants or prosperous workers, particularly for their Sunday dress. It was already traditional for the laboring population who worked in direct contact with the upper classes (servants, dressmakers, modistes, etc.) to follow, imitatively, a rather rapid tempo of change. During the Second Empire, new material and social conditions extended the right and the duty of fashion to increasingly numerous social strata. Their distinctive traits were not blurred, however, so that petty-bourgeois and provincial fashions were immediately recognizable because they exaggerated or misunderstood[47] the legitimate definitions mastered by all parts of the dominant classes.

These pretensions to elegance, at first laughable, often acquired some legitimacy so that the copy sometimes closely resembled the model. At that point, the distinguished became first banal then, quickly, common. The objects of this overly successful imitation had to transform the identifying article that no longer differentiated them. A woman would give her cook or chambermaid a dress socially worn out, and then adopt, in simplified and subdued versions, the fashions launched by the demimonde.

Topographically, this process manifested itself as waves that radiate outward from a central point and succeed one another without meeting. "When a fashion leaves the rue de la Paix," wrote Coffignon, "it needs a year to get beyond the outer boulevards and spread into the suburbs; when it is general enough to become common, it has long been forgotten at the center of Paris."[48]

Men's fashions, though sluggish, followed approximately the same itinerary through less official relays, such as the Boulevard des Italiens, the Tortoni or the Jockey Clubs. There was no male equivalent of the demimondaine to launch new fashions, but certain figures who stood out because of their excesses unwittingly launched fads more successfully than did men of distinction. "A *cocodès* dresses as he pleases, providing it is different. They invented the part in the middle, huge buttons, and open vests. They abandon the styles they launch when they become popular, trying to outdo last season's follies the better to astonish the season about to begin."[49]

In the park: the beaux of the department.

As white as pierrots, in the fashion of tomorrow or the day before yesterday: trousers too short, pulling at the knee. Hair coiled with curling irons and paunchy at eighteen years of age. Come to town to show these pretentious Parisiennes what a real man is, making their choices to the tune of

"And I've been seen everywhere
Courting brunettes and blondes."

—Let's court, messieurs, let's court, but do not go farther.—Don't worry, ladies: basically, most of them are quite nice young men who've come to Vichy to drink the water with their daddies."

FASHION'S DURATION

Linked to the passage of time that ineluctably depreciated them, the ex-change-value and the sign-value of fashion stocks were determined by their duration. And the differences in these durations defined a hierarchy that affected roughly all social categories and their topography.

Different rates of circulation corresponded to the fashion channels just described, and, accordingly, different time-lags corresponded to different social and geographical spaces. Fashion news, traveling along more or less the same circuits, underwent the same decelerations: what was outmoded in Paris and in high society was still fashionable elsewhere, to the great profit of business that found a market for its surplus. Fashion journalism short-circuited the mechanism by warning distant readers: "Merchants in the provinces often dupe their customers and make them accept what we call 'old-fashioned stuff' here. For example, bunches of Malaga grapes in white pearls, considered so lovely on hats two years ago, are now packed up or given to chambermaids. Yet, I am sure that in some provincial town they are sold as the 'latest thing.'"[50]

The provinces in Paris

Fashion, everywhere present, was everywhere different: here moribund, there hardly born. Thus one should not mistake the accelerated mobility of signs for real social mobility. To speak of the "democratization of clothing" is to overlook new subtle strategies born from the different use of temporal marks, strategies that reveal the static underlying economic, social, and cultural structures. This is true even though fashion appears only when a certain stage of surplus wealth was reached and sometimes seemed to indict a sociopolitical order.

The place an article of clothing occupies along the aging process, which corresponds to a place along the price scale, indicates the status of its wearer, just as surely as the intrinsic quality of the fabric, one confirming the other. Wearing a black taffeta dress in 1860, for example, represented an attempt to appear both fashionable and wealthy—inextricable equivalents in terms of signs because of what the dress vainly tried to express:

> It used to be the fashionable, ceremonial formal dress, the indispensable dress for the comme il faut woman, but [it] lost its aristocratic cachet to become the classic dress, and from a classic it declined to the most common of commons. To wear a black taffeta dress on social calls or for promenades is to advertise a precarious budget or imposed thrift. It is also to affect the luxurious elegance of a silk dress one is not used to wearing. It betrays a lack of experience in dressing well, an effort to be all gussied up in one's Sunday best. It requires silk to serve for every occasion, to render unalterable, undying service.

A black taffeta dress is nevertheless the dream of the young girl who counts on its sparkling reflections to attract the young suitor who, alas, would not be enticed by a meager dowry. It is the dream of the modest working woman who can accept it unblushingly from the honest worker who will give her his name. . . . Today, a woman dressed in a black taffeta dress . . . is the humble assistant manager of a middle-class boarding house who after many years of deprivation has been able to reach this decent, almost showy dress. She is the working mother who momentarily leaves her daily routine to solicit powerful protectors for the son who is her sole hope for comfort in her old age. . . . Sometimes it is the dress that one wears out, uses up, and ends up in.[51]

Good taste required one to distance oneself from the too-recent fashions of parvenus and demimondaines and the outdated fashions of the middle and lower classes. For fashion could become a sign of acceptable social standing only when one played with it skillfully, by choosing the appropriate place in the sequence between the excessively rapid innovation of eccentric fashions and the excessively slow tempo of ready-to-wear imitations.

Fashion existed within this hierarchy of life spans and acquired its value in comparison with the "unfashionable." It was consequently forced to change continuously. As a product of labor, fashion was material wealth. But it was also symbolic wealth created by destruction. The same process that brought it into being repudiated its earlier manifestations by creating an ever-changing, prestigious scarcity.

Fashion was necessarily more expensive and changeable in the upper reaches of society, and understandably, the mechanism of supply and demand pushed those who profited from it to increase the tempo of change even more and gradually shorten a fashion's life span for all social classes. The inherent logic of industrial production, which already deliberately limited the physical life expectancy of clothing, reduced its social life expectancy as well. Accelerated fashion created ephemera, profit, social wear and tear, and thus inequality. Fashion's cycles—which made and unmade prices—substituted "temporal" for physical scarcity.

FASHION GOODS

Made-to-measure and ready-to-wear had become the modes of clothing production, and the former could achieve success only by defining itself in opposition to the other.

For the tailor, profit or loss would depend on his ability and understanding of the new rules: "He cannot remain a simple artisan but must become an artist; his domain must be that of elegance, just as vulgarity is the domain of 'ready-made.' Their roles are distinct, answering to different needs. The latter must be made inexpensive by skillful commercial operations and the use of industrial techniques. The tailor must have knowledge, taste and initiative to fulfill and preserve his own role.[52]

The birth of *grande couture* (the future haute couture) was not unrelated to the expansion of the ready-to-wear industry. On the one hand, its luxury and refinement distinguished it from ready-to-wear without ambiguity; on the other, it borrowed some of the former's methods. Charles Frederick Worth, the Englishman who went to Paris as the head clerk at Gagelin's (a fashionable clothier) was the real founder of *grande couture*. He set up shop in 1858 at 7, rue de la Paix, a neighborhood in upheaval that had not yet been invaded by luxury shops. There he realized his ambition, the creation of designs no longer unique but reproduced in limited numbers. The designs were varied, adapted, and altered to fit the wearer, and he gave his enterprise a quasi-industrial dimension by stocking fabrics, enlarging his staff, and multiplying the fitting rooms. He rapidly gained a clientele among celebrities and, thanks to Princess Metternich,[53] whom he convinced of his talents, supplied the Imperial court as well. After 1860 his authority was considerable.[54] "The autocrat of taste . . . and spiritual director in matters of fit,"[55] noted for his arrogance, as much as for his professional qualities, treated even the wealthiest women with an incredible condescension. He received them only if they were properly introduced and presented,[56] made them wait for hours, then admitted them, a cigar in his mouth, to his boudoirs, where, indolent and majestic, surrounded by piles of fabric carelessly thrown on the furniture, he would look them over in silence until the judgment fell and an order was given:

> She was like a schoolgirl standing before her teacher, in her new gala outfit, waiting for the oracle to speak. "Very good," said the god. "Except for the belt, which is hideous. Get another one!" She obeys. Another young woman takes her place and tells him in a caressing manner: . . . "I would like a dress for walking about." He replies imperturbably: "You don't walk about. Here's what you need." He points to a dress in white faille, embroidered with straw. She submits.[57]

To revolt against his insolence or protest against his tyranny meant excommunication, and a formal invitation to leave the profaned sanctuary. To be dressed by Worth the haughtiest women swallowed insults and concealed their anger, which only heightened his prestige. His stupefying bills[58] were paid by a clientele in whom the fear of losing his services silenced all protest. The master enlarged his store on the rue de la Paix and surrounded it with a luxury as outrageous as his behavior. In 1870 *La Vie Parisienne* described this in an anonymous article entitled "Monsieur Chose," or "Mr. What's-His-Name:

> We enter through a double door and climb a padded, lined staircase, warm as a greenhouse. From the first steps, it smelled of pretty women. Green plants, dracenas, camellias, procession of charming women—in a word, angels! Jacob's ladder, and at the first landing, a coming and going, scents, rustling of silk, and a vague perfume of *high life* hanging in the air.
>
> To the left and right the doors were wide open, and lovely, bareheaded girls walked to and fro, rather extraordinary silhouettes dressed in the day after tomorrow's fashions, coiffed in original chignons. Frightfully up to date, they escorted customers to the door while taking leave of others and greeting still others. . . . They walked about the salons in model dresses, living examples of the celebrated What's-His-Name's art. For his clients, this was a living temptation, the materialization of what his scissors could do with the fabrics that were still nothing but promises.
>
> By pointing to a skirt that undulated before her, a woman could choose the style of her bustle, her bodice, or her belt, worn by a live model. It was ingenious, convenient, and extraordinarily up to date.[59]

The fashion "parade" was still informal, but the "mannequin" had been invented: an anonymous vessel presenting the new designs in a canonical manner.

Chez Chose

A genius at harmonizing, fitting, and constantly varying forms, inventing new trimmings, skillfully playing his haughty role, continuously in demand, Worth convinced his clients—each of whom he treated as unique cases—to innovate audaciously. Struggling against inertia, always insisting on the quality and richness of materials, he revived the vogue of Lyon velvets and silks, encouraged manufacturers to diversify their products, stimulated the trimmings and fur industries, and encouraged the manufacturing of *articles de Paris*, fancy goods essential for individualizing an outfit.

But because he revived the intermittent tradition of the woman's tailor, the *couturier* stirred up anger, the same protests that in 1675 had deprived tailors, as we have seen, of the right to dress women and children, and during the Revolution discredited male involvement in fashion.[60] The Larousse *Encyclopedia* was scandalized:

Here, under the Second Empire we see the reappearance of those unspeakably peculiar men (are they really men?) presiding over the clothing of women, the most fashionable women, crumpling gauze on the bosoms of princesses, placing ribbons and flowers on the bodices of duchesses, and becoming arbiters of dress designs or fabric choices. This is a trend we sincerely hope will not become a general practice, one that might spread to include unaffected and upright women. Let feminine hands have the privilege of constructing clothing for mothers, wives, and sisters. To them leave the delicate tasks that require a skillful touch, not an athlete's strength, if they are to be done well and above all decently.[61]

Worth nevertheless gained widespread acceptance, even though until the 1880s he remained the exception to the couturière's monopoly. But for the entire period, no couturière equaled the prestige or charged the prices of the English master, their most expensive dresses ranging between 500 and 2,000 francs—a considerable enough expenditure.[62]

For its part, men's made-to-measure clothing, thanks to a few great names, perpetuated a long tradition of taste and elegance, even if it did not acquire the magic aura of *haute couture*, an aura strengthened by the role Paris played in the diffusion of fashion. Nor did it equal the British tailoring that it held up as a model. Like a couturière, a good tailor found himself assigned a role that was as essential to appearance as it was delicate. He was the body's confidant, an accomplice in artifice, and a counselor in exploitation and camouflage. "For one tailor who understands, shapes, and corrects nature, I would give three classical sculptors," wrote Michelet.[63] In fact, a career, marriage, or reputation could hang on his skill and style.[64]

The value of made-to-measure clothing, created and confirmed by the oligopoly of tailors and celebrated couturières, increasingly confronted ready-to-wear clothing, a typical result of mass production in that it represented the industrialized, mechanical reproduction of an already-existing model. This opposition was nevertheless more complementary than antagonistic in that it both produced and reproduced the interplay of distinctive signs within the same hierarchy, differentiating the authenticity of made-to-measure from the approximation of ready-to-wear. These two products would soon exist only in conjunction with each other because their respective markets were interdependent.[65] But the contest between the *façon* or fit of a great tailor who gave his products an incomparable finish and individuality and the *contre-façon* or counterfeit of the ready-to-wear manufacturers who sacrificed quality for quick production was always unequal. It always had the same outcome, since the needs and tastes dominated by the commercialization of inexpensive ready-to-wear clothing were related to and existed only in reference to the dominant model—the tailor-made garment—which could acquire its own meaning and distinctive values only in

relation to the demand for inferior ready-to-wear and through details all
the more important because they were minute.[66] A *Figaro* journalist noted
that

> between M. Rotschild's [*sic*] black suit and the black suit of his lowly clerk
> there are imperceptible details that only a tailor's apprentice could appreciate.
> M. Rotschild's suit probably comes from Renard's and cost him 180 francs.
> The clerk's was probably purchased at *La Belle Jardinière* for 35 francs. There
> is all the difference. M. Rotschild's suit will stay black, and his clerk's will turn
> blue and then a dirty gray. M. Rotschild is also a little freer in his move-
> ments.[67]

Renard's prestige thus was fueled by the contrast with the approximate
copies, devoid of chic, from *La Belle Jardinière* or *Le Printemps*, copies differentiated from the original only by a superior dye or better fit. And these
copies existed only because they plagiarized the great tailors.

Conclusion

TOCQUEVILLE NOTED THE PARADOX: the citizens who "swept away the privileges of some of their fellow creatures . . . have opened the door to universal competition; the barrier has changed its shape rather than its position."[1] We have seen how dress translates these opposing tendencies: the traditional order, based on differences that excluded any large-scale pretensions, was succeeded by a modern one that sought to remove differences but, in fact, multiplied them.

Today in the age of universal, multipolarized ready-to-wear, rivalry in appearances continues—less noisily but more tortuously than before—following a system of distinction inherited from the nineteenth century, with new, often ineffable, details. Sometimes context helps to fix meaning. A novelty necktie can signify two distinct worlds, depending on whether it is worn in the first or second degree, displayed with a satisfaction a little too marked by a traveling salesman or sported with derision by a "distanced" intellectual. A detail can throw everything off balance: the bag with or without an *H*, the shirt with or without a crocodile say different things, though there is elegance in not participating in a conflict where the stakes—a sign that is rare because expensive—matter only to nouveaux riches or their impecunious plagiarists.

In the cleavage separating age groups and genders, contemporary dress suggests the onset of new trends. Juvenile dress situates itself so forcefully between adult and children's styles that it encroaches below and above its age bracket, covering not only adolescents but also adults and young children. Like the bourgeois suit donned by both aristocrat and proletarian in his Sunday best, "junior" styles now shape and crystalize new representations, notably those of a prestigious adolescence, which is experienced as a promotion for the child to enter and a disgrace for the adult to leave. Linked to a postwar demographic surge and the extensive market it created,[2] the phenomenon has led children to adopt, in miniature, the appearance of adults who are themselves "juvenilized." In fact, clothing established and reinforced—by making it visible—the social and cultural conflict between an interminable adolescence and an indefinitely postponed maturity, a moral and political conflict between the "young" and the "old."

As this movement grew, however, the sexual dimorphism in place for centuries subsided dramatically. As early as 1900, a slender, less massive and hieratic figure emerged in fashion plates. Thenceforth the bust and the hips would be less developed, and clothes, closer to the body, would emphasize the change. Picking up the trend, advertising enjoined something unprecedented: lose weight, lose weight with *oriental pills*, lose weight with *aromatic baths*. In his novel *Fécondité*, Zola castigated the "malthusian" idea of slender beauty, embodied in "sterile women with tall, spindly figures and shrunken flanks";[3] however, as Countess Tramar exclaimed, "What a lovely revenge [thin women] have had on their rivals with full, opulent figures who have always been held up to them and who, on the contrary, are now out of fashion."[4] The women who conformed to the new canons could even do without a corset, which Poiret, moreover, removed from his designs. The new thin figure as yet affected only the upper fringe of society, the erotic, healthy body remaining resolutely ample.[5] After the Great War, on the other hand, when corsets disappeared in great numbers, having mutated into girdles, the urban population became obsessed with *taille*, no longer as a strangled space between the bust and hips, but *taille* as defined by the Robert Dictionary: "size, weight and conformation of the body in relation to clothing." The envelope that had concretely, physically tortured its contents became a moral precept, an accusatory finger pointed at the new anatomical defect: overweight. First, fitted short dresses and then, in the 1960s, pants revealed previously hidden regions of women's bodies. The new forms, idealized by leptosomatic mannequins in display windows and magazines, reproved plump members, condemned generous contours, and stigmatized outsized figures, excluding or converting

Poiret design, 1914

heretics. Entering slacks meant quite often entering into the religion of slimness, with its martyrdom of diets, its vows and lapses, its mystics and its apostates.

"Difficult passage, 1932" (A. Guillaume)

The transformation of fat into muscle and the resulting attenuation of secondary sexual characteristics had not been the only results of moral constraint, mental orthopedics, and an internalized corset. Work, and less sedentary leisure activities such as tennis, bicycling, walking, and skiing, gradually relieved women of their textile monument. Diminished, simplified, and lightened, modern clothes led women to discover looks and styles inconceivable earlier. Gestures became freer for new activities, gaits more supple for the new spaces. The "virilized" female was all the more easily accepted because she came after two decades that glorified a "feminized" boy who had rediscovered long hair, finery, and bright colors. At the same time there was a spectacular growth of interchangeable garments like blue jeans, pullovers, and jackets, even though certain articles like the dress or the three-piece suit remained strongly sexed.

We should nuance this general sketch of broad currents below social disparities and the froth of fashion. For example, certain feminine attributes are accentuated when contained within a masculine garment because of the paradoxical simulation. After all, never had buttocks—admittedly slimmed—been displayed in so straightforward a fashion before jeans molded them. Sexual signs can survive in other ways, such as the hobbling found in the cyclical resurgence of high heels and tight skirts, the permanence of neckties and trouser creases, even though relaxation and functionalism has replaced stiffness and formality as a mark of prestige. The new ease that has led to better-tolerated deviations has neither inverted the traditional pattern of fashion diffusion nor reversed the orders of distinctive signs. Soft collars, rolled collars, pea jackets, cloth caps, and, more recently, tank tops, overalls, and clogs are articles borrowed by the bourgeoisie from sailors, workers, and peasants. But like other sports, military, or exotic clothes, they were adopted only after being duly diverted, denatured, and emptied of their original meaning, or ironically parodied and reinterpreted. In short, nothing is farther from the *worker's* blue overalls than a sky-blue jumpsuit. The history of appearances must be wary of appearances: the nineteenth century still insidiously haunts our armoires.

"Woman of the year 2000,
viewed from 1888"

Notes

INTRODUCTION

1. On the historiography of dress see the criticisms and the methodological suggestions of Hilaire and Meyer Hiler in the preface to their monumental *Bibliography of Costume* (New York, 1939), pp. xi–xxxix; and also those of Roland Barthes in his article "Histoire et sociologie du vêtement: quelques observations methodologiques," *Annales E.S.C.* 3 (1957): 430–441.

We should note that the materials collected in histories of dress nevertheless provide us with valuable information. See, among others, Jules-Étienne Joseph Quicherat, *Histoire du costume en France depuis les temps les plus reculés jusqu' à la fin du XVIIIe siècle* (Paris, 1875); Albert Racinet, *Le Costume historique* (Paris, 1875–88), 6 vols.; Germain Demay, *Le Costume au Moyen Age d'après les sceaux* (Paris 1880); Augustin Challamel, *Histoire de la mode en France* (Paris, 1881); Camille Enlart, *Manuel d'archéologie française depuis les temps mérovingiens jusqu' à la Renaissance*, vol. 3: *Le costume* (Paris, 1916); Cecil Willett Cunnington, *Handbook of English Costume in the Sixteenth Century* (London, 1945–57), 3 vols.; and Max von Boehn, *Die Mode* (Munich, 1963), 8 vols. We should also note that some histories of costume now attempt to go beyond the purely taxonomic erudition that describes, dates, and indexes clothing. See, for example, James Laver, *Taste and Fashion: From the French Revolution to the Present Day* (London, 1948); see also his *Modesty in Dress: An Inquiry into the Fundamentals of Fashion* (London, 1969); François Boucher, *Histoire du costume en Occident de l'Antiquité à nos jours* (Paris, 1965); and Yvonne Deslandres, *Le Costume, image de l'homme* (Paris, 1976).

2. From the perspective of this book, which first appeared in 1981, it is nevertheless incontestable that the history of clothing has taken on a new vigor. Witness, for example, the impressive synthesis of Daniel Roche, *La Culture des apparences, une histoire du vêtement, XVIIe–XVIIIe siècle* (Paris, 1989); and other more narrowly focused works such as Michel Pastoureau, *L'Etoffe du diable: une histoire des rayures et des tissus rayés* (Paris, 1991); and several articles on clothing and appearance in the special issue on "Parure, pudeur, étiquette" of *Communications* 46 (1987).

3. Nevertheless, before the nineteenth century clothing played only a minor role in literature. "I remember," writes L. P. Fargue, "a course taught by M. Charles Brun, professor at the Collège Libre des Sciences Sociales, on 'women's fashion and French literature.' We were astonished when he demonstrated that writers did not engage in detailed descriptions of their heroines' clothing before the XIXth century. Boileau or Molière, he pointed out, rarely did this, except when making a critical point, or as in Molière's case, to call attention, for example, to Don Juan's libertine turn of mind when he encountered Elvire again. The triumphal arrival of fashion in the novel begins with Balzac. A true innovator,

Balzac enlarged the novel's frame and introduced formerly neglected elements." *De la mode* (Paris, 1945), p. 34.

4. Herbert Spencer, "Manners and Fashion," in *Essays Scientific, Political, and Speculative*, vol. 3 (New York, 1892), pp. 1–51; by the same author, *The Principles of Sociology*, vol. 2, part 4 (London, 1879), pp. 174–192; Thorstein Veblen, *The Theory of the Leisure Class* (New York, 1899), in particular chap. 7, "Dress as an Expression of the Pecuniary Culture"; William Graham Sumner, *Folkways: A Study of the Sociological Importance of Usages, Manners, Custom, Mores, and Morals* (New York, 1906), in particular pp. 184–186, 188–189, 194–220, 426–428, 444–446; Georg Simmel, *Philosophie der Mode* (Berlin, 1905); by the same author, "Fashion," *International Quarterly* 10 (1904–5): 130–155, reproduced in *American Journal of Sociology* 62, no. 6 (May 1957): 541–558; and Werner Sombart, *Wirtschaft und Mode, ein Beitrag zur Theorie der modernen Bedarfsgestaltung* (Wiesbaden, 1902).

Since then sociologists and social psychologists have examined the question primarily through the phenomenon of fashion. A few recent theses and syntheses are: Olivier Burgelin, "Mode" (sociology), *Encyclopedia Universalis*, vol. 2 (1968), pp. 118–220; Marc-Alain Descamps, *Psychosociologie de la mode* (Paris, 1969); René Koenig, *Sociologie de la mode* (Paris, 1969), originally published as *Kleider und Mode, Zur Soziologie der Mode* (Frankfurt, 1967); Ted Polhemus and Lynn Procter, *Fashion and Anti-Fashion: An Anthropology of Clothing and Adornment* (London, 1978); Paul Yonnet, *Jeux, modes et masses* (Paris, 1985), especially pp. 295–366; and Gilles Lipovetsky, *L'Empire de l' éphémère, la mode et son destin dans les sociétés modernes* (Paris, 1987).

Journals have published issues devoted to problems of fashion: "La mode l'invention," *Change* 4 (1969); "La mode," *Traverses* 3 (February 1976); "A propos de la mode," *Revue de l'Institut de sociologie* 2 (1977); and "Modes," *Sociétés* 13 (March–April 1987).

The contributions of ethnologists are equally significant. See, for example, Yves Delaporte, "Le Signe vestimentaire," *L'Homme* (July–September 1980) 109–142; "Teddies, Rockers, Punks, et Cie: quelques codes vestimentaires urbains," *L'Homme* (October–December 1982) 49–62; "Vêtement et sociétés, Actes du colloque national CNRS, Vers une anthropolige du vêtement," held at the Musée de l'Homme, 9–11 March 1983, special issue of *L'Ethnographie* (1984): 92–94; in the special numbers of *Ethnologie française*, "Linge de corps et linge de maison," in vol. 3 (1986); "L'enveloppe textile," in vol. 1 (1989); "L'apparence physique," in vol. 2 (1989); and also the collective work published under the direction of Jean Cuisenier, *Mille ans de costume français* (Paris, 1991).

A number of works have contributed to the elaboration of a sociology of signs. The hypotheses, results, and theoretical implications resulting from this sociology of signs should overlap any new approaches to the history of clothing. Jean Baudrillard's works on consumption: *Le Système des objets: Ses mythes, ses structures* (Paris, 1968); *La Société de consommation* (Paris, 1970); or *For a Critique of the Political Economy of the Sign*, trans. with an intro. by Charles Levin (St. Louis, 1981); Pierre Bourdieu's studies of taste, such as, among others, *Distinction: A Social Critique of the Judgement of Taste*, translated by Richard Nice (Cambridge, Mass., 1984). Finally, differentiating themselves from this hypercritical sociology, Paul Yonnet's and Gilles Lipovetsky's works on fashion properly speaking (cited above in this note) have contributed to wide-ranging reflections on signs as discriminative, liberating, or playful.

5. *Traité de la vie élégante* (1830; reprint, Paris, 1922), p. 105.

6. Surviving examples of Second-Empire clothing are rare. Preserved mainly for their aesthetic value, they reveal the exceptional rather than the ordinary. With the advent of photography, images of clothing convey a reality altered by the absence of color and the very long poses that made the models appear stiff. Drawing, however, restored a sense of movement, whereas official painting underlined the shimmering of fabrics at a time synthetic dyes had just been discovered. Unfortunately, the persons painted are socially homogenous, almost always members of the upper classes, even in the canvasses of impressionists like Monet, Manet, and Degas who only rarely portrayed the common people or the petty bourgeoisie. Fashion plates contrast with this body of evidence because they sought not to depict clothing known to the public but to promote an intentionally accentuated modernity. They therefore indicated tendencies in fashion, even though these were never generally adopted, either immediately or completely. Caricature, on the other hand, exaggerated fashions already adopted. It is thus an invaluable source on how people really dressed and what was considered ridiculous. Moreover, since it emphasized faces, it helps to establish a typology—the grisette, the parvenu, the provincial, the dandy, etc.

Finally, aside from the novel, writing about clothing is a tangled mixture of discourses, discontinuous, ephemeral, odd, waggish, and curious. It belongs to the subliterature that people read only once—news reports, pamphlets, satires, lampoons, fashion articles, writing about the body—or that certain people read again and again—etiquette manuals, works of household advice, or health treatises.

7. Fernand Braudel, *Civilization and Capitalism, 15th–18th Century*, vol. 1: *The Structures of Everyday Life: The Limits of the Possible*, orig. trans. of Miriam Kochan, rev. Siân Reynolds (New York, 1981), p. 333.

CHAPTER I

1. See, for example, Pierre Daubert, *Du port illégal de costume et de décoration* (Paris, 1904).

2. In a chapter devoted to clothes-making processes in different periods and places, André Leroi-Gourhan points out that "up to a point, technological inertia makes it possible to use dress as historical evidence of real movements of men, of true invasions. For, although fabrics have always been imported, only the presence of a conqueror can make fashion abandon its traditional forms." *Milieux et Techniques*, "Sciences d'aujourd'hui" (Paris, 1973), p. 203.

3. In fact there are no "national costumes" but rather local, regional, or international costumes. It would be fruitless to confine them within political boundaries. See François Boucher, "Géopolitique du costume," *L'Amour de l'art* (1er trimestre, 1952): 69.

4. On the problems of vestimentary acculturation see, for example, Patrick O'Reilly and Jean Poirier, "L'evolution du costume," *Journal de la société des océanistes* 9, no. 9 (December 1953): 151–169. The article deals with the modifications

in New Caledonian dress under the influence of colonization; or Ali A. Mazrui, "The Robes of Rebellion: Sex, Dress and Politics in Africa," *Encounter* 34, no. 2 (February 1970): 19–30.

5. See Charles Darwin's account in *The Voyage of the Beagle* (New York, 1909), chap. 9.

6. "Bald and naked, the women deportees were unrecognizable. Most of them broke into hysterical laughter that ended in weeping or in a stupor that sounded like a death sentence. How else can one explain the fact that some of them died within a few days although they were not sick, not yet weakened, other than by the horror they felt when they found themselves naked, shorn, reduced to a number, to beasts of burden, to 'nothing'?

'It was very important for morale to care for one's physical appearance,' Lise Lesèvre recalls. 'You knew that the end was near when a girl let herself go. Young girls stole chalk from the factory to rouge their lips. I myself stole carbonate of soda to wash my hair.'" Ania Francos, *Il était des femmes dans la Résistance* (Paris, 1978), p. 239.

7. Maurice Leenhardt, "Pourquoi se vêtir?" *L'Amour de l'art* (1er trimestre, 1952): 14.

8. Robert K. Merton, *Social Theory and Social Structure*, 2d ed. (Glencoe, Ill., 1957), pp. 60–82.

9. Roland Barthes, "Éléments de sémiologie," *Communications* 4 (1964): 106.

10. See the *Oxford English Dictionary* and the *Dictionnaire Robert* for this version of the etymology of *cravat*.

11. George H. Darwin, "Development in Dress," *Macmillan's Magazine* (September 1872), quoted by Wilfred Mark Webb, *The Heritage of Dress* (London, 1907), p. 3. Webb's work itself should also be consulted on this subject.

12. The end of the thirties introduced "a technical revolution that made it possible to reinforce the trouble spots of jeans with a simple stitch. Now at last rivets were out of date, useless! . . . But the buyers of jeans still demanded their beloved rivets." John Brooks, "Petite encyclopédie du blue-jeans," *Jardin des Modes* 31 (April 1980): 32.

13. Clothing's role as a clear hierarchical sign is still important within groups in uniform as well as in their relations with civilians. Uniforms are vital means of identification for a hierarchical group. As James Laver writes, "It is clothes that make it possible for governments to obtain obedience, religions reverence, judiciaries a respect for law, and armies discipline." See his preface to Lawrence Langer, *The Importance of Wearing Clothes* (New York, 1959), p. xiv. But uniforms as instruments and expressions of power can also reveal and instigate conflicts. See Nathan Joseph and Nicholas Alex, "The Uniform: A Sociological Perspective," *American Journal of Sociology* 4, no. 77 (January 1972): 719–730

14. For example, when Paul Post compared the evolution of garments to that of the arts between 1350 and 1475, he concluded that during this period dress was subject to and manifested the same stylistic laws. *Die französisich-niederländische Männertracht einschliesslich der Ritterüstung im Zeitalter der Spätgotik, 1350 bis 1475. Ein Rekonstruktionversuch auf Grund der Zeitgenössischen Darstellungen* (Berlin, 1910).

15. "Fashion managed to modify even the form, color, and expression of the face. The neck of a Romantic-era belle bowed like a swan's, but Marlene Dietrich's

cheeks were hollow and the corners of her disillusioned mouth turned down. The red cheeks of Nattier's women were followed by Madame de Pompadour's rosy complexion, Malibran's ivory skin, Suzy Solidor's deep bister, and Juliette Greco's pale coloring." Jacques Wilhelm, *Histoire de la Mode* (Paris, 1955), p. 5. On this subject see Philippe Perrot, *Le Travail des apparences, ou les transformations du corps feminin, XVIIIe–XIXe siècle* (Paris, 1984).

Male silhouettes also reflect changes in erotic detail: broad shoulders, massive chests, narrow waists, or prominent genitals. Facial hair has also varied considerably.

16. On the variations in time and space of the body's zones of modesty and desire, see, among others, William Graham Sumner, *Folkways*, pp. 429–435, 453–459; and Havelock Ellis, *Studies in the Psychology of Sex* (New York, 1936), chap. 1, "The Evolution of Modesty."

The differences in practices and sensibilities concerning the body from one society to another or from one period to the following have been more closely studied than the synchronic variations within a single society. Such a study could show how the oppositions among these variants differ and explain their functions within concrete social reality.

17. "Everyone knows—but the manufacturers of corsets know it better than anyone else—that women are built differently in every European country. Different models must be designed for each nation. Spanish women have wide hips and flat abdomens. Their short and cambered corsets free the natural protuberance of the bust. English women on the contrary are straight and prefer to stand erect. They require corsets that are laced tightly from top to bottom. Russian and Scandanavian women have long figures with few prominent lines. German and Dutch women, being naturally massive, need corsets that are confining, sturdily constructed.

These differences among ethnic groups, well known to the clothing industry, extend to all the parts of the body, from the calf—higher up on British women than on our compatriots—, to the bust, usually situated lower across the Channel than on this side of the Ocean." Georges d'Avenel, *Le Mécanisme de la vie moderne*, 4th ser. (Paris, 1902), pp. 64–65.

18. Fashion is a means of updating "sexual information," to use André Martinet's expression from his article "La fonction sexuelle de la mode," *Linguistique* 10 (1974): 5–19. For the psychoanalyst Edmund Bergler, the entire evolution of fashion is determined by the "shifting erogenous zone." *Fashion and the Unconscious* (New York, 1953).

19. Lo Duca wrote as late as 1963, "Among so much softness, so many means and curves, breasts enjoy an indisputable prestige. They have definitively dethroned not only the thigh, which had its day in the era of the can-can, but also the behind, whose double, silvery sphere swayed slowly, insolently, and mischievously in the erotic firmament of our fathers." But later he admits that "it nevertheless seems that for young people these sweet objects have lost much of their power to fascinate. The overall figure and the legs are generally more appealing. They are cited 7,219 times in 14,000 responses." *L'Amour aujourd'hui* (Paris, 1963), pp. 22–24.

20. *The Complete Essays of Montaigne*, trans. Donald M. Frame (Stanford, 1958), book 2, chap. 15: "That Our Desire Is Increased by Difficulty," p. 465. This led

Rétif de la Bretonne to say: "The modesty of women is nothing but their own politics. Everything they hide or disguise is disguised or hidden only to raise the price—when they are ready to sell." Cited by Adolphe Ricard [pseud. of Gustave Sandré], *L'Amour, les femmes et le mariage* (Paris, 1857), p. 452.

21. "Father," cried Magis [the monk who had been sent by the saint to clothe the penguin population], "you must admire how each of them advances with his nose pointed toward the center of gravity of that young lady, now that this center is veiled in pink. Spheres inspire the meditations of geometers because of the number of their properties; when the sphere proceeds from physical, living nature it acquires new qualities. And so that the interest of this form might be fully revealed to the penguins, it was necessary, because they could no longer see it distinctly with their eyes, they be led to represent it to themselves in their minds. I myself feel at this moment irresistibly attracted toward that penguin. Is it because her skirt lends more importance to her ass and that, by simplifying it magnificently, invests it with a general and synthetic character, and allows only the pure idea, the divine principle of it to appear? I can't say, but it seems to me that if I embraced her I would hold in my arms the heaven of human pleasure." *Penguin Island*, trans. A. W. Evans (New York, 1933), p. 41. Evans's translation has been slightly modified.

22. *L'Érotisme* (Paris, 1965), p. 159.

23. For example, a study by André Handricourt proves that a relationship exists between unshaped garments such as the tunic or the poncho and the way loads are carried, namely, slung across the shoulder or carried by a band across the forehead. The same relationship exists between shaped clothing such as the jacket and the way in which the same burdens are carried—in a backpack or in a two-strapped basket. "Rélations entre gestes habituels, forme des vêtements et manières de porter les charges," *Revue de géographie humaine et d'ethnologie* 3 (July–September 1948): 32–48.

24. See Robert Mandrou, *Introduction to Modern France, 1500–1640: An Essay in Historical Psychology*, trans. R. E. Hallmark (New York, 1977), pp. 27–28.

25. Robert Rouquette, "Une centenaire: la soutane," *Études* 314 (July–August 1962): 32–48.

26. Augustin Cabanès, *Le Costume du médecin en France*, 2 vols. (Paris, 1921); Françoise Lehoux, *Le Cadre de vie des médecins parisiens aux XVIᵉ et XVIIᵉ siècles* (Paris, 1976), pp. 237–246; and Nicole Pellegrin, "L'Uniforme de la santé: Les médecins et la réforme du costume au XVIIIᵉ siècle," *XVIIIᵉ Siècle* (1989).

27. W. N. Hargreaves-Mawdsley, *A History of Legal Dress in Europe until the End of the Eighteenth Century* (Oxford, 1963); E. Glasson, "Les origines du costume de la magistrature," *Nouvelle revue historique du Droit français et étranger* 8 (1884): 109–137; Louis Marchand, *Du costume de l'avocat à travers les ages* (Poitiers, 1919); and Sophie Loubriat, "Robe judiciaire et justice enrobée: histoire d'un costume professionnel," *L'Ethnographie* (1984): 227–336.

28. W. N. Hargreaves-Mawdsley, *A History of Academical Dress in Europe until the End of the Eighteenth Century*. (Oxford, 1963).

29. An article of clothing does not always generate the same gestures. Bernard Koechlin has discovered a profound sexual differentiation in the technique of removing a sweater. "A woman crosses her arms in front, grips the bottom of the sweater and raises her arms far enough to free her head, then, grasping the arms of the sweater, she turns it right-side out. A man reaches back over his shoulders, grips

the neck of the sweater and pulls until his head is freed." "Techniques corporelles et leur notation symbolique," *Langages* 10 (June 1968): 38. W. M. Webb has also noted that men and women have specific ways of buttoning garments. *The Heritage of Dress*, p. 21.

30. Robert Devleeshouwer, "Costume et société," *Revue de l'Institut de Sociologie*, 2 (1977): 183.

31. Geoffrey Gorer and John Rickman, *The People of Great Russia: A Psychological Study* (New York, 1962). See chap. 1, "Character and Developments," and appendix 1, "Development of the Swaddling Hypothesis."

32. *Journal intime, année 1857* (Paris, 1965), p. 135.

33. Cited by Merton, *Social Theory and Social Structure*, p. 31.

CHAPTER II

1. As Max Weber writes, "'Luxury' in the sense of rejecting purposive-rational control of consumption is for the dominant feudal strata not something 'superfluous,' it is a means of social self-assertion." *Economy and Society: An Outline of Interpretive Sociology*, ed. Guenther Roth and Claus Wittich, vol. 2 (Berkeley, 1978), p. 1106. Translation slightly modified.

2. Jean Baudrillard, *L'Échange symbolique et la Mort* (Paris, 1976), p. 78.

3. See, among others, Ulysse Robert, *Les Signes d'infamie au Moyen âge* (Paris, 1891); Henri Marcel Fay, *Histoire de la lèpre en France: lépreux et Cagots du Sud-Ouest* (Paris, 1910); and G. De Matos Sequeira, "Le costume défendu," *Actes du Ier Congrès International d'histoire du costume* (Venice, 1955), pp. 64–68.

This powerful symbolic order was revived during the Second World War in a pitiless way by the pink triangles, yellow stars, etc. of the concentration camps. It would be very interesting to study the genealogy of yellow in particular, for it seems to have been totally discredited in the West, and to establish the historical topography of its use against marginalized populations.

4. Fernand Braudel, *Civilisation matérielle et Capitalisme, XVe–XVIIIe siècle* (Paris, 1967), p. 242.

5. See François Boucher, "Les conditions de l'apparition du costume court en France vers le milieu du xive siècle," *Recueil de travaux offert à M. Clovis Brunel* (Paris, 1955), pp. 183–192.

6. Philippe Ariès, *Centuries of Childhood: A Social History of Family Life*, trans. Robert Baldick (New York, 1962), p. 50.

7. See, for example, Henry Aragon, *Les Lois somptuaires en France* (Perpignan, 1921).

8. On sumptuary laws during the reign of Louis XIV see, among others, Nicolas de Lamare, *Traité de la police*, vol. 1 (Paris, 1705), pp. 339–426.

For example, materials were prescribed according to the season: in the summer, taffeta; light fabrics in the fall or spring; furs were allowed only on All Saints Day or at Easter. Women over forty could not appear at court without a black lace cap, etc.

9. Norbert Elias notes that "in a society in which every outward manifestation of a person has special significance, expenditure on prestige is for the upper classes a necessity that they cannot avoid. They are an indispensable instrument in main-

taining their social position, especially when—as is actually the case in court society—all members of the society are involved in a ceaseless struggle for status and
prestige." *The Court Society*, trans. Edmund Jephcott (New York, 1983), p. 63. For
an exorbitant price Louis XIV granted a few favorite courtiers the wearing of a
jerkin similar to his own—blue moiré lined in red and embroidered with silver.
The privileged courtiers received a *brevet*, or warrant, authorizing them to wear
their jerkin at all times except during periods of deep mourning, hence its name of
justaucorps à brevet. See Saint-Simon, *Mémoires*, vol. 12 (Paris, 1874), p. 69; or Nicolas de Lamare, *Traité de la police*, p. 406.

10. Symptomatically, this meaning replaced the earlier one that Furetière still
gave as the first definition of "fashion" in his 1690 *Dictionnaire*.

11. Louis A. de Caraccioli, *Voyage de la raison en Europe* (Compiègne, 1772), p.
256.

12. Montesquieu wrote in 1717: "A woman who leaves Paris to spend six
months in the country returns as antiquated as though she had mouldered there for
thirty years. A son can't recognize a portrait of his mother, so strange do the clothes
in which she is painted appear to him. He imagines that some American lady is
pictured, or that the painter has tried to represent one of his flights of fancy."
Charles Louis de Secondat, Baron de la Brède et de Montesquieu, *The Persian
Letters*, ed. and trans. J. Robert Loy (Cleveland, 1961), letter 99, p. 187.

13. The last ordinances against bourgeois luxury date from the years 1700 and
1720: *Royal Edict against Luxury Stating Regulations for Fabrics, Braids, Furnishings
Dishes, Plates and Other Silver or Gold Utensils etc., Given the Month of March, 1700*
(Paris, 1700); and *Royal Declaration Prohibiting the Wearing of Diamonds, Given at
Paris the Fourth of February, 1720* (Paris, 1720). The first was partially amended by
an edict of 1702, *Declaration of the King Which Permits Women and Girls Who Were
Forbidden to Do So by the Edict of the Month of March, 1700, to Wear Jewels, Given at
Versailles the 25th of February, 1702* (Paris, 1702). It allowed the wives and daughters
of notaries, prosecutors, government officials, clerks of court, and merchants to
wear earrings and other ornaments, "provided that together they were not worth
more than 2,000 livres" (p. 5). But the second forbade everyone to wear diamonds,
pearls, and precious stones, "with the exception of those [subjects] who have obtained our written permission" (p. 4).

14. Jean François Barbier, *Journal historique et anecdotique du règne de Louis XV*,
vol. 2 (Paris, 1849), pp. 440–441.

15. In 1765 Diderot defined *petit-maître* in his *Encyclopédie*: "Name given to
young men madly in love with themselves, conceited in their speech, affected in
their manners, and elaborate in their attire. Someone has defined the *petit-maître* as
an insignificant insect distinguished by its ephemeral beauty who flits about waving
its powdery wings."

16. See Norbert Elias, *The Civilizing Process*, vol. 1: *The History of Manners*,
trans. Edmund Jephcott, (New York, 1978), pp. 9–10; and Jean-V. Alter, *Les Origines de la satire antibourgeoise en France*, vol. 2: *L'Esprit antibourgeois sous l'Ancien
Régime* (Geneva, 1970). See especially pp. 106–109.

17. L'Abbé Gabriel François Coyer, *Année merveilleuse* (n.p., 1748), pp. 1–2. As
this sketch indicates, the point was to internalize the norms of a class that distanced
itself from the Third Estate to affirm its own status by avoiding the stigma of

laborious and mercenary activities. To be ostentatiously unproductive implied "a loss of time" in the economic sphere and a corollary increase of honor and prestige in the symbolic sphere.

18. As Norbert Elias has pointed out, "The contradiction within the social existence of this court aristocracy, all the more perceptible the more the French economy develops into a network of people practising rational economics, lies in the fact that while their expenses are dictated by their rank and obligations within society, their income is not. This situation is further aggravated for the nobility throughout the eighteenth century by increasing competition from rising bourgeois strata, above all the financiers, as regards outward appearances.... But the style of life of the financiers has a retroactive effect on that of the grands seigneurs. The whip of fashion, now wielded by the former as well, is also felt by the latter. At the same time prices are going up while the nobility's income from rents remains the same, their need for money increases." *The Court Society*, pp. 64–65.

19. Rabaut Saint-Étienne, a Protestant deputy of the Third Estate, attested to this: "The upper clergy, glittering with gold, and the great nobles of the kingdom, crowded around the canopy, displayed the utmost magnificence, while the Third Estate looked as if they were dressed in mourning. Yet their long line represented the nation, and the people were so conscious of this that they overwhelmed them with applause. They shouted, "Long live the Third Estate!" just as since then they have shouted, "Long live the Nation!" This impolitic distinction had produced an effect contrary to the intentions of the court. The Third Estate recognized their defenders and their fathers in the men in black coats and high cravats and its enemies in the others.... These men, who had never before traveled beyond their own provinces and who had just left behind them the spectacle of poverty in the towns and in the countryside, now saw evidence with their own eyes of the extravagant expenditure of Louis XIV and Louis XV and of the new court's quest for pleasure." *Précis historique de la révolution française* (Paris, 1792), pp. 68–69. Translation by Barbara Bray; cited in full at the end of this note.

Citing this text, Jean Starobinski underlines the importance of this moment "when," as he writes, "for the onlookers who had learned to count, the magic of pomp and circumstance ceased to work: mere expense no longer inspired wonder and respect.... The humble people, without whom brilliant society would not have had its decor of illusion, were about to make their grievances heard.

For those who condemned it and wanted to do away with it, the world now coming to an end took on the aspect of evil itself. It was the expression of an active determination to reject universal good, shutting itself up senselessly in its own pleasures and so becoming the equivalent of a natural accident, an affliction that sensible people ought to bring under control." *1789, The Emblems of Reason*, trans. Barbara Bray (Charlottesville, 1982), pp. 17–18.

20. *Le Moniteur universel*, no. 39, 1re décade de Brumaire, l'an II (30 October 1793).

21. On this subject see Laure-Paul Flobert, *La Femme et le costume masculin* (Lille, 1911).

22. André Malraux wrote: "I have never clarified what I think about fashion, ... the centuries during which men must wear beards, the centuries during which they must shave." *Les Chênes qu'on abat* (Paris, 1971), p. 183. For a quantitative study—if

not of the "why," at least of the "how" of these fluctuations—see Dwight E. Robinson, "Fashions in Shaving and Trimming of the Beard: The Men of the *Illustrated London News*, 1842–1972," *American Journal of Sociology* 81, no. 5 (March 1976): 1133–1141. On the general topic of pilosity Jean-Louis Soulavie notes an interesting fact in his *Mémoires historiques et politiques du règne de Louis XVI*. On the occasion of the secret marriage between the duke of Orleans and Madame de Montesson in 1773, etiquette required that the marquis of Valençay present the nuptial shirt. The prince removed "his shirt, and naked to waist showed himself completely epilated. Here he followed the rules of the most exquisite gallantry of the time. Princes and the great nobles neither consummated marriages nor received the first favors of mistresses without undergoing this operation." vol. 2 (Paris, 1801), p. 99.

23. "Three Centuries of Women's Dress Fashion: A Quantitative Analysis," *Anthropological Records* 5, no. 2 (1940): 111–154. Kroeber had previously established series for the period 1844–1919: "On the Principle of Order in Civilization as Exemplified by Changes of Fashion," *American Anthropologist*, n.s. 21 (July 1919): 235–263

24. "Histoire des sciences sociales: la longue durée," *Annales: Economies, Sociétés, Civilisations* 4 (October–December 1958): 725–753. Reprinted in *Écrits sur l'histoire* (Paris, 1969), pp. 41–83, and as "History and the Social Sciences," *On History*, trans. Sarah Matthews, (Chicago, 1980), pp. 25–54.

25. Of course the forms of clothing, like the forms of the body, do not all evolve at the same speed. Hats, like hairstyles, can change very rapidly. Shoes, like body contours, are modified more slowly. Age, and social and civil status also influence the pace of these variations.

26. Agnes Brooks Young, *Recurring Cycles of Fashion 1760–1937* (1937; reprint, New York, 1966).

27. "Because we change so suddenly and promptly in fashion, the inventiveness of all the tailors in the world could never furnish us enough novelties; it is inevitable that despised fashions very often return into favor, and those very ones soon after fall back again into contempt." Montaigne, "Of Ancient Customs," *Essays*, p. 216.

28. Traditional societies undergoing acculturation retain certain historical forms. In this regard see, for example, Jacques Berque, *Le Maghreb entre deux guerres* (Paris, 1962), pp. 90–92.

29. See, among others, Bernard Rudofsky, *Are Clothes Modern?* (Chicago, 1947).

30. Up to the end of the sixteenth century, the role of sight appears to have been less important than those of hearing, touch, taste, and smell. See Lucien Febvre, *The Problem of Unbelief in the Sixteenth Century: The Religion of Rabelais*, trans. Beatrice Gottlieb, (Cambridge, Mass., 1982), pp. 424–429; and Robert Mandrou, *Introduction to Modern France*, trans. R. E. Hallmark (New York, 1975), pp. 50–55.

CHAPTER III

1. Princess Marthe Bibesco, *Noblesse de Robe* (Paris, 1928), pp. 212–213.

2. Alfred Franklin, *La Vie privée d'autrefois*, vol. 16: *Les Magasins de nouveautés* (Paris, 1894), p. 267.

3. Thirifocq, "Du costume dans ses rapports avec les moeurs et avec la civilisation," *Journal des modes d'hommes* 1 (January, 1867).

4. On this subject see Amelia Mott Gummere, *The Quaker: A Study of Costume* (Philadelphia, 1901).

5. On these themes—already set during the Reformation—see John Calvin, *Sermon où il est montré quelle doit être la modestie des femmes en leurs habillements* (1561; reprint, Geneva, 1945); or the anonymous *Traité de l'estat honneste des chrestiens en leur accoustrement*, (Geneva, 1580). On this subject see Philippe Perrot, "La Richesse cachée: pour une généalogie de l'austérité des apparences," *Communications*, 46 (1987): 157–179.

As Max Weber notes, "This profound tendency toward the uniformity of life, which today so manifestly aids capitalism's interest in the standardization of production, had its foundation in the repudiation of all idolatry of the flesh." *The Protestant Ethic and the Spirit of Capitalism*, trans. Talcott Parsons (New York, 1958), p. 169. Parsons's translation has been slightly modified.

Neutral dress and obligatory dark, anonymous, all-purpose colors are profoundly anchored traditions in Northern Europe. This puritanical influence is stronger in France than in other Catholic countries.

6. On these questions see, for example, Aileen Ribeiro, *Fashion in the French Revolution* (New York, 1988), a very richly illustrated introduction to the subject by a fashion historian; and Nicole Pellegrin, *Les Vêtements de la liberté. Abécédaire des pratiques vestimentaires en France de 1780 à 1800* (Paris, 1989), with a postface by Daniel Roche.

7. "Because clothing is the most powerful symbol, the Revolution became . . . a debate between silk and plain cloth," wrote Balzac in his *Traité de la vie élégante*, p. 60. Silk makes colors glisten; wool dulls them.

8. Republican bourgeois in search of patriotic clothing but repelled by the all-too-plebeian sans-culottes' pink-striped grey trousers or the carmagnole jacket, decorated their vests with bowdlerized and muted patriotic signs—red, white, and blue emblems woven, embroidered, or printed—and symbols such as the phrygian cap and the cocade. To demonstrate its hostility to the Revolution the aristocracy wore black—mourning for the monarchy. Then it more discreetly adopted cravats or tails of green, the color of Louis XVI's brother, the Count of Artois, or white—the Bourbons' color—or wore vests made from cloth with faint fleurs-de-lis patterns.

9. "Our clothes are made of iron," proclaimed Bernhard Christoph Faust in 1792. "They are the invention of barbarian and gothic centuries. To be free and happy, break these irons." *Sur le vêtement libre, unique et à l'usage des enfants* (n.p.), pp. 1–2. Proposals for a national costume proliferated. Inspired by recommendations for the reform of clothing—Rousseau's was the most famous—a number of physicians before and after Rousseau also propounded theories, such as Jacob B. Winslow, "Mémoire sur les mauvais effets de l'usage des corps à baleines," *Mémoires de l'Académie des Sciences* (Paris, 1741); Jean C. Desessartz, *Traité de l'éducation corporelle des enfants en bas âge* (Paris, 1760); Alphonse Leroy, *Recherches sur les habillements des femmes et des enfants* (Paris, 1803); and L. G. Clairian, *Recherches et considérations médicales sur les vêtements des hommes particulièrement sur les culottes* (Paris, 1803).

Proposals, especially for a national costume, multiplied. The Marquis de Vilette suggested: "In revolutionary times when civil society is being regenerated throughout the kingdom, we could institute a 'new fashion' for men.

Begin by suppressing the stiffness and affectation of French clothing, and outlaw the very words 'dressy dress.'

Adopt the round hat, to be called 'liberty hat,' with the addition of two flowing feathers in red, white, and blue; and finally renounce the three-cornered hat whose bizarre form offends and afflicts the eye.

Wear short hair, gracefully and naturally curled, that will complete the headgear. Rosettes on shoes, knees, and the cravat.

Women will wear long, blue gowns and the cocade. Because gold must be sent to the Mint, they will wear epaulettes woven from corded silk. Materials and notions will be supplied by our own factories.

Let a single one of our young soldiers appear dressed this way, with his youthful grace, and this sole example will be worth more than all I can say.

With this new uniform, we could recover both French values and French manners. It would become the hallmark of our well-tempered revolution, and through it we would have accomplished more than the English." *Lettres choisies* (Montargis, 1790), pp. 19–20.

The "Popular and Republican Society of the Arts" celebrated even more enthusiastically the virtues of a national costume: "Under the rule of despotism, the useless class of idle rich determined the form of clothing; engrossed by its puerile games, it dictated injudiciously the vicissitudes of fashion, taking as its sole rule the caprice of its imagination or the impulses of its conceit. Free men will not follow the footsteps of such frivolous creatures. That adornment and baubles absorbed these vain slaves, however, does not mean that what a nation chooses to wear is unimportant or futile. Clothing presents physical and political considerations worthy of a reasonable republican's attention. . . . Dressed in more sensible clothing than our own, men would become healthier, stronger, swifter, better able to defend liberty; women would give the state healthier children. A national costume would fulfill functions truly deserving of a free man's consideration, such as constantly proclaiming and recalling *la patrie*, and distinguishing French citizens from nationals of countries still stigmatized by the chains of servitude. It would make it easy to signal the age and public functions of citizens, without tampering with the sacred foundations of equality." From "Considération sur les avantages de changer le costume françois," *La Décade philosophique, littéraire et politique*, 10 Floréal l'an II, Ier année [29 April 1794], pp. 60–62.

10. As will be seen later, the top hat can also be considered as a reincarnation of a Revolutionary hairstyle.

11. Extract from an article by Gustave Claudin in *Le Petit Moniteur du soir*, cited in the *Journal des modes de l'hommes* (March 1869).

12. Jean Baudrillard, *Le Système des objets*, pp. 43–44.

13. *De la mode* (Paris, 1858), pp. 5–6.

14. On this subject see Jean-Paul Aron and Roger Kempf, *Le Pénis et la démoralisation de l'Occident* (Paris, 1978), especially the chapter dedicated to "bodily defects," pp. 249–286.

15. "For men in modern attire, the proper bearing is having none. This is not to condemn elegance of bearing—apart from clothing—which means walking elegantly or presenting oneself easily. But just as in earlier times men were considered uncouth who neglected their carriage, so today they would appear ridiculous when trying to strike poses in a frock coat or a suit. In these clothes the less affected the manners, the more one avoids a silly, awkward contrast between clothes and the man." Gabriel Prevost, *Le Nu, le vêtement, la parure chez l'homme et chez la femme* (Paris, 1883), pp. 379–380. Significantly, the word *pose* acquired its pejorative sense in the nineteenth century. The *Dictionnaire Robert* dates this acceptation from 1835; the *Oxford English Dictionary* gives 1840.

16. In the eighteenth century the *maîtres d'agrément* trained young people to please others through elegant manners. "These teachers," Sébastien Mercier tells us, "train them how to smile cleverly before a mirror, to take snuff gracefully, to cast subtle glances, to roll their *r*'s like actors, to imitate stage players without actually copying them, and to show their teeth without grimacing. One would devote two or three hours a day, closeted with one's teacher, to perfecting these important matters." *Tableau de Paris*, vol. 2 (Amsterdam, 1782), p. 217.

17. "As for eccentrics once easily betrayed by their use of harsh, violent colors," notes Baudelaire in his *Curiosités esthétiques*, "nowadays they turn to nuances of design, and cut rather than color." *Oeuvres complètes* (Paris, 1968), p. 260.

18. "Strange to note that while the coat is victim of epidemic gravity and scientific airs, vest fabrics shimmer with luxury. Nothing is too rich, too brilliant for this ancillary item of attire, which is hidden completely or partially under one's coat; mixtures of silks and wools with gold and silver threads, silk cloths embroidered in assorted shades completely eclipse the somber melancholy of the funeral suit!" *L'Élégant 18* (1 January 1853).

19. Anonymous, *Écho des tailleurs, journal de mode pour hommes*, 2ᵉ année 19 (August 1858).

20. *Fashion-Théorie* 34, no. 267 (June 1862)

21. *Écho des tailleurs* 8, no. 84 (January 1864).

22. Nestor Roqueplan, *Parisine* (Paris, 1869), p. 43.

23. In his *Theory of the Leisure Class.*

24. *La Femme et la Mode* (Paris, 1893), p. 227.

25. Georges d'Avenel, *Le Mécanisme de la vie moderne*, pp. 60–61.

26. "Some scant remains of shame and fear of censure have kept us from resuming the use of powdered wigs, which we reinstituted for high-class servants, along with rouge. Servants powdered and rouged in the mid–nineteenth century, after the storming of the Bastille and the Oath of the Tennis Court! Great-grandchildren of ours, what will you say about us!" Arnould Frémy, *Les Moeurs de notre temps* (Paris, 1860), p. 62.

27. In the nineteenth century, uniforms acquired an unprecedented prestige and not only because they made a brilliant show in contrast to the drab black suit. Even more important was the fact that the bourgeois had conquered the right to military glory and death, finally gaining an aristocratic privilege denied them since the Crusades.

CHAPTER IV

1. The guild of tailors was not organized until 1402, when, clothing having become sexualized, men and women stopped dressing alike in robes and loose coats. The earlier garments required only rudimentary skills on the part of the *robarum sciores* or "garment cutters." By creating new imperatives in design, cut, sizes, pressing, and sewing methods, the shift from the loose and floating system to a fitted one thus gave rise to the new craft of "tailor."

2. Mercers were the only retail corporation of retailers not specialized in a specific product. Their statutes allowed them to sell a very large number of articles—gloves, mittens, ribbons, lacings, belts, makeup, powder, perfumes, jewels, flowers, feathers, etc. The only restriction was that they could not make what they sold. "Dealers in everything, makers of nothing," was the saying.

3. Alongside the strong and influential tailors' guild there were innumerable communities of workers, established and designated according to the specific part of the garment they made. They appeared and disappeared, joining or breaking away from the tailors and other groups in the trade as fashion evolved. The *doubletier* cut and sewed doublets, the *pourpointier* made short garments, the hosier fabricated *haut de chausse et bas*, the furrier worked with furs, etc.

On this subject see René de Lespinasse, *Histoire générale de Paris, Les métiers et corporations de la ville de Paris*, vol. 3: *Tissus, étoffes, vêtements, cuirs et peaux, métiers divers* (Paris, 1897); and Pierre Vidal, *Histoire de la corporation des travailleurs d'habits, de la ville de Paris d'après des documents originaux* (Mimeographed publication, Paris, 1923).

4. *Statuts Ordonnances et Déclaration du Roy confirmative d'iceux pour la communauté des courturières de la ville, Fauxbourgs et banlieue de Paris, Verifié en Parlement le 7 octobre 1675* (Paris, 1678), pp. 14–15.

5. See Jean-Paul Desaive's article "Le nu hurluberlu," *Ethnologie française* 6, no. 314 (1976): 219–226; and Norbert Elias, *The Civilizing Process*, pp. 164–165.

6. Cited by Henri Bouchot, *Les Femmes de Brantôme* (Paris, 1890), p. 234.

7. *Mémoires sur Voltaire, et sur ses ouvrages, par Longchamp et Wagnière, ses secrétaires*, vol 2 (Paris, 1862), pp. 119–121.

During the Regency Father La Rue reproached women who were "served by valets their own age and who dressed in front of them." *Sermons* (Lyon, 1719), p. 277. "A woman of quality," adds Balzac, "gets dressed in front of her servants as though they were oxen." *Traité*, p. 52.

8. The fame of one Langlé, a tailor at the court of Louis XIV, mentioned by the Marquis de Dangeau, the Duc de Saint-Simon, and Madame de Sévigné, seems to be the exception that proves the rule.

9. During the Middle Ages clothing was the product of numerous independent operations. In 1656, suit tailors, master merchants, pourpoint makers, and hosiers united, as did mercers and drapers in 1776.

10. On Rose Bertin and Mme Éloffe, see, for example, Pierre de Nouvion and Émile Liez, *Un ministre des modes sous Louis XVI, Mademoiselle Bertin, marchande de modes de la reine, 1747–1813* (Paris, 1911), which includes an inventory from the Doucet archives of articles made for the queen; Émile Langlade, *La*

Marchande de modes de Marie-Antoinette, Rose Bertin, (Paris, 1911); and Comte de Reiset, *Modes et usages au temps de Marie-Antoinette, Livre-journal de Madame Éloffe, marchande de modes, couturière, lingère de la reine et des dames de sa cour*, 2 vols. (Paris, 1885).

11. *Tableau de Paris*, vol. 1, p. 183.

12. Savary counted 1,882 master tailors, 1,700 dressmakers, 700 fripperer merchants, 659 linen drapers, 1,820 shoemakers, 1,300 cobblers, and 319 hatters in Paris around 1750. Cited by René de Lespinasse, *Les Métiers*, p. 181.

13. Witness this *Épître à Beaulard*:

> Faut-il compte seize quartiers
> Pour oser prétendre à la gloire?
> N'est-ce qu'aux champs de la victoire
> Qu'on peut moissonner des lauriers?
> Beaulard, plus de mille sentiers
> Mènent au temple de mémoire.
> Poursuis; calcule nos travers:
> Déjà ton riche répertoire
> Est l'entrepôt de l'Univers.
> L'Artiste, en son laboratoire,
> De l'art sondant les pronfondeurs
> Saura bien même dans nos moeurs
> Meriter un rang dans l'Histoire.
> Tant de chefs-d'oeuvre si brillants
> Dont tu decoras ta Patrie
> Prouvent assez tes grands talents.
>
> Does one need sixteen quarterings
> To dare to pretend to glory?
> Is it only on battlefields
> That one harvests wreaths of laurel?
> Beaulard, over a thousand paths
> Can lead one to the Hall of Fame.
> Continue and measure our failings:
> Add to your rich repertory
> The warehouse of the Universe.
> In his laboratory, the artist who
> Plumbs the depths of his talent
> Even according to our views
> Merits a place in History.
> Your many bright masterpieces
> Which embellish your Fatherland
> Are proof enough of your talents.
> —Anonymous, (n.p., n.d.), Bibliothèque Nationale, Pièce 8° Ye 5328

14. On the social history of the fashion trades properly speaking, from 1830 to 1870, see especially the work by Henriette Vanier, *La Mode et ses métiers. Frivolités et luttes des classes, 1830–1870* (Paris, 1960).

15. *Tableau de Paris*, vol. 10, p. 162.

16. Roger de Beauvoir, "Le Tailleur," *Les Français peints par eux-mêmes*, p. 239.

17. *Physiologie du tailleur* (Paris, 1840), p. 49.

18. Ibid., p. 49.

19. Huart's figures, which are only approximate, generally confirm those published a few years later by the Paris Chamber of Commerce. In 1847 there were:

3,012	custom manufacturers
9,765	custom workers
233	ready-to-wear manufacturers
7,440	ready-to-wear workers
3,393	manufacturing tailor-assemblers
4,560	wage-earning tailor-assemblers

The assembling tailor was a worker employed by a custom tailor or a ready-to-wear tailor. The crisis of 1848, therefore, struck a population of at least 25,158 employees. *Statistiques de l'industrie à Paris résultant de l'enquête faite par la Chambre de commerce pour les années 1847–1848* (Paris, 1851).

20. "Le tailleur," *Les Français peints par eux-mêmes*, pp. 239–240.

21. For his bills see *Le Grand Livre de Leroy* (his accounts), deposited in the Bibliothèque Nationale (Fonds Français 5932). For more on Leroy, a "braggart, counterjumper, gambler, misogynist, it was said, because he had seen too many shoulders; haughty toward the lowly, craven before the powerful, a procurer, a usurer, and on the whole a crook," see Henri Bouchot, *La Toilette à la cour de Napoléon, chiffons et politiques de grandes dames (1810–1815)* (Paris, 1895).

22. "I often observed this old countess," he wrote, "because of the charming Victorine dresses she wore. I love well-made dresses to distraction. For me this is a sensual pleasure." *Oeuvres complètes*, vol. 36 (Geneva, 1970), p. 120.

23. For example, when Mme de Bargenton becomes Countess du Châtelet, she wears a "silk dress with a pointed bodice, delectably fringed, whose design—by the famous Victorine—really set off her figure." "Illusions perdues," *Oeuvres complètes*, vol. 8 (Paris, 1843), p. 497.

24. Roger de Beauvoir, "Le tailleur," p. 250.

25. "A suit by Buisson, . . ." he said, "is enough to make a man king of the drawing room." *Oeuvres complètes*, vol. 16 (Paris, 1846), p. 369.

26. A writer for *Petits-Paris* reported, "Chevreuil admitted that he knew only one man who could measure up to him, Blain, under whom, moreover, he had served his apprenticeship. 'And, even then,' he immediately added, 'I feel sure that I've surpassed him.' The few people in Paris who could appreciate the cut of a garment said: 'Blain is knowledgeable and distinguished; Chevreuil is supreme.'" Taxile Delord, Arnould Frémy, and Edmond Texier, *Paris Viveur* (Paris, 1854), p. 32.

27. A census was taken in 1847–48 of the streets in which the greatest number of custom tailors had set up shop:

Number of Tailors	Street
106	rue de Richelieu
96	Saint-Honoré
61	Neuve-des-Petits-Champs
58	Vivienne
49	Fontaine-Molière
43	Sainte-Anne
43	Saint-Marc
43	Montmartre
28	faubourg-Saint-Martin
24	faubourg-Saint-Antoine
23	Neuve-Saint-Augustin

The rest were scattered throughout the city. *Statistiques de l'industrie à Paris*, p. 268.

28. Louis Huart, *Statistiques de l'industrie à Paris*, p. 86. For his part, Roger de Beauvoir writes: "In Paris, where one can find anything, there are honest tailors who claim to sell at half the price what their colleagues sell at double its worth. Such were the tailors of the Palais-Royal and the various covered passages in Paris. But don't these honorable producers have to pay rent, and aren't their rents higher than anywhere else? Almost all the tailors in the *passages* display a dressed manne-quin at the door, like the London tailors; and besides astounding dressing gowns, most of which are of Lyon silk, and which they sell at very high prices, they offer vests as well, made of gold and silver cloth to please the 'beaux' from Carpentras." "Le tailleur," p. 244.

29. Of the 5,181 couturières recorded by the Paris Chamber of Commerce, 3,203 worked alone, and only 86 employed more than 10 workers. And of the 3,012 custom tailors counted, 870 worked alone. *Statistiques de l'industrie à Paris* (1851), pp. 249, 286.

30. Nestor Roqueplan, *Parisine* (Paris, 1869), p. 166.

31. There were 180 female and 271 male fripperers listed by the Paris Chamber of Commerce in 1847–48. Of these, 164 females and 165 males lived in what was then the sixth arrondissement, and of these, 160 females and 149 males lived in the quarter of the Temple itself. See *Statistiques de l'industrie à Paris*, pp. 256, 306.

32. The various *Almanachs du commerce de Paris* published by Sébastien Bottin during the first half of the nineteenth century recorded a number of fripperers on the odd-numbered side of the rue de la Tonnellerie.

33. *Tableau de Paris*, vol. 9, p. 174.

34. When Panurge stole the paternosters (the beads of a rosary) from the great lady of Paris, he "took them to the fripperers." Rabelais, *Pantagruel*, book 2, chap. 21 (Paris, 1955), p. 262. Fripperers were also suspected of buying the belongings of executed criminals and deceased persons:

> Tous les habits qu'avez vienne de ces penduz,
> Ou bien de ceux qui sont sur la roüe rompuz,
> Ou bien de quelque noble, qui pour un coup d'espée,

Dessus un eschaffaut à la teste tranchée,
Ou bien d'un vérole, qui se faisant suër:
Est mort entre les mains, de Monsieur le Barbier.

All the clothing you have comes from hanged persons,
From those who have on the wheel been broken,
From noble felons decapitated
For using their swords in duels outlawed,
From syphilitics who induced such a sweat
That they gave up the ghost while the barber bled them.
—*Discours de deux marchands fripiers et de deux maîtres tailleur*s (n.p., 1614), p. 6

35. *Les piliers des Halles*:

Tandis que j'ay la verve rogue,
Point de quartiers à ces gens cy,
Voila l'enfer en racourcy
C'est à dire, la sinagogue
Hé quoy fripiers rabinisez
Seigneurs Chrétiens Jusaysez
Osez-vous bien icy paraistre?
Engeance de Mathusalem,
Juifs baptisez, croyez, vous estre
Encore dans Hiérusalem?

As long as I've any fight left
I give no quarter to those folks.
This is a hell in miniature
That is to say, a synagogue:
Hey there, rabbinized fripperers,
Jewified Christian Lords you are.
Dare you show your faces here,
Methuselah's worthless brood,
Baptized Jews, do you believe
Yourselves in Jerusalem?

—Claude Le Petit, *La Chronique scandaleuse, ou Paris ridicule* (Cologne, 1668), p. 13

Or:
"Tailors find it more difficult to design than to sew, and when a garment lasts longer than a flower, it begins to look decrepit. From this has sprung a tribe of fripperers, a vile race descended from what was once Israel; they buy and sell old rags and used clothing, and live splendidly by stripping some to dress others." Giovanni Paolo Marana, *Lettre d'un Sicilien à un de ses amis, contenant une agréable Critique de Paris et des Français* (Chambéri, 1714), pp. 18–19. Translated from the Italian.
    36. *Tableau de Paris*, vol. 5 (Paris, 1852), p. 15.
    37. Edmond Texier, vol. 1 *Tableau de Paris*, p. 146.
    38. Marc Fournier, "La Rotonde du Temple," *La Grande Ville, Nouveau Tableau de Paris*, vol. 2 (Paris, 1842), p. 45.
    39. Texier, vol. 1 *Tableau de Paris*, p. 148.

40. Ibid.

41. "Although the halles du Temple were established fairly recently, the practices of old-fashioned commerce have taken refuge there. . . . A *half-light* that barely penetrates the dank atmosphere hovers over a world unto itself and strikes groups and faces worthy of a Flemish painting," writes Marc Fournier, "La Rotonde," p. 45 (emphasis added).

42. See the "Short Lexicon of the Secondhand Clothes Trade," p. 57.

43. Marc Fournier, "La Rotonde," pp. 43–44.

44. Edmond Texier, *Tableau de Paris*, vol. 1, p. 148.

45. Marc Fournier, "La Rotonde," p. 47.

46. Edmond Texier, *Tableau de Paris*, vol. 1, p. 150.

47. Taxile Delord, Arnould Frémy, and Edmond Texier, "Paris-Gagne-Petit," *Les Petits Paris* (nos. 6–10), p. 41. For the number of rag-pickers, their trade, traditions, rules, history, social milieu, and, above all, habitat in the nineteenth century, see Alain Faure, "Classe malpropre, classe dangereuse, *Recherches* 29 (December 1977): 79–102; and L. A. Berthaud's monograph "Les chiffoniers," *Les Français peints par eux-mêmes*, vol. 3 (Paris, 1841), pp. 333–344.

48. "Chiffoniers," *Grand Dictionnaire universel du xix* siècle, vol. 4 (Paris, n.d.), p. 96.

49. Ibid.

50. Ibid.

51. Joseph Mainzer, "Le marchand d'habits," *Les Français peints par eux-mêmes*, vol. 1 (Paris, 1841), p. 363.

52. Arnould Frémy, "La Revendeuse à la toilette," *Les Français peints par eux-mêmes*, vol. 1 (Paris, 1841), p. 362.

53. Ibid., p. 363.

54. Comtesse Dash, *Les Femmes à Paris et en province* (Paris, 1868), p. 102.

55. Arnould Frémy, "La Revendeuse," p. 364.

56. Edmond Texier, *Tableau de Paris*, p. 150.

57. Ibid., p. 147.

58. F. d'Antonelle, "Le marché aux vieux linges," *Nouveau Tableau de Paris au xix siècle*, vol. 1 (Paris, 1834), p. 355.

59. The cycle of wear and the degradation of clothing as a social sign followed essentially the same paths in England: "In every newspaper," Hippolyte Taine noted, "I have found the addresses of merchants who will call on you to buy your slightly out-of-date clothing; a gentleman's dress must be beyond reproach; his suit, once it is passé, goes to a man of the lower classes and ends as a rag on the back of a poor person and thus marks the social rank of its owner. Nowhere else is the distance between social conditions written so visibly on men's exteriors. Imagine the evening dress of an elegant gentleman or the pink, flowered hat of a "lady"; you will encounter them again: one will be on a miserable drunk crouched on the steps leading to the Thames, the other at Shadwell, on the head of an old woman digging in garbage." *Notes sur l'Angleterre* (Paris, 1872), p. 24.

60. F. d'Antonelle, "Le marché aux vieux linges," pp. 358–359.

61. Ibid., pp. 359–360.

62. Alfred Franklin, in his *Vie privée d'autrefois*, believes that he had discovered the creator of ready-made clothing. He quotes a notice from a 1770 newspaper:

"The sieur Dartigalongue, master and merchant tailor in Paris, has opened a store where he sells new clothes in all sizes and in the latest fashions. If his wares do not suit the taste of those who want to be clothed quickly, he can supply what they want almost at once because of the numerous workers he employs. . . . His address is *A la Renomée*, rue de Savoye, faub. Saint-Germain, near the rue des Grands-Augustins." *Les magasins de nouveautés*, vol. 15, p. 265.

But what he sold was probably *almost*-ready-to-wear clothing kept in inventory and altered "almost-at-once," according to the customers' needs. The guild regulations would not have permitted anything else.

63. See Georges d'Avenel, "Les grands magasin," *Revue des Deux-Mondes* 4 (1894): 343.

64. Charles Eck, *Histoire chronologique du vêtement (homme) ou, Jadis et aujourd'hui, suivi de l'art de se vêtir au XIX siècle* (Paris, 1867), p. 66.

65. Lemann [a ready-to-wear manufacturer and dealer], *De l'industrie des vêtements confectionnés en France, réponse aux questions de la commission permanente des valeurs relativement à cette industrie* (Paris, 1857), p. 14.

66. Jules Simon, *L'Ouvrière* (Paris, 1861), p. 235. On the organization of work in ready-to-wear companies, see Albert Aftalion, *Le Développement de la fabrique et le travail à domicile dans les industries de l'habillement* (Paris, 1906); and Émile Dorchies, *L'Industrie à domicile de la confection de vêtements pour hommes dans la campagne lilloise* (Lille, 1907).

67. "Because it was taking longer and longer to have clothes made, customers were led to buy ready-made garments; workers and employees wanted and needed their clothes as soon as they had the money in hand." *Le Journal des tailleurs* 19, no. 12 (1 July 1848).

68. *Statistiques de l'industrie à Paris* (1851), p. 297.

69. Vol. 22, no. 24 (16 December 1851).

70. Previously, "Only a provincial newly arrived in town or a phony man of fashion went to ready-to-wear shops whose products could be recognized at a glance. Since 1848 ready-to-wear has made enormous strides; it has killed off the domestic tailor who used to work for the middle class." Kerckhoff, *Le Costume*, pp. 209–210.

During his stay in Paris, Richard Wagner sent these typical details in a 9 February 1850 letter to his wife, Minna: "And then I also had to outfit myself: 1. hat; 2. umbrella (indispensable); 3. black cravat; 4. gloves; 5. two pairs of underpants; 6. a wallet; and finally, 7. a *ready-made* paletot (author's italics), *Lettres de Richard Wagner à Minna Wagner* (Paris, 1943), pp. 58–59. In 1848, "The ready-to-wear industry discovered new business opportunities in export trade and from then on gained in importance. The February Revolution completely halted the manufacture of cloth: the warehouses of the Elbeuf factories contained quantities of fancy goods but had no market for them; M. Victor Grandin proposed that the government raise the export subsidy from the 9 percent at that time allocated to exported woolen cloth to 13.5 percent. This measure, ratified by a decree of 10 June 1848, enabled the manufacturers to lower their prices, dispose of their products abroad, and continue production with wool that they bought cheaply." *Statistiques de l'industrie à Paris* (1860), p. 307.

71. Auguste Dusautoy, *Rapport du Jury international de l'Exposition de 1867, 35e classe* (Paris, 1867), p. 29.

72. *Statistiques de l'industrie à Paris* (1851), p. 223.

73. Gaston Worth, *La Couture et la Confection des vêtements de femme* (Paris, 1895), pp. 19–20.

74. A keen observer of the evolution of Parisian business during the first half of the nineteenth century, Balzac describes in *La Maison du Chat-qui-pelote* one of these shops from another age, with its prudent and routine activity, its outward lack of appeal. "Many a passer-by," he writes, "would have found it difficult to guess the class of trade carried on by Monsieur Guillaume. Between the strong iron bars which protected his shop windows on the outside, certain packages, wrapped in brown linen, were hardly visible, though as numerous as herrings swimming in a shoal." *"At the Sign of the Cat and Racket" and Other Stories* (1829; reprint, London, 1944), p. 21.
The absence of a real shop window was always attributed to the old mercantile preference for deceptive darkness: "Some stores are somber; the casement windows have wooden panes at the bottom and dirty glass elsewhere; a half-open jalousie lets in enough daylight to embellish the colors, and once outside you no longer recognize the color you bought." Louis Prudhomme, *Voyage descriptif et philosophique de l'ancien et du nouveau Paris* (Paris, 1821), p. 102, not to mention Zola and his descriptions (in *Au Bonheur des Dames*) of the shops of Baudu the draper, Robineau the silk merchant, and Bourras the umbrella merchant.

75. *Le Petit Matelot*, which opened in 1790 on the Ile Saint-Louis at the corner of the quai d'Anjou, seems to have been the first "fancy goods store," said Balzac, who had Constance Pillerault, César Birotteau's future wife, work there. This was "the first of many of its kind to be set up in Paris, all of them characterized by painted signs, floating streamers, window displays of shawls suspended in air, ties arranged like houses of cards, and endless other attractions, such as price tags, fancy wrappings, and show-cards, the optical effect of which was to transform storefronts into commercial poems. The low prices of all the *Petit Matelot*'s wares, known as "novelties," made it unprecedentedly successful." *César Birotteau*, trans. Frances Frenaye (1837; reprint, New York, 1955), p. 27. Translation slightly altered.

76. Arnould Frémy, "La revendeuse à la toilette," p. 360.

77. However, honesty did not challenge commercial practices: "There is nothing," writes Prudhomme, "that merchants won't do to get customers into their stores. The merchants selling at set prices who distribute on the Pont-Neuf and at theater entrances and publish in the newspaper lists of goods they claim to be available at their shops at certain prices are often embarrassed when asked for the advertised items. But they explain: 'We sold the last one—less than two hours ago. But, the one you asked for wouldn't have suited you; here is what you need. This is quite superior cloth; ordinary material isn't for a man like you.'" *Voyage descriptif*, p. 101.

78. "Les Magasins de Paris," *Paris, ou le livre des Cent-et-un*, vol. 15 (Paris, 1844), p. 243.

79. "Magasins de nouveautés," *La Grande Ville, Nouveau Tableau de Paris, comique, critique, et philosophique*, vol. 1 (Paris, 1844), pp. 241–242.

80. The textile sector was still dispersed, but compared to other industrial sectors, it was the most modern. The privileged position of textiles, a light industry producing consumer goods, showed that mechanization proceeded slowly. It was

characteristic of a stage in economic development in which oil, steel, railroads, and heavy machinery were yet undeveloped.

81. Au Trois Quartiers, born in 1829, is one of the rare "fancy goods stores" that, transformed into a department store, survives into the present.

CHAPTER V

1. For detailed studies of two exemplary cases, see Michael B. Miller, *The Bon Marché, Bourgeois Culture and the Department Store, 1869–1920* (Princeton, 1981); and François Faraut, *Histoire de la Belle Jardinière* (Paris, 1987).

2. Documents on their origins are rare. On this subject see Bertrand Gille, "Recherches sur l'origine des grands magasins parisiens, notes d'orientation," *Fédération des sociétés historiques et archéologiques de Paris et de l'Ile-de-France*, Mémoire VII (1955), pp. 308–321.

3. Chauchard entered into a partnership with Heriot, head of the silk fabric department at La Ville de Paris, and Faret, the owner of La Belle Française, and the brothers Pereire, who owned the building and adjacent property, invested 1,100,000 francs in the Louvre.

4. Boucicaut went into partnership with Videau, who owned a small store, the Bon Marché, on the rue du Bac. Jaluzot received the sum of 300,000 francs from his wife. In 1863, Videau ceded his share to Boucicault.

5. Zola's fictional department store, *Au Bonheur des Dames*, was, for example, a transformed "fancy goods store." Before its metamorphosis, he gave the following description of it in *Pot-Bouille*:

"There was a fancy goods store at the corner of the rue Neuve-Saint-Augustin and the rue Michodière. Its door opened onto the narrow triangle of the Place Gaillon. Barring two of the windows of the entresol was a sign in decorated letters: '*Au Bonheur des Dames*, firm founded in 1822.' While, on the plate glass of the windows, one could read, painted in red, the firm's corporate name: *Deleuze, Hedoin and Co.* . . . The young man spent two hours in the store. He found it ill-lit, small, cluttered with merchandise that spilled out from the basement and accumulated in the corners, leaving only narrow passages between walls of stacked-up bundles." Émile Zola, *Pot Bouille* (Paris, 1957), pp. 20–21.

6. On this subject see Claude Fohlen's thesis, *L'Industrie textile au temps du Second Empire* (Paris, 1956).

7. "At the head of each subdivision, the store equivalent of ministries in a government, there is a '*chef de rayon*,' or 'department head,' who stands in the same relationship to his superior as a minister toward his sovereign. The department head is both ship captain and ambassador. He is captain in that he has absolute, discretionary power over the crew that sell under his direction, and responsibility. He is ambassador in that he takes daily inventory of his stock in his department and is fully empowered to make the purchases necessary to fill the gaps left by customers. Since he often must be out on business most of the day, he delegates the sales supervision to a steady, reliable lieutenant who bears the title of "Second." For this second-in-command, as well as the "Thirds" and "Fourths" who merge under the title of "clerk," the department head is a "premier." Eugène Muller, *La Boutique du*

marchand de nouveautés (Paris, 1868), p. 17. The department is the constitutive unit of the department store.

8. Maxime du Camp, "Les voitures publiques dans la ville de Paris," *Revue des Deux-Mondes* 37 (15 May 1867): 343.

9. "La revendeuse à la toilette," p. 360.

10. "*E probitate decus*" became, for example, the motto of Printemps and the core of its advertising. Fixed prices, inaugurated by "fancy goods stores" and adopted by department stores, were forced upon most establishments above a certain size and a certain level.

"Nothing was more unpleasant or made one more irritated and suspicious than having to constantly bargain as shoppers were once forced to do," noted Countess Drohojowska in 1860. "Thank God, all respectable stores today buy and sell at marked prices." *De la politesse et du bon ton ou devoir d'une femme chrétienne dans le monde* (Paris, 1860), pp. 98–99.

11. On their working conditions see Claudie Lesselier, "Employées de grands magasins à Paris (avant 1914)," *Le Mouvement social* 105 (October–December 1978): 109–126; and Miller, *The Bon Marché*.

12. *Ladies' Delight*, trans. April Fitzlyon (London, 1957), p. 10.

13. The *Bon Marché* increased its gross as follows (amounts in francs):

1852	450,000
1860	5,600,000
1863	7,000,000
1866	12,000,000
1869	21,000,000
1877	67,000,000

See Georges d'Avenel, "Les grands magasins," *La Revue des Deux-Mondes* 4 (1894): 335–336; and Auguste Dusautoy, *Rapport*, p. 44.

14. Cast iron and glass construction, which we think characteristic of the department store, did not appear until the Third Republic. For these technical aspects, see the magnificently illustrated book by Bernard Marrey, *Les Grands Magasins: des origines à 1939* (Paris, 1979).

15. *Au Bonheur des Dames*, p. 277.

16. The *Bon Marché* had 4,300 gas jets in 1882. Zola's preparatory dossier for *Au Bonheur des Dames* (manuscript, Bibliothèque nationale, Nouvelle Acquisitions françaises, N° 10278).

17. *La Joie du foyer* 2, no. 3 (1 December 1865).

18. *Ladies' Delight*, pp. 226–227.

19. Vol. 2, no. 7 (1 April l868).

20. Zola's preparatory dossier for *Au Bonheur des Dames*.

21. *Ladies' Delight*, p. 402.

22. *Les Grands Bazars* (Paris, 1882), p. 62.

23. Zola's Mouret must certainly be numbered among these ingenious topographers; he divulged his concept of labyrinthine commercial space to a skeptical Bourdoncle: "First, the continual coming and going of the customers disperses them a bit everywhere, increases their number and makes them lose their sense of direction; second, we must be able to lead them from one end of the store to the other;

if, for example, they want to buy lining after they've bought a dress, these trips in every direction will make the store seem three times as big; third, because they are forced to go through departments they've never seen before, they will be ensnared as they pass through, and they will succumb." *Au Bonheur des Dames*, p. 279.

24. Zola, *Ladies' Delight*, p. 402.

25. Ibid., p. 299.

26. "Ravaged by a furious, irresistible need, Madame de Bove had been stealing like that for a year. The attacks had been growing more acute, increasing until they had become a sensual pleasure necessary to her existence, sweeping away all the reasonings of prudence and indulged in with an enjoyment which was all the more keen because she was risking her name, her pride, and her husband's important position, under the very eyes of the crowd. Now that her husband let her take money from his drawers, she was stealing with her pockets full of money, stealing for stealing's sake as people love for the sake of loving, spurred on by desire, unhinged by the neurosis which had been developed within her in the past by her unassuaged desire for luxury when faced with the enormous, ruthless temptation of big stores." *Ladies' Delight*, p. 398.

27. "From 1868 to 1881," wrote Dr. Legrand du Saulle, at the central police station I questioned 104 women accused of theft. As we shall see, the greatest number were hysterics and belonged to the category which I discuss.

Here is the breakdown of my statistics; among 104 pathological or semipathological thieves, I found:

"Pathological" Thefts

Very feebleminded	4
Hysterical lunatics	9
Hemiplegic lunatics	2
Totally paralyzed lunatics	5
Senile lunatics	5
Total	25

"Semipathological" Thefts

Hysterics, 15–42 years old, apprehended at the time of their menstrual periods	35
Hysterics of the same age but not in their menstrual periods	6
Girls or women hereditarily predisposed to mental illness (with a greater or lesser number of hysterical symptoms)	24
Women at menopause or seriously weakened by uterine hemorrhages	10
Pregnant women	5
Total	80

Les hystériques, état physique et état mental, actes insolites, délictueux et criminels (Paris, 1883), pp. 449–450.

28. "By now Madame Marty had the animated and hysterical face of a child that has drunk undiluted wine. She had come into the shop, her eyes clear and her skin fresh from the cold of the street, and her eyes and skin had gradually become scorched by the sight of all the luxury of those violent colours, the continual succession of which inflamed her passion. When she finally left, after having said that she would pay at home, terrified by the figures on her bill, her features were drawn and she had the dilated eyes of a sick woman. . . . Then, outside on the pavement, . . . the keen air made her shiver, and she was still frightened, unhinged by the neurosis caused by big shops." *Ladies' Delight*, pp. 254–255.

29. Gustave Macé, *Un Joli monde* (Paris, 1887), pp. 262–268.

30. See, for example, Alexandre Weill, *Un Fléau national, les grands magasins de Paris et les Moyens de les combattre* (Paris, 1888).

31. Zola clearly overdid the image of the Second Empire monster—gigantic and luminous—that devoured the small, dark, damp, low-ceilinged shops, expropriating, bulldozing everything in sight, annihilating Baudus, Vincards, Bourras, and consorts, and flourishing amidst their ruins. Jeanne Gaillard indicates that "in a survey of one-tenth of the Paris bankruptcies during the Second Empire, the department store was named only twice as the cause of the failure of fancy goods merchants." In fact, she concludes later, "the department store–shop feud . . . picked up speed only during periods of economic crisis. Thus, in 1882, when Zola wrote *Au Bonheur des Dames*, all businesses in Paris were shaken by the crash of the Union générale." *Paris, La Ville* (Paris, 1977).

32. As Jeanne Gaillard notes, the history of the department store is also a history of "lost illusions and resounding setbacks." *Paris, La Ville*, pp. 544–547.

33. *La Corbeille* (fashion magazine), vol. 1 (1 January 1854).

34. Auguste Dusautoy, *Rapport du Jury international de l'Exposition de 1867, 35^e classe*, p. 49.

35. Preparatory dossier.

36. *La Joie du foyer* 11 (1 April 1867).

37. The ready-made firms in Paris grew in the following way:

Year	Number	Volume (in francs)
1846	190	30 million
1849	180	25 million
1855	180	42 million; and 2 million for military clothing
1860	322	50 million; and 6 million for military clothing
1866	420	100 million; and 9 million for military clothing

Dusautoy, *Rapport du Jury*, p. 28.

38. For the technical particulars, see G. Bardin, "Machines servant à la confection des vêtements," *Études sur l'Exposition de 1867*, 8th ser. (Paris, 1869), pp. 37–100.

39. In the 1860s a Singer sewing machine cost between 300 and 1,000 francs, depending on its features. On its social history—not well known—see Michelle Perrot's "Machine à coudre et travail à domicile," *Le Mouvement social* 105 (October–December 1978): 161–164.

40. Dusautoy, *Rapport du Jury*, pp. 15–16. Henri Despaigne described another factory of the period:

"M. Dusautoy was kind enough to take me recently on a visit to one of the immense workshops producing military clothing that he has established in the Rochechouart quarter. I realized what mechanical processes and the sewing machine can do in cutting and assembling clothes. A man needs only to direct the automatic movement of the machines; the task is precisely and solidly accomplished with extreme rapidity and economy. And far from depriving the worker of his work or diminishing his wages, machines have increased both. The factory of this eminent industrialist provides jobs for an entire population." *Le Code de la mode* (Paris, 1866), p. 50.

41. *Le Coupeur* [a tailors' journal], vol. 5, no. 2 (15 February 1853).

42. *Histoire chronologique du vêtement*, pp. 68–69.

Speaking of Gavarni, Edmond and Jules de Goncourt mention in their journal the cheapness and convenience of ready-to-wear clothes:

"Friday, 28 January 1859. . . . Walking by a ready-to-wear on the rue Montesquieu: 'Look, I'm going to buy a pair of pants.' He goes in: 'A warm pair of pants in a dark color.' They take his measurements: 'I don't mean to say anything, but really! It does suit you.' 'Do you think so? How much?' 'Twenty-six francs.' He pays and carries away his pants under his arm." *Journal, Mémoires de la vie littéraire*, vol. 3 (Monaco, 1957), pp. 99–100.

Of course such speed in buying clothes was derided, as though it lacked caution and solemnity: "Let us leave roses to the rosebush, theatrical farces to M. de Girardin, the literary guillotine to M. Gagne, and American-style advertising to dentists and ready-to-wear merchants, who for 33 francs will provide a fiancé with:

black cashmere trousers;
a coat;
a vest;
boots;
a hat;
and two witnesses—for the civil ceremony.

Le Club 2, no. 16 (8 January 1865).

43. Pp. 11–12.

44. *Report to Internal Jury*, p. 14.

45. On this subject see Jeanne Gaillard, *Paris, La Ville*, pp. 537–539.

46. *Statistiques de l'industrie à Paris* (1864), p. 274.

47. *Le Costume à la cour et à la ville*, pp. 205–206.

48. "One of the trades killed by progress was that of the rags peddler. His cry—'Any old clothes?'—so familiar to our ears, is almost never heard anymore," observed Georges d'Avenel in 1894. "Les Grands magasins," p. 342.

49. "It is known that the contagious miasmas of illnesses particularly breed in woolen cloth. The effects of people who died from phthisis, pneumonia, and consumption are sold instead of being burned. The fripperer buys them for resale, and the infected garment is placed on the body of a poor worker who knows nothing about science and catches the illness from the fabric. Hidden diseases are spread among the masses by this imprudent exchange of clothes, and the working class

does not know whence the illness came. Louis Sébastien Mercier, *Tableau de Paris*, vol. 9, pp. 175–176.

50. *Traité d'hygiène publique et privée*, 4th ed., vol. 2 (Paris, 1862), pp. 784–785.

51. *Traité d'hygiène publique et privée*, p. 785.

52. Adolphe Joanne, *Paris illustré en 1870. Guide de l'étranger et du parisien*, 3d ed. (Paris, 1870), p. 1017.

53. Marcel Charlot, "Fripier," *La Grande Encyclopédie*, vol. 18 (Paris, 1886–1902).

54. The stalls were, moreover, deserted in a dramatic fashion. From 188 vacant stalls in 1866, the figure grew to 626 in 1876. Soon reduced to a third of its area, the market lived on until 1905, when its pavilions were torn down except for two, located where the Rotonde and the first *carreau* used to be. It is under this roof, which creates one vast hangar, that the present Temple market is held, though secondhand clothing was banished from it shortly after World War II. For figures and a detailed analysis of the beginning of this decline, see *Rapport du Conseil municipal de Paris, présenteé par M. Georges Villain, au nom de la 2ᵉ Commission, sur diverse pétitions rélatives au marchée du Temple* (Paris, 1892).

55. In today's Paris, Third World immigrants seem to have replaced the nineteenth-century working class as clientele for secondhand clothing. See Bernard Feuillet and Anne-Marie Vasseur, *Le Marché d'occasion de l'électro-ménager et du vêtement* (mimeographed publication, Paris, 1979).

56. Marcel Charlot, "Fripier," p. 181.

57. After 1850 the overproduction crises required that more money be spent on internal consumption and less on investment. Levels of production and profits were sustained, therefore, by the rise (which varied greatly) of relative and real wages. See Jacques Rougerie, "Remarque sur l'histoire des salaires à Paris," *Mouvement social* 63 (April–June 1968), pp. 71–108.

58. This was not true for leather shoes. See Georges Duveau, *La Vie ouvrière en France sous le Second Empire* (Paris, 1946), p. 363.

59. The 1855 Universal Exposition in Paris received 5,163,000 visitors, and the 1867 fair 15,000,000—enormous figures for the period. See Jacques Lacour-Gayet, *Historie du commerce*, vol. 2 (Paris, 1952), p. 132.

60. In 1855, for example, La Belle Jardinière offered "all kinds of clothing within the reach of people of modest means under these three headings: work clothes, daily wear, Sunday clothes, from pea jackets at 4.75 francs, *cuir-laine* trousers at 5 francs, trousers at 20 francs, all the way to frock coats at 60 francs." *Journal des tailleurs* 26, no. 618 (16 November 1855).

61. "It was open season on old houses, small towns, and thatched cottages. Mahogany, which was once favored, was shamefully relegated to the attic in disgrace. And anything old found there was triumphantly retrieved from the dust.

When old furniture ran out and the usual lodes were exhausted, 'old' furniture was manufactured everywhere: imitation-old.

The cabinetmakers of the faubourg Saint-Antoine eagerly carved Henri II and Louis XIII chests. The chair-joiners began turning twisted legs for medieval tables. Artisans from the Marais outdid Boulle, Gouttière, and Riesener.

Clocks, copper plates, Venetian mirrors, flagons, candelabras, swords, armoires, antique fabrics, and chandeliers poured out of the workshops.

Once fabricated, the objects were endowed with a patina and antique coloration. Small and delicate gimlets imitated worm borings, acids cleverly altered bronzes and blunted the sharp edges of the new." Bertall, *La Comédie de notre temps*, vol. 1 (Paris, 1874), p. 494.

The contemporary proliferation of "second homes" inescapably "rustic" has brought a repetition, on a greater scale, of the rarefication and valorization of antiques and consequently the industrial production of "old-new."

62. Moreover, social critics quickly attacked women who trangressed standards of propriety in dress that guaranteed semantic clarity. A working-class woman who "scorns the title of wife and mother," wrote Stanilas Martin, "requires eccentric, gaudy outfits above her station; she wants artificial flowers, marabous, lace, and *exaggeratedly wide crinolines*. In factories that employ only women one can see this passion for dress carried to the extreme" (emphasis added). *La Joie du foyer* 5 (1 January 1866).

63. The Peugeot works at Valentigney (in the Doubs department) specialized in the manufacture of turnspits, clock springs, and rolled-out corset stays. Set back by the economic crisis engendered by the 1848 revolution, it turned after 1855 to the production of "cages" of steel strips. So many orders poured in that Peugeot built a new factory that began full production by 1858. See, especially, René Sédillot, *Peugeot—De la crinoline à la 404* (Paris, 1960).

64. Statistic from "Crinoline," *La Grande Encyclopédie*, vol. 13.

65. "It has required the combined efforts of science and art to force rebellious and ungrateful cotton fabrics to undergo every day so many brilliant transformations and to spread them everywhere within the reach of the poor. Every woman used to wear a blue or black dress that she kept for ten years without washing, for fear it might tear to pieces." Jules Michelet, *The People*, trans. and with an intro. by John P. McKay (Chicago, 1973), p. 44.

66. "Tailleur," *Grand Dictionnaire universel du XIXᵉ siècle*. The Larousse encyclopedia overgeneralizes in contending that workers wore smocks even on Sunday. An 1842 description indicates otherwise: "The worker who gets on well with his wife and has no bad acquaintances takes his wife and his children on Sunday excursions. . . . The family dresses up as well as its means permit; a madras fichu and a new apron may be all that the wife can add to her weekday dress; the husband wears a white shirt and tie; and his children have socks and shoes, which they do not wear every day." Paul de Kock, "Le Dimanche à Paris," *La Grande Ville. Nouveau tableau de Paris* (Paris, 1842), p. 223.

67. See my article "Aspects socio-culturels des debuts de la confection parisienne au XIXᵉ siècle," *Revue de l'Institut de sociologie* 2 (1977): 185–202.

68. Georges Duveau, *La Vie ouvrière*, pp. 366–367.

69. Kerckhoff, *Le Costume à la cour et à la ville*, pp. 210–211.

70. Lemann, *De l'industre des vêtements*, pp. 34–35.

71. Michelet, *The People*, p. 45. The following expression of the belief that "the beautiful," namely the "clean," "proper," "respectable," "tasteful," and "discreet" as defined by the bourgeois, could improve morals illustrates the nineteenth century's ideology of appearances:

"One can safely say that this willful disorder pushed to an extreme and this cynically displayed filth augur ill.

Those who wantonly choose ugliness display their lack of self-respect; they try to shock by not caring for their person; they insult public opinion, which they know is based on appearance; they are at least guilty of self-contempt, if not of contempt for others. . . .

Everything is connected. Aesthetic education, which teaches us to hate ugliness in any form, is indirectly moral education. Are not self-respect and love of home derived from beautifying oneself and one's home? Does not vice cause physical ugliness as much as moral ugliness? Few artists appear in criminal statistics because beauty is one and indivisible whether in thought or deed.

In calling for a more aesthetic education, we do not advocate the Florentine enervation that produces a population of artists absorbed in pointless pursuits but a people sensitive to beauty that enables the individual, such enoblement being, after all, the purpose of all progress." Gabriel Prévost, *Le Nu, le vêtement, la parure*, pp. 21–23.

72. *La Mode des enfants* (A women's magazine that gave advice on children's clothing), vol. 1, no. 2 (1 May 1853).

73. Brittany, possessing a long tradition of clans with distinctive costumes, seems, on the other hand, to have derived the complexity and originality of its regional garb from a very distant past. See René-Yves Creston, *Le Costume breton* (Paris, 1974).

74. The country tailor who went from village to village and farm to farm, stayed with families, became part of their life, and sat around the fire with them. His role consisted as much in enriching sociability by transmitting news as in making clothes:

"Newsmonger, living legend of the canton, he had to tell stories remarkably well and to answer tactfully indiscreet questions without revealing the family secrets he ordinarily learned. When necessary he had to gossip about neighbors without being branded a slanderer. He had to know the local customs and habits and to show manners suitable for one who had seen the world and spent several days a year in the bosom of the province's most exalted families.

He watched the boys grow, cut bodices for the girls, made clothing for baptisms, weddings, and mourning. Like the church, he participated in all of life's important events. No solemn occasion affecting the individual, the family, or the community could do without him. . . .

Wandering from home to home and learning everything about the family's wealth, origins, and members, he inevitably became a natural marriage-broker. Before M. Foy invented the matrimonial profession, this upright and shrewd artisan, the country tailor, practiced throughout France and Navarre. How eagerly he was received by boys and girls alike, how closely fathers and mothers watched the secret conversations they had with him! As he fitted the bodice that would sparkle at Easter, he knew that before Lent he would return to make a wedding dress." Émile Kerckhoff, *Le Costume*, pp. 201–202.

75. In 1850 there were 3,010 kilometers of tracks; in 1860 there were 9,439; and in 1870, 17,733. *Annuaire statistique de la France* (Paris, 1910).

76. *Les Lois de l'imitation* (Paris, 1890), pp. 245–246.

77. On the character of the traveling salesman and his cultural role during the July Monarchy, consult Balzac's masterful study. "No one in France," he wrote,

"doubts the incredible power incessantly deployed by the Travelers, these intrepid opponents of negation who in the remotest villages represent the genius of civilization and Parisian inventions, battling provincial good sense, ignorance, and routine. How can one forget the admirable maneuvers that mold the intelligence of populations by entertaining the most refractory masses with words and that resemble the indefatigable polishers whose files burnish the hardest porphyry?" *L'Illustre Gaudissart* (1833; reprint, Paris, 1971), pp. 27–28.

See also Raoul Perrin's monograph "Le commis-voyageur," *Les Français peints par eux-mêmes*, vol. 1 (Paris, 1841), pp. 549–558.

As early as 1845, Fernand Wagnien observed that "scheming and harassing, the peddlers and traveling salesmen who flood the countryside with their products will soon destroy its originality. In their own way they assist the process of centralization so that in twenty years or less all of France will dress the same." Cited by Guy Thuillier, "Le couleurs," *Pour une histoire du quotidien au XIXe siècle en Nivernais* (Paris, 1977), p. 299.

The hair merchant also spread urban elegance. "He would arrive in the village in a cabriolet like the dentist . . . and bartered scarves, bonnets, shawls, ribbons, and plated earrings in exchange for hair." But "contemporary peasant girls . . . prefer good money. Hair 'on the hoof,' (or rather on the head!) sells for around ten francs. The market operates on the spot. The girl climbs into the carriage, and in five minutes she is sheared, paid and gone, her head wrapped up because the lads would poke fun at her." Louis Lemercier de Neuville, *Physiologie du coiffeur* (Paris, 1862), p. 123.

78. "Formerly" (a word that denotes different periods depending on the social strata involved), notes Werner Sombart, "sturdy merchandise was needed, useful goods had to be durable and 'solid.' Clothing was made of heavy, durable materials: wool, linen, felt, satin, and fur. . . .

Shoes were made of horsehide or cowhide, with high, turned up uppers.

Body, table, and bed linens were of heavy cloth or heavy damask so that they could last for centuries. Today our armoires still contain tablecloths and napkins that date from the eighteenth century. And all gigantic: chemises fell to the ankles, napkins were as large as tablecloths, and handkerchiefs had the dimensions of a fichu.

In keeping with the durability of clothing, the used-clothing trade was one of the characteristic phenomena of these periods.

Today? . . .

Clothes are made of light fabrics that wear out quickly and cannot be repaired. The transformation of women's dress dates back to the nineteenth century with the appearance of mousseline, which became 'lighter' and 'lighter.' Dresses, underwear, and stockings are made of cotton, batiste, light silk. Ceremonial dresses are in lace. The same is true of men's clothing: 'cheviot,' a light wool and cotton blend, has eliminated all heavy woolen fabrics. Shoes are made of calf or goatskin, cloth or silk." *L'Apogée du capitalisme*, vol. 2, trans. S. Jankélévitch (Paris, 1932), pp. 116–118.

Thus, during the nineteenth century, the peasant world gradually assented to the ephemeralization of goods transformed into merchandise, a process that Frédéric Soulié considered the hallmark of his century:

"Today's fancy goods merchant who provides antique lace, resuscitates heavy fabrics and dresses women in flimsy rags that wear out in two days, embodies our period, an age that turns out shoddy goods, begs from the past ideas ill-suited to the present, and creates only rags in literature, painting, and government. Nothing is stable, be it the form of sovereign power or the shape of a woman's bonnet; nothing is made to last, be it the throne or an embroidered tulle fichu. Damask and epic poems are contemporaries; penny dreadfuls and six-franc dresses are born on the same day." "Les marchands de nouveautés," *Nouveau Tableau de Paris au XIXe siècle*, vol. 2 (Paris, 1843), p. 151.

79. *"Fashion and Modernity*. Wherever," wrote Nietzsche, "ignorance, uncleanliness and superstition are still rife, where communication is backward, agriculture poor, and the priesthood powerful, national costumes are still worn. Fashion, on the other hand, rules where the opposite conditions prevail. Fashion is accordingly to be found next to the virtues in modern Europe." *Complete Works*, vol. 7: *The Wanderer and His Shadow*, trans. Paul V. Cohn (New York, 1964), p. 303.

80. *L'Art de relever sa robe* (Paris, 1862), p. 70.

81. *Manuel de l'homme et de la femme comme il faut*, 5th ed. (Paris, 1862), p. 138.

82. Arnold Gennep, *Manuel du folklore français contemporain*, part 1, vol. 2 (Paris, 1949), pp. 390–392.

83. Bertall, *La Comédie de notre temps*, vol.1, p. 412. Bourgeois dress enjoyed such prestige because it signified a certain status in the rural world. Traditionalist movements and Catholic Leagues considered it a factor contributing to emigration. To dissuade peasants from leaving the land, Adolphe Leroy described the economic constraints imposed by bourgeois clothes and flayed the illusions it fostered:

"Their position [office workers] forces them to dress up. They must wear 'presentable dress.' They must also on piddling salaries feed and support wife and children, pay for room and board. And God knows what it costs to live in the city. Never mind your stomach's grumbling, you must have a good-looking suit for every day and a splendid one for Sundays. For so-and-so's clerks and employees will not be outdone by the elegance of the rich, lively, and brilliant world.

We see these fugitives from the countryside wearing fine clothes that are like peacock feathers stuck on bodies consumed by poverty! If you did not know who they are and what privation and misery they suffer at home, you might keep calling them 'sir,' but this title that flatters their vanity won't put food on their table." *La Vie des champs comparée à la vie des villes ou la désertion de nos campagnes* (Paris, 1864), pp. 48–49.

84. See, for example, Alain Corbin, *Archaïsme et Modernité en Limousin au XIXe siècle, 1845–1880*, vol. 1 (Paris, 1975), pp. 78–81; Maurice Aghulon, "La société paysanne et la vie à la campagne," *Histoire de la France rurale* (Paris, 1976), pp. 323–325.

85. The numerous travelers who crisscrossed Europe by rail before the First World War confirmed this observation. For example, Dr. Ricord wrote: "As I set foot [in Naples] I eagerly searched for the classic and picturesque costumes that please us so much in the charming paintings of Léopold Robert and of my lamented friend Papéty: nothing remains. The railroads not only carry Paris fashions throughout the world but also level the population. Neapolitan working-class women look just like those in the faubourg Saint-Antoine. I hoped for better luck

with the *lazzaroni* but found Seine bargemen from the Bercy dock. I'll make up for this, however. The next time they perform *La Muette de Portici* at the opera, I shall go!" *De Paris à Meaux en passant par Venise, Vienne, Pesth, La Roumanie, Constantinople, Athènes* (Paris, 1873), p. 23.

86. *Le Journal des tailleurs* 26, no. 613 (1 September 1855).

87. Lemann, *De l'industre des vêtements*, pp. 26–27.

88. Cited by Jacques Mousseau, *L'Amour à refaire* (Paris, 1969), p. 99.

CHAPTER VI

1. "The object of art—like every other product—creates," wrote Marx, "a public which is sensitive to art and enjoys beauty. Production thus not only creates an object for the subject, but also a subject for the object. Thus production produces consumption (1) by creating the material for it; (2) by determining the manner of consumption; and (3) by creating the products initially posited by it as objects, in the form of a need felt by the consumer. It thus produces the object of consumption, the manner of consumption and the motive of consumption. Consumption likewise produces the producer's *inclination* by beckoning to him as an aim-determined need." *Gründrisse: Introduction to the Critique of Political Economy*, trans. Martin Nicolaus (New York, 1973), p. 92.

2. *Le Système des objets*, p. 183.

3. *Les Moeurs de notre temps* (Paris, 1860), p. 82.

4. *Manuel de l'homme et de la femme comme-il-faut*, pp. 109–110, 133–134.

5. "Distinction: that which in dress has the characteristics of elegance, nobility and good manners. . . . *This meaning seems to be recent, for it is not to be found in earlier authors.*" The *Littré* Dictionary. "Distinction: (widely used in the nineteenth century): elegance and reserve in dress and manners." The *Robert* Dictionary (emphasis added).

6. *Theory of the Leisure Class*, p. 186.

7. *The Wanderer*, p. 304.

8. See Adeline Daumard, *Les Fortunes françaises au XIXᵉ siècle* (Paris, 1973).

9. Jean-Paul Aron, *Le Mangeur du XIXᵉ siècle* (Paris, 1973).

10. "The villa's originality obscured its ancestors [Italian villas and eighteenth-century French and English country houses] and left it with only one progenitor, that is, the nineteenth-century bourgeoisie for whom it was the ideal dwelling. Marked by a taste for representing the signs of opulence, shaped by a desire for comfort and a certain functionalism, and placed at the center of the town/country debate, the villa, as César Daly insisted in 1864, manifests the genius and the character of modern civilization." Patrick Favardin, "La villa ou l'avénement d'un nouveau mode d'habitation," *Monuments historiques* 102 (April 1979): 57.

11. For a discussion of these problems, see, of course, Max Weber, *Wirtschaft und Gesellschaft*.

12. The symbolic and economic profitability of the effect of "essence" can also be seen in the labels, signatures, and trade names that increased the value of commercial products like perfumes, designer fashions, etc.

13. The hybrid character of this kind of imitation became apparent, for example, when the bourgeoisie tried to re-create chateau living or its degraded forms. They succeeded, in fact, only in mimicking a few of its elements, without wanting or being able really to take over its primary implication: the total condemnation of the moral and economic ideology of thrift.

"Chateau life," wrote Arnould Frémy in 1860, "is very much a fragment of the old society that we are trying to revive, after having razed all of the old chateaus, puerile and illogical generation that we are!

The chateau craze has engendered rustic vainglory, which has spread even among the most petty of the petty-bourgeois and has contributed more than a little to the general breakdown of social relations, to sowing isolation and boredom in all ranks of the aristocracy. . . .

This taste for country living, which nowadays begins with the gothic castle of the moneybags and ends with the chalet of varnished pine of the small merchant in retirement is, above all, when it isn't hiding parsimony or stinginess, a matter of the parvenu's vanity and ostentation. He loves the appearance of living off one's land to ape the aristocracy. Since one can no longer say "my peasants," or "my vassals," one loves to be able to say "my warden," "my farmer," and "my gardener."

"At the same time," Frémy continues, "one can see people who live in grand chateaus with magnificent grounds and sell their fruit, vegetables, and poultry themselves."

As for Madame: "Any time she can look like the lady of the manor, the heroine of charitable deeds, the great lady, she gloats and really believes in the role she plays!

And then, through all of this display, one can discern remarkable calculations on the cost of a pot-au-feu, dissertations on the cost of poultry, butter, and game, suddenly broached amidst brilliantly gilded panels!" *Les Moeurs de notre temps*, pp. 64–66, 70. On this question see also the subtle analysis of Guy Chaussinand-Nogaret, "La Noblesse, Ministère de l'idéal," *Autrement* 89 (April 1987): 88–95.

14. *Le Messager des modes et de l'industrie* 4, no. 3 (1855).

15. Émile Kerckhoff, *Le Costume à la cour et à la ville*, p. iii.

16. The trend toward imitation goods increasingly resembling authentic made vestimentary discrimination in women's wear, as in men's wear, as much cultural as economic. For example, as early as 1883, Gabriel Prevost wrote:

"There was a time when only the Queens of France could wear woven stockings. Fabric has become incredibly cheap so that the most luxurious finery is imitated so well as to fool the most acute observer. This trend will only increase.

Some people deplore this in the name of art. They are wrong: the more we advance, the more people can adorn themselves inexpensively. And the more they need art to adorn themselves, the less people will be satisfied to resemble the ass bearing relics and wrapping themselves in randomly selected costly objects." *Le Nu, le vêtement, la parure*, pp. 392–393.

17. *Fashion-Théorie* 29, no. 201 (May 1857).

18. Ibid.

19. "De la mode et du bon goût," *Le Messager des modes et de l'industrie* 1, no. 2 (1853).

CHAPTER VII

1. Comtesse de Bassanville, *La Science du monde: politesse, usages, bien-être* (Paris, 1859), p. 5.

2. Otto Lorenz, *Catalogue général de la librairie française depuis 1840*, vol. 8 (Paris, 1924), pp. 465–466 (2d vol. of the table of contents, 1840–75).

3. Pierre Boitard, *Manuel-physiologie de la bonne compagnie, du bon ton et de la politesse* (Paris, 1862), pp. 5–6.

4. Edmond Goblot, *La Barrière et le niveau* (1925; new ed. Paris, 1967).

5. Eliane de Sérieul, *Le Diable rose* 3, no. 4 (20 July 1862). This analogy between clothing and language, both of which class an individual socially, remains relatively unexploited by sociologists or anthropologists. However, Charles Bally, a disciple of Saussure, did discuss it as early as 1909:

"Consider fashion: it too classes and makes distinctions; it too gives rise to agreeable or disagreeable feelings that result from the observance or the nonobservance of tacit and unconscious social conventions. And just as the cut of a suit can be a social mark—an imperfect one, I willingly admit, but still a social mark—for the person who wears the suit, so too a way of speaking places an individual who talks in a certain way and assigns him to a certain class. And just as a worker's smock is shocking when it is worn amongst tailcoats and décolleté dresses, so too a slang word appears out of place in a conversation among 'proper' people." *Traité de stylistique française* vol. 1 (1909; reprint, Geneva, 1970), pp. 11–12.

6. Madame la Comtesse de B. . . . , *Du savoir-vivre en France au xixe siècle, ou Instruction d'un père à ses enfants* (Paris, 1838), p. 11.

7. The following remarks appear in a treatise on civility: "It is in bad taste for a man to display on his person or in his appearance things that belong to a profession other than his own; to wear moustaches like military men when he is not a soldier makes him look ridiculous; to grow the kind of beard worn by men of letters and artists is a foolish mistake for a man who is not a member of these two professions, and so on." Bassanville, *Science du Monde*, p. 14.

8. Balzac, *Traité de la vie élégante*, pp. 41–42. Excluded from elegant life because of their work, men who lived active lives did not for all that share the same opprobrium. Balzac classified the levels of inelegance hierarchically as functions of their socioprofessional status and on the basis of the degree of physical labor involved. See pp. 37–39.

9. Comtesse Dash, *Les Femmes à Paris et en province*, p. 15.

10. Ibid., p. 66.

11. Thus, depending on whether it produces or consumes, the body is shaped differently: "Long necks, fine shoulders and small, white, tapered hands are considered to be pretty and elegant because these are the characteristics associated with noble origins, inactivity, and great wealth. . . . A man of toil, one who must constantly call on his muscular strength, will have a short neck and a head sunken between his shoulders." Eugène Chapus, *Manuel de l'homme et de la femme comme-il-faut*, pp. 63–64.

12. The activity of fashion did not modify the foundation of these norms: "Its ascendancy ends where that of etiquette begins. Above all, etiquette sets up taste,

good manners, and distinction as limits to fashion's caprices." Despaigne, *Le Code de la mode*, p. 85.

13. Ibid., p. 58.

14. Alfred de Meilheurat, *Manuel de savoir-vivre ou l'Art de se conduire selon les convenances et les usages du monde dans toutes les circonstances de la vie et dans les diverses régions de la société* (Paris, 1852), p. 22.

15. Comtesse Dash, *Comment on fait son chemin dans le monde* (Paris, 1868), p. 63.

16. Mme Celnart, *Nouveau manuel complet de la bonne compagnie ou guide de la politesse et de la biénseance destiné à tous les âges et à tous les conditions* (Paris, 1863), p. 22.

17. Comtesse Dash, *Comment on fait son chemin*, p. 5.

18. Celnart, *Nouveau Manuel*, p. 22.

19. This is why "one should never call on anyone before noon, above all if you are paying a visit to a lady; a woman's morning must always be respected." Meilheurat, *Manuel de savoir-vivre*, p. 25

20. Comtesse Dash, *Comment on fait son chemin*, p. 65.

21. Celnart, *Nouveau Manuel*, p. 23.

22. Chapus, *Manuel de l'homme et de la femme*, p. 15.

23. Bassanville, *Science du monde*, p. 16

24. *Code du cérémonial* (Paris, 1868), p. 12.

25. Comtesse Drohojowska, *De la politesse et du bon ton ou devoirs d'une femme chrétienne dans le monde*, 2d ed. (Paris, 1860), p. 110.

26. Bassanville, *La Science du monde*, p. 17.

27. Drohojowska, *De la politesse*, pp. 109–110.

28. Dash, *Les Femmes à Paris*, p. 64

29. *La Corbeille*, 14th year, no. 7 (1 July 1853), p. 101.

30. Drohojowska, *De la politesse*, p. 87.

31. Bassanville, *La science du monde*, p. 11.

32. Celnart, *Nouveau manuel*, pp. 56–57.

33. *Ferragus, Oeuvres complètes*, vol. 11 (1833; reprint, Paris, 1843), p. 11. That one sentence states the entire argument of his *Théorie de la démarche*.

34. "If you live in a provincial city in which people don't use carriages," noted Mme Celnart in 1863, "you must be taken about in a sedan chair. Who cannot feel how laughable it is to see a woman dressed in satin, blond lace, or velvet, trudging in dust or through the mud?" *Nouveau manuel*, p. 28. In fact, the *Grande Encyclopédie* confirmed that "in certain provincial towns [sedan chairs] are still used." See the article "Chaise," written in 1888.

35. Bassanville, *La science du monde*, p. 7.

36. "Whatever degree of luxury you may be obliged to adopt, you should never depart from the greatest simplicity when you receive guests. Would it not be an unpardonable lack of tact if you, the mistress of the house, outshone the other women because of your finery? You should therefore dress so that your toilette will always be the most simple." Drohojowska (writing under the pseudonym of the Chevalier A. de Doncourt), *La Verité aux femmes sur l'excentricité des modes et de la toilette* (Paris, 1858), pp. 35–36.

37. Despaigne, *Code de la mode*, p. 66.

38. Ibid., p. 207.

39. Vicomtesse de Renneville, "Les bals," *La Sylphide* (20 January 1854), p. 26.

40. "A very pretty toilette night before last; a waist of blue silk, close-fitting and showing her figure; rising a little in front upon the bosom; above, a soft nest of lace. Very modest and still very young, her dress is cut quite high in the neck; a simple rose in her hair. But this delicate figure so closely fitted, this sweet virginal white hiding and indicating the bosom, is a skillful invention; the invention is not hers, she follows the fashion; her mother dresses her; she is still too young to suspect the exact effect of her toilette; her ideas are too vague and too new; it is I who at this moment am explaining this effect as a sculptor, as a man of the world; she would blush to hear my explanation—and yet, in the half daylight of her thoughts, she has some suspicion of it; she knows that it is becoming to her, that another style of waist would not be so becoming, that she pleases, and that the eye is attracted to her figure. She goes no further; she half sees, in a diaphanous and golden mist, a whole aurora of things. A very rose asleep while the vapors of morning are vanishing, and masses of luminous whiteness are spreading over the pearly sky, she listens, motionless and as in a dream, to the beatings of distant wings, the indistinct rustle of a whole world of insects which will soon come buzzing and murmuring around her heart." Hippolyte Taine, *Notes on Paris, The Life and Opinions of M. Frédéric-Thomas Graindorge*, trans. John Austin Stevens (1867; reprint, New York, 1875), pp. 159–160.

41. Michel Lévy, *Traité d'hygiène publique et privée*, vol. 2, p. 254.

42. "It is almost always when they leave ballrooms where they have spent most of the night that they contract, because of the effects of extremes of temperature, the diseases that overwhelm their bitter lives. Upon leaving these brilliant gatherings, in which fashion, like Pandora's box, exhales calamities of all kinds, how many young women have contracted either those nervous afflictions that are, as Boerhaave says, the scourge of humanity and of medicine, or leukorrhea, which dries up the wellsprings of fecundity, or skin diseases, which hide the sweetest and most pleasant traits beneath hideous eruptions. Fortunate is the young woman who does not carry deadly germs home with her, and in the springtime of her life does not catch the principle of that terrible sickness that decomposes the body little by little, after establishing its seat in the extremely delicate organ of respiration." J. A. Goullin, *La Mode sous le point de vue hygiénique*, pp. 34–35.

43. Comtesse de Bassanville, *La Science du monde*, p. 6.

44. Ibid.

45. Drohojowska, *De la politesse*, pp. 80–81.

46. Bassanville, *La Science du monde*, p. 8.

47. Ibid., p. 13.

48. "During the first months of mourning all clothing should be woolen; ornaments and cut must be very simple, sleeves closely fitted, with cuffs and collars in smooth braided crepe or, better, in quilled embossed tulle. For the head, a cashmere hat or a crepe hood with a soft crepe veil somewhat longer than ordinary. A plain cashmere shawl or a mantelet similar to the dress. For the first days a scarf would be quite unsuitable. "Des usages," *Le Magasin des demoiselles* 9, no. 10 (25 July 1853).

49. Celnart, *Nouveau manuel*, p. 25.

50. Louis Verardi, *Manuel du bon ton et de la politesse française* (Paris, 1853), p. 101. Writing for a working-class public, the anonymous author of a *Catéchisme des grandes filles qui souhaitent se marier* (Paris, 1865), produced the following question-and-answer:

"Q. When a girl does not have a suitor, how should she behave so that someone notices her?

A. "Rich or poor . . . it is essential that she appear to be perfectly tidy and not at all flirtatious. She would be very ill-advised to want to shine in a way inappropriate to her station, for this would repulse rather than attract wooers." Pp. 2–3.

51. Bassanville, *La Science du monde*, p. 12.

52. Ibid., p. 11.

53. Celnart, *Nouveau manuel*, p. 26.

54. Although the Empress Eugénie was accused of having "imperiously imposed her turbulent, loud or, in a word, Spanish taste on France," in fact these brutal tonalities could be found throughout Europe during that period. Octave Uzanne, *Les Modes de Paris* (Paris, 1898), p. 168. And, as Taine noted, perhaps in an exacerbated way in England: "Beauty and adornment are abundant; but there is a want of taste. The colours are outrageously crude, and lines ungraceful. Crinolines too full, or the fullness badly draped, like geometrical cones or else dented; ribbons and scarves, green; gold lacing; bold, flower-patterned materials; a profusion of floating gauze; hair bunched, falling or curled. The whole display surmounted by tiny hats, much trimmed but hardly perceptible. The hats are over trimmed, the hair too shiny and clamped to the temples with too hard a line; the *mantelet* or *casaque* hangs shapeless to the hips, the skirt is monstrously overfull and the whole of this scaffolding is badly put, badly matched, striped, fussed, overdone, loud, excessively numerous colours, each swearing at the others.

In sunshine particularly, the day before yesterday at Hampton Court, among shop-keepers' wives, the spectacle was wildly ridiculous. There was a quantity of violet dresses, of a really feröcious [*sic*] violet, encircled at the waist by a gold belt. It would have made a painter weep. I said to one lady, 'Your clothes here are more "showy" than in France.' 'But our dresses come from Paris!'

I was careful not to reply, 'But it's you who choose them.'" *Notes on England*, pp. 19–20.

55. Vol. 7 (April, 1851).

56. Meilheurat, *Manuel de savoir-vivre*, p. 23.

57. "The same is true," the author goes on to say, "for the color of gemstones used for decoration: brunettes should choose turquoise, topaz and rubies; blondes will prefer amethysts, corals, pearls, emeralds and garnets. Settings of brilliants are suitable for any woman." (Paris, 1857), p. 267.

58. "The electrifying bath of M. J.-A. Pennes, 1, rue de la Fontaine-Saint-Georges, lightens and perfumes the skin (1 franc per dose)." *Le Favori des dames*, February 1854.

"This year at the seashore we saw the astonishing results of a freckle-removing lotion used on the faces of young children who—to the great despair of their young mothers—looked like true pickaninnies thanks to the ocean air and sun. A few applications of the lotion diluted with water removed the masks, and its continued use provided protection against the effects of sunlight." *Le Diable rose* 5 (1 November 1863): 1. These advertisements, which touted all kinds of "demelanization" techniques or tricks to camouflage freckles, abounded in women's magazines.

59. Fashion magazines encouraged other refinements in which even temperament had a role to play: "Thus women of an indolent, nonchalant nature, who are pleasantly lazy and whose life is nothing but a long dream, whose useless occupations enable them to spend an entire day in the same place and for whom moving is laborious if not fatiguing, these women could and, indeed, should dress in the liveliest and most varied colors: floral patterns on a floor strike us as charming only because they are immobile. . . .

For the dainty, nimble young woman who is as lively as a bird and whose life is one of constant bustle, only soft, muted, nearly plain colors are suitable. A cloud escaping into the infinite inspires in us a sweet reverie only because of its vaporous form, its indefinite and nearly uniform color." Eliane de Sérieul, *Le Diable rose* 3, no. 6 (20 September 1854).

60. Ibid.

61. Marc Constantin, *Almanach des belles manières ou l'Art du bon ton, de la politesse, etc.* (Paris, 1854), p. 24.

62. Ly'onell, *L'Art de relever sa robe*, p. 22.

63. See William A. Rossi, *The Sex Life of the Foot and Shoe* (London, 1977).

64. Ly'onell, *L'Art de relever sa robe*, pp. 33–34. Frenetically seeking out dazzling visions, our author did not hesitate to scour the countryside tracking down peasant women dressed in rustic crinolines:

"When it is muddy and they have to walk down a wet stairway, they hitch up their dress in the back. . . . This has the advantage of lifting up the skirt high enough, as one might expect, so that if the woman has a shapely leg, which is almost always the case during the first year of marriage when her body has reached its fullest development but has not yet been deformed by overwork in the fields, the connoisseur can enjoy a sight that is all the prettier since they almost never wear stockings. What's to be said when they bend down to gather grapes or pick up nuts? My word!" Ibid., pp. 71–72.

65. *Le Code de la mode*, p. 70.

66. Ernest Feydeau evoked all of its eroticism: "A young and pretty woman taking a siesta on her divan during the long, hot summer days should be able to amuse herself by playing with her mules. With her naked feet she throws them up into the air one after the other with a very lively kick, catches them on the fly with her toes, slips them on again—without using her hands—and then starts all over again. If a slipper falls to the floor, she is permitted to beg a kind friend, who is there just at the right moment, to pick it up. I was told of a beautiful dark-eyed creole who, from laziness or disdain for human beings, had trained her husband, a serious man, to play this little game." *L'Art de plaire, Études d'hygiène, de goût et de toilettes* (Paris, 1873), p. 48.

67. *De la politesse*, p. 59.

68. Ibid.

69. Despaigne, *Code de la mode*, p. 70.

70. An example: "Short blunt fingers are the unambiguous signs of low origins

and mediocre intelligence. Long and narrow fingertips indicate distinguished breeding and superior intelligence." *Physiologie du gant*, (Paris, 1843), p. 28.

71. François-Jérôme-Léonard de Mortemart-Boisse, *La Vie élégante à Paris*, pp. 45–46.

72. "This ballooning out keeps husbands at a distance—-perhaps this explains their coldness these days," wrote Raoul de Lamorillière. He also noted: "A mother has become an impregnable tower to her children who have to climb up her flounces as though they were ladders when they want to kiss her." *Crinolines et volants* (Bordeaux, 1855), p. 42.

73. The "cage" seems to have been inspired less by the panniers of the eighteenth century than by advances in ferrous technology. Thus the Crystal Palace of the 1851 Exposition in London is not unlike a monumental crinoline.

74. The cage itself also underwent several improvements. For example, the metallic armatures were made more flexible, and a drawstring was added so that it could be raised like a window blind.

75. Marie-Elisabeth Cavé, *La Femme aujourd'hui, la femme autrefois* (Paris, 1863), pp. 157–58.

76. Nestor Roqueplan, *Parisine*, p. 44.

77. Raoul de Lamorillière, *Crinolines et Volants*, p. 22.

78. *Défense de la Crinoline par un médecin de campagne* (Paris, 1867), pp. 60–62.

79. *De la mode* (Paris, 1858), pp. 24–25.

80. *De la politesse*, p. 111.

81. Ibid., p. 56.

82. Charles Coligny, cited in the *Grande Encyclopédie*, vol. 10, S. V. "Châle."

83. Actually, in addition to those from India, mouzaia shawls from Tunisia, with green and red or blue and white stripes, and burnose shawls from Algeria, which had goat-hair tassels, were also imported.

84. "The role of the shawl has been . . . very much reduced by the vogue of ready-made. It has become an article whose presence is required more in a trousseau than on the shoulders." Despaignes, *Code de la mode*, p. 40.

85. *L'Art dans la parure et dans le vêtement*, p. 239.

86. See Denis Diderot, *Regrets on Parting With my Old Dressing Gown*, in *Rameau's Nephew and Other Works*, trans. Jacques Barzun and Ralph H. Bowen (Indianapolis, 1964).

This is how Balzac describes his sumptuous termolama to Laure Surville:

> When I was sick I had a dressing gown that has definitively deposed the Carthusians' white robes. It is a dressing gown made of termolama. Now, I must tell you that for me this Persian or Circassian fabric was something fabulous, and that, ever since 1834, when I had the occasion to admire some samples of it in Geneva, I imagined that only queens could wear it. It is a fabric made entirely of silk, its weave displays all of the miraculous working characteristic of Indian cashmeres. It is like a shawl executed in silk, but it's even more brilliant. It lasts for years. It's like wearing the sun. It's warm and light. My *termolama* is black, sprinkled with pressed palmettes surrounded by flowers of an admirable delicacy with glints of gold. It's hand-made and resembles Venetian brocade, for brocade is made of silk, gold and silver thread. My illness has turned me into a child,

because I've had one of those delights you can have only when you're eighteen—because then you're really only twelve. I walk about in the glory of my palms like a sultan and I am writing to you in the aforementioned *termolama*.

(Letter of 20 October 1849), *Correspondances, 1819–1850*, vol. 2 (Paris, 1876), pp. 418–419.

87. *Hygiène vestimentaire*, p. 158.

88. Mortemart-Boisse, *La Vie élégante*, p. 34.

89. Kerckhoff, *Le Costume à la cour et à la ville*, p. 159.

90. Verardi, *Manuel du bon ton*, pp. 95–96.

91. Barbier, who mentions "riding coat" in his *Journal* in September 1725, gives this definition: "a garment of English origin that is now very common here for cold weather, rain and especially for horseback riding." vol. 1, p. 228.

92. As early as 1862, the *Echo des tailleurs* called attention to the English fashion of knickerbockers (a name taken from Washington Irving's *Knickerbocker Tales*): "No man of taste would dare be without knickerbockers in his wardrobe," he said. "This is especially appropriate for château life. Perhaps it will be worn elsewhere, but we don't yet know. The knickerbocker is the indispensible complement of a *gentleman's* wardrobe. A gentleman who prepares for a country excursion, or a visit to several manors, tells his servant—emphatically: *mind you do not forget my knicker-bocker.*" vol. 6, no. 50 (January 1862).

The case of the knickerbocker is an example of sartorial forms, originally used by aristocrats or the grand bourgeois, which were gradually popularized until they became after 1920 faddish among common people. (See the cartoon character "Tintin.")

93. Bassanville, *La Science du monde*, pp. 11–12

94. *Tableau de Paris*, p. 337.

95. During the day a man who wears a street suit is ill-dressed, unless he wears a paletot." Bassanville, *Science de la mode*, p. 11.

96. *Manuel de l'homme*, pp. 111–112

97. Mr. Lachenaud, "Du paletot," *L'Elégant* 18, no. 214 (1 July 1853).

98. On this subject, see Alfred Franklin, *La Vie privée d'autrefois: les magasins de nouveautés*, vol. 15, p. 263.

99. *Mémoires*, (1789; reprint, Paris, 1970), p. 478.

100. Constantin, *Almanach des belles manières*, p. 23.

101. Ibid.

102. Verardi, *Manuel du bon ton*, p. 96.

103. "Physiologie de la toilete," *La Silhouette* 2, no. 11 (June 1830).

104. The cravat does not seem to have been borrowed from the dress of German cavalrymen called Croats, a regiment that entered the French service of France around 1600, which has generally been credited with the spread of the cravat. See A. Verron's richly documented article "La cravate en dentelle," *Cahier Ciba* 3, no. 31 (September 1950): 1065–1068.

105. On the history of the cravat during the Revolution and at the beginning of the nineteenth century, see another article by A. Verron, "La cravate, emblème politique," *Cahier Ciba* 3, no. 31 (September 1950), pp. 1071–1076.

106. See, for example, the anonymous *Code de la cravate, traité complet des formes, de la mise, des couleurs de la cravate* (Paris, 1828); *Cravatiana, ou traité général des cravates considerées dans leur origine, leur influence politique, physique et morale, leurs formes, leurs couleurs et leurs espèces. Traduit de l'anglais* (Paris, 1823); and Baron Emile de l'Empesé, *L'Art de mettre sa cravate de toutes les manières connues et usitées, enseigné et demontré en seize leçons, précédé de l'histoire complète de la cravate* (Paris, 1827). Attributed to Balzac or his friend Marco Saint-Hilaire, this small duodecimo volume went through at least eleven editions.

And, during the Second Empire, Gr. de M., *Histoire philosophique, anecdotique et critique de la cravate et du col* (Paris, 1854).

107. For example, "tying the gordian knot, recommended to fledgling diplomats," required the kind of talent and patience that enables us to grasp the meaning of the assertion that "to seize a *comme il faut* man by his tie is as cruel an insult as slapping him in the face. Strictly speaking neither man could cleanse himself without bloodshed." Baron de l'Empesé, *L'Art de mettre sa cravate*, p. 11.

108. *Cravatiana*, p. 40.

109. "With ties you have neither aid nor stay: you are left on your own. . . . And to tell the truth, the necktie is the man; it is by his tie that a man reveals himself and makes himself known." Balzac, "Physiologie de la toilette."

110. "Around 1830," notes Roger Kempf, "the *Art de la toilette* listed seventy-two ways to knot a tie. It was up to the dandy to invent the seventy-third." *Dandies, Baudelaire et Cie*, (Paris, 1977), p. 179.

111. Baron de l'Empesé, *L'Art de mettre sa cravate*, pp. 9–10.

112. Ibid., publisher's note, p. viii.

113. Ibid., p. 142.

114. As the following advice on sartorial hygiene shows, the necktie was still a constricting object: "It is more wholesome to wear only ties of simple and light fabrics, without frames of cardboard, boar bristle, or whalebone, which imprison the neck like an iron collar. Refrain from tightening the tie too much, and remove it when your neck perspires. You should loosen the knot before singing, declaiming, etc., and remove it completely when you go to sleep." Debay, *Hygiène vestimentaire*, pp. 293–294

115. Kerckhoff, *Le costume à la cour*, p. 143.

116. Debay, *Hygiène vestimentaire*, pp. 144–145.

117. Muller, *La Boutique du marchand de nouveautés*, p. 10.

118. "One must always wear gloves to go out. This is one of the distinctive marks of a well-bred man." Meilheurat, *Manuel de savoir vivre*, p. 21. On the history of gloves and their use, see Alfred Franklin, *La Vie privée d'autrefois: les magasins de nouveautés*, vol. 16, pp. 1–14, 55–56, 111–112.

119. *La Comédie de notre temps*, vol. 1, p. 54.

120. Georges Guénot-Lecointe, *Physiologie du gant* (Paris, 1841), pp. 24–25.

121. Because of the provincial connotations of green shades, they were discredited after the July Monarchy. "At the present," wrote Guénot-Lecointe, "only good souls, obviously provincial from a mile away, have remained loyal to the color green." *Physiologie du gant*, p. 46. Thirty years later, however, Bertall repeated the warning: "Never wear green gloves." *La Comédie de notre temps*, vol. 1, p. 58.

122. Bassanville, *La Science du monde*, p. 9.
123. Chapus, *Manuel de l'homme*, p. 84.
124. Ibid., p. 83.
125. Muller, *La Boutique*, p. 10.
126. Debay, *Hygiène vestimentaire*, p. 155.
127. Ibid.

CHAPTER VIII

1. *The Old Regime and the French Revolution*, trans. Stuart Gilbert (New York, 1955), p. 81.

2. Important work on all these subjects has been undertaken. See Alain Corbin, *The Foul and the Fragrant: Odor and the French Social Imagination* (Cambridge, Mass., 1986); Georges Vigarello, *Concepts of Cleanliness: Changing Attitudes in France since the Middle Ages*, trans. Jean Birrell (Cambridge, 1988); and Julia Csergo, *Liberté, Egalité, Propreté: La morale de l'hygiène au XIXe siècle* (Paris, 1988).

3. On this subject see, for example, Guy Thuillier, "Pour une histoire de l'hygiène corporelle," *Revue d'histoire économique et sociale* 2 (1968): 232–253.

4. "It cannot be denied that since the Revolution the people of Paris have made great gains in cleanliness and consequently in health. Rancid pomade and dirty powder no longer hide handsome black or silver-blonde hair. The people change their underwear more often, frequent public baths more often, and prefer simple and comfortable clothes to the stiff clothes that twelve years ago transformed a 'citizen' who was quite well dressed the whole week long into an awkward 'monsieur' on Sundays because they hindered his movements." P. J. Marie de Saint-Ursin, *L'Ami des femmes ou Lettres d'un médecin concernant l'influence de l'habillement des femmes sur leurs moeurs et leur santé et la nécessité de l'usage habituel des bains en conservant leur costume actuel. Dédié a Mme Bonaparte* (Paris, 1804), p. 115.

5. Although there were only eight to ten public baths in Paris around 1780, from 1817 to 1831 inclusively thirty-seven of these establishments were founded. In 1832 Paris could in fact count seventy-eight establishments using 2,364 fixed bathtubs, not counting the portable tubs that were transported to private dwellings. See P. S. Girard, *Recherches sur les établissements de bains publics à Paris* (Paris, 1832), pp. 41–48, 51. Around 1900 the capital had more than five hundred public baths, but, as Georges Vacher de Lapouge wrote in 1896, "the majority of women died without having taken a single bath. The same would be true for men were it not for military bathing." *Les Sélections sociales* (Paris, 1896), p. 316.

6. Two accounts will suffice to show that in spite of the the Third Republic's hygiene policies an enormous resistance to cleanliness persisted, above all in the country and in religious institutions.

Henri Napias, who visited several provincial asylums and hospitals around 1880, described their sanitary conditions: "What made the situation even more disturbing was that baths were given only at the express prescription of the doctor in certified pathological cases and that the patients did not ask for baths because they generally brought to the institution a holy terror of water. In addition, in almost all of the hospitals and asylums the bathing facilities were very rudimentary; one small institution in the principal town of a canton had twenty-four beds in all but only one bathtub, in which the gardener stored his vegetable seeds, flower bulbs, and a few changes of work clothes to keep them dry." *L'Assistance publique dans le département de Sambre-et-Loire* [*sic*] (Paris, 1890), p. 10.

Twenty years later, the legal proceedings against the Bon Pasteur orphanage in Nancy revealed a virtually total deficiency in care of the body: "The inmates, who never took baths, did not even have cloths to wash their faces and hands; they had to use a chamber pot. They washed their feet every three months in the winter and every six weeks in summer! Nor was there ever any soap, either: soap would have been too expensive. Towels and underwear were changed as seldom as possible." And, questioned about this as a witness, Mlle Laurent declared: "They made us afraid in every possible way by telling us that it was a mortal sin to wash certain parts of the body."

This identification of cleanliness with indecency, which made it possible to avoid linen expenses, led to "repugnant practices" which were denounced by the prosecution: "Young girls, young women are in this institution. Therefore there are accidents of their sex. . . . Underwear is necessary during these accidents. Did they have underwear? No. Each was given one—I say: one—old skirt so worn out as to be completely unserviceable, a useless rag. Were these washed at least? No. Before the war, they were washed only once every six months; since the war they lavishly wash them every three months. And what was done with them in this condition? Where were they put? Everyone had to put 'her skirt' between her mattress and pallet, where it dried out!" Maître Eugène Prévost, *Le Procès du Bon Pasteur* (Paris, 1903), pp. 82–85.

7. "Even today in Rennes," Vacher de Lapouge wrote in 1896, "thirty bathtubs are adequate for an urban population of seventy thousand inhabitants, and two private houses had bathrooms." *Les Selections sociales*, p. 316. On the history of the bathroom and the water closet, see Lawrence Wright, *Clean and Decent: The Fascinating History of the Bathroom and the Water Closet* (London, 1960). The author compares French to English and American hygiene, which, in the nineteenth century, were no better.

8. *De la politesse*, p. 56. It seems that the menstrual cycle above all timed these baths: "At the time of the monthly tribute," wrote Dr. A. Debay, "increase personal hygiene, change underwear often in order to be completely free of odor, and take a general bath the morning after the last day." *Hygiène des mains et des pieds, de la poitrine et de la taille* (Paris, 1860), p. 114.

9. *La Mode sous le point de vue hygiénique, médical et historique*, pp. 81–82

10. The word "shampooing," imported from India by way of England, dates from 1877. Before then similar products (eau-de-vie, extract of quilliai bark, or a mixture of rum and egg yolks)—were used on rare occasions.

11. Drohojowska, *La Verité aux femmes*, p. 56.

12. Muller, *La Politesse française*, pp. 2–3.

13. *Délassements permis aux personnes pieuses appelées à vivre dans le monde* (Lyon, 1856), p. 220.

14. Ibid., p. 217

15. The modern definition of cleanliness—"the quality of that which is clean and free of dirt" or "quality of a person whose body and clothes are perfectly clean

and who is careful in the way he handles objects"—always strongly connotes, more-over, its classical definition: "Propriety in the way one behaves, dresses, furnishes one's home, sober and tasteful elegance." *Grand Larousse de la langue française* (Paris, 1971).

16. *La Science du monde*, p. 18.

17. *Medical Dissertation* (Paris, 1817).

18. *The Begum's Fortune* (New York, 1958), p. 125.

19. Dr. Cabanès noted that at the very beginning of the nineteenth century, in a lecture on physical cleanliness delivered at Charleville, M. Secheret was able to compile the following statistics: "In a working-class population taken as a whole, among one hundred individuals, two took baths in a tub; eighteen washed their feet when they changed socks; fifty-two washed only their feet twice a winter, their faces and necks every Saturday, their scalps never; twenty-four never washed at all." *Moeurs intimes du passé, la vie au bains*, vol. 2 (Paris, 1885), p. 372.

20. For the Nivernais, see Guy Thuiller's article "Pour une histoire de l'hygiène corporelle."

21. During the Third Republic the medical and educational establishments, aware that their mission was completely legitimate, spread increasingly imperative and systematic hygienic rules. These gradually drew the traditionally "dirty" classes into the dominant system of value-signs where they were continued to be held at a distance, but more subtly. On the other hand, these health rules, which were identi-fied with moral rules and perceived and internalized as such, functioned as supple-mentary social controls.

22. *Beyond Good and Evil: The Complete Works of Friedrich Nietzsche*, ed. Oscar Levy, trans. Helen Zimmern, vol. 12 (New York, 1964), p. 248.

23. Verardi, *Manuel du bon ton*, p. 94

24. Celnart, *Nouveau manuel*, p. 20.

25. "The eighteenth century favored the domestic arts. One can be convinced of this by reading the articles on home economics in the *Encyclopédie*: "Laundering," "Washing linen," and "Linen maid." How many laundresses are there in paintings and novels: Greuze's laundress—an untrustworthy strumpet, Diderot contends; Mme Dutour, Toinon, and Marianne in Marivaux, and Cunegonde in *Candide*, washing a Bulgarian captain's linen against her will. The runaway nun in Diderot's *La Réligieuse* also went to work for a laundress." Roger Kempf, *Diderot et le roman* (Paris, 1964), p. 165.

26. In this regard see Guy Thuillier, "Pour une histoire de la lessive," *Annales: Économies, Sociétés, Civilisations* 3 (1969): 377–390; and Yvonne Verdier, *Façons de dire, façons de faire* (Paris, 1979), pp. 108–149.

27. Valuable figures on the cost of living have been furnished by Gustave Beinaymé in his article "Le coût de la vie à Paris à diverse époques: le blan-chissage," *Journal de la Société de statistique de Paris* (January 1903): 20–29; and ibid. (February 1903): 40–56.

28. For urban laundry techniques, their concomitant fatigue, burns, rheuma-tism, and infectious diseases (tuberculosis, typhoid fever, etc.), and the laundry's very peculiar kind of sociability, see, of course, Zola's *Assomoir*.

For laundering procedures and chemical and mechanical innovations, see, for example, Alfred Bourgeois d'Orvanne, *Lavoirs et Bains publics gratuits et à prix réduits* (Paris, 1854); and Julia de Fontenelle, *Nouveau Manuel complet du blanchissage, nettoyage et dégraissage*, 2 vols. (Paris, 1855).

29. Mme Amet d'Abrantès, "De la mode et du bon goût," *Le Messager des modes et de l'industrie* 1, no. 2 (1853).

30. *Le Complexe de droite* (Paris, 1969), p. 23

31. Comtesse Dash, *Les Femmes à Paris et en province*, pp. 68–69.

32. *La Vie élégante à Paris*, pp. 38–39.

33. *Oeuvres complètes*, vol. 4: *Lettres parisiennes, années 1836–1840* (Paris, 1860), pp. 379–380.

34. *Les Petites Filles modèles* (Paris, 1858), pp. 63–65.

35. "In fact, when a vulgar rich woman travels she reveals that her dress is very affected. Unsure of herself when she buys or orders clothes, she shops where one pays dearly, and when she receives many things in return for a great deal of money, she thinks that she is elegant because what she has is beyond people of modest means. A woman of high birth, on the contrary, distinguishes herself by the simplicity of her dress, by the modest shawl or coat that covers her; in fact, this woman dressed that way has a certain aura of gracefulness, a bearing whose significance escapes only those of very ordinary judgment." *Le Diable rose* 2, no. 4 (20 July 1861).

36. *Physiologie du gant* (Paris, 1843), pp. 50–51.

37. *Le Diable rose* 1, no. 4 (20 July 1860).

38. Hippolyte Taine, *Notes on Paris*, trans. J. A. Stephens (New York, 1875), p. 160

39. *Du luxe, des femmes, des moeurs, de la littérature et de la vertu* (Paris, 1866), pp. 107–108.

40. Eugène Chapus, *Manuel de l'homme et de la femme comme-il-faut*, pp. 150–151. Mme de Girardin had already written: "Beware of women of modest means who have magnificent diamonds. You do not know what it cost them to attain that glamour. They deprive themselves of everything, even children; they have a cook for chambermaid, a servant who comes in once a week to dust their apartment, and a husband badly nourished with potatoes and beans to give them their arm and take them out in society, covered with diamonds." *Lettres parisiennes, années, 1836–1840, Oeuvres complètes*, vol. 4, p. 381.

41. Celnart, *Nouveau manuel*, p. 25.

42. Comtesse Dash, *Comment on fait son chemin dans le monde*, p. 73.

43. Bassanville, *La Science du monde*.

44. Mme la Baronne de Fresne, *De l'usage et de la politesse dans le monde* (Paris, 1858), p. 34. But in turn this self effacement should not overstep certain limits, for "the affectation of simplicity could well become food for pride," recalled the Rev. Father Huguet, thinking perhaps of the Protestants' haughty simplicity. "An austere simplicity is a refinement of vanity: in this case grandeur is renounced but in a spectacular manner." *Délassements*, p. 221.

45. On these problems see George Vigarello's handsome book, *Le Corps redressé* (Paris, 1978).

46. "Our bearing should be easy, natural; if unfortunately you are nervous, you will appear awkward. In that case you should try to calm yourself, master your

appearance, and especially your face, for fear of betraying your emotions." Th. Bourgeau, *Les usages du monde ou ce qui s'observe dans la bonne compagnie* (Paris, 1864), p. 51.

47. Achille Tola-Poix, *Les Ceintures qui parlent* (Paris, 1861), pp. 26–27.

48. Comtesse de B——, *Du savoir-vivre en France au XIXe siècle*, p. 3.

49. Bassanville, *La Science du monde*, p. 3.

50. *Le Magasin des demoiselles* 6 (1849–50): 34.

51. As Marcel Pagnol recalled, a certain slovenliness connoting seniority notably in schools, as well as indifference to the school discipline, long seemed to constitute a prestigious sign of "historical legitimacy" and admired rebelliousness in the culture of children: "I locked up the new smock my mother had made and put on last year's rag I had secretly brought along: its tears and the silent softness of the fabric that had become fluffy indicated my standing. My entry into the schoolyard was triumphant: I was no longer the disoriented, immobile, and solitary 'new boy' looking all around for a smile, and perhaps a friendship. I moved forward in my tattered smock and immediately Lagneau, Nelps, and Vigilanti dashed toward me shouting." *Le Temps des amours* (Paris, 1977), pp. 16–17.

52. In the nineteenth century, dolls, and the novels, tales, or playlets that presented them, played an important role in the vestimentary and physical education of little girls. On this subject see Leïla Sibbar-Pignon's article "Mlle Lili ou l'ordre des poupées," *Les Temps modernes* 358 (May 1976): 1796–1828. She writes: "The doll, docile, stiff, and mute, is always the irreplaceable ally of mothers in the education of little girls. She is not a toy, and she is not a doll. She is a 'person'—rigid, orderly, reasonable—who teaches the little girl that she must control her body and that desire and pleasure do not exist and should not exist in the house. The little girl, trained like the doll and through the doll manipulated by her mother, will be like a doll at the end of the performance: stiff, reserved, clean, silent, submissive." P. 1796.

53. *La Modes des enfants* [a periodical that informed mothers about children's clothing], vol. 1, no. 2 (1 May 1853).

54. Bassanville, *La Science du monde*, p. 8.

55. *Traité de la vie élégante*, pp. 104–105.

56. *Vie élégante*, p. 114.

57. Bassanville, *La Science du monde*, p. 8.

58. For each kind of garment worn during the day, that is, according to its intended place or activity, there was a corresponding propriety that itself inspired a type of mood: "Observe the same man in casual clothing, or a short frock coat, jacket, or sack paletot, etc. In the first outfit he was at ease, gay, natural, witty, depending on his condition and his means. In the second, though, he retains his nature, his manners will be different; his thoughts might be the same, but their expression will undergo perceptible changes, and gaiety dare not show itself without a rather serious surface." *L'Echo des tailleurs* 4, no. 4 (4 July 1860).

59. *Traité de la vie élégante*, p. 96

60. *Manuel de l'homme et de la femme comme-il-faut*, p. 119.

61. Paul de Saint-Victor, *La Presse*, 21 August 1859.

62. P. 50.

63. "Anything that strives for effect is in bad taste, like anything that is noisy. Brummel has, in addition, left us the most admirable maxim on this subject, which England's approbation has consecrated: 'If people look closely at you, you are not well dressed: you are too well dressed, too affected, or too recherché.'" Balzac, *Traité de la vie élégante*, pp. 111–112.

64. "Mon coeur mis à nu," *Oeuvres complètes*, p. 630.

65. J. P. Martinon, "Mythe du Dandy," *Encyclopedia Universalis* (1980 supplement), p. 447.

66. But among the Romantics, scorn for bourgeois conventions became considerably more restrained during the Second Empire. And the traditional bearded, longhaired, flashy, and hirsute battle against respectability did not reach the excesses and the eccentricity of the "Jeunes-France," with their Renaissance doublets and Spanish ruffs. "That extravagance in dress would seem strange now," wrote Théophile Gautier in 1865, "but then they were considered natural: the word 'artist' excused everything, and everyone pretty much followed his own whims." Cited by Louis Maigron, *Le Romantisme et la Mode* (Paris, 1911), p. 57.

67. Paul de Saint-Victor, *La Presse*, 21 August 1859.

CHAPTER IX

1. We should immediately call attention to exceptions to this historiographical deficiency, at least on a scholarly and descriptive level: C. Willet and Phillis Cunnington, *The History of Underclothes* (London, 1951); and, for its illustrations, Cecil Saint-Laurent, *A History of Ladies' Underwear* (London, 1968).

2. Octave Uzanne's lyrical remarks confirm this: "For a sensitive being, what is being done today with the various parts of women's intimate envelope partakes of a rare perfection in the most absolute sybaritism. I know nothing more disturbing, more cajoling to the eye, more supple, adorable, and titillating to the touch than these flimsy, brilliant, and superfine veils, veritable works of art that would challenge an artist to experience the soft and evanescent colorations, to admire their transparency, to handle their supremely fine and delicate fabrics." *L'Art et les Artifices de la Beauté* (Paris, 1902), pp. 214–215.

3. Suggestive dishabille was one of the principal themes of the newspaper *La Vie Parisienne*, founded in 1863.

4. In *Orlando* (New York, 1928) Virginia Woolf recalled the beginnings of this fanatical practice in England:

"Thus, stealthily, and imperceptibly, none marking the exact day or hour of the change, the constitution of England was altered and nobody knew it. Everywhere the effects were felt. The hardy country gentleman, who had sat down gladly to a meal of ale and beef in a room designed, perhaps by the brothers Adam, with classic dignity, now felt chilly. Rugs appeared, beards were grown and trousers fastened tight under the instep. The chill which he felt in his legs he soon transferred to his house; furniture was muffled; walls and tables were covered too.

Outside the house—it was another effect of the damp—ivy grew in unparalleled profusion. Houses that had been of bare stone were smothered in greenery. . . .

What light penetrated to the bedrooms where children were born was naturally of an obfusc green and what light penetrated to the drawing-rooms where grown men and women lived came through curtains of brown and purple plush." Pp. 228–229.

5. This modesty, which really indicated a fascination with sex and an erotic imaginary that has nothing in common with our time was so exaggerated—in England—that chicken drumsticks were left for the servants so that they would not be displayed on the table.

6. Countess de Tramar, *Le Bréviaire de la femme, pratiques secrètes de la beauté*, 8th ed. (Paris, 1903), p. 115.

7. *L'Art de la toilette chez la femme* (Paris, 1885), p. 41.

8. *Journal de la Société de statistique de Paris*, p. 54.

9. Thus, in the first discourse of his *Dames galantes* (Lausanne, 1968), Brantôme speaks of "two large women, their skirts hitched up all the way, their drawers down, sleeping one on top of the other."

10. For the history of women's pantaloons through the ages see Pierre Duffay's erudite study *Le Pantalon féminin* (Paris, 1979).

11. The painting dates from 1767.

12. See, for example, a detail in Deuret's painting *L'Air*, at the Musée d'Orléans.

13. "If I only had your pleasure in view, I might choose the story of Mlle Lambercier's backside, which owing to an unfortunate somersault at the bottom of the meadow, was exhibited in full view to the King of Sardinia who happened to be passing by." Jean-Jacques Rousseau, *The Confessions* (New York, n.d.), p. 30.

14. "At Lyons, on Easter-day, 1791, as the people are leaving the six o'clock mass, a troop, armed with whips, falls upon the women. Stripped, bruised, prostrated, with their heads in the dirt, they are not left until they are bleeding and half-dead; one young girl died from the beating, and this sort of outrage occurs so frequently that even ladies attending the orthodox mass in Paris dare not go out without sewing up their garments around them in the shape of drawers." Hippolyte Adolphe Taine, *The Origins of Contemporary France: The French Revolution*, vol. 1, trans. John Durand (New York, 1931), p. 342. Translation slightly altered.

15. Pierre Antoine de La Mésangère, *Dictionnaire des proverbes français* (Paris, 1823), p. 459. In his opinion, this fashion for children dates from 1807.

16. Under Louis XV a decree made it obligatory for these performers. See Pierre Dufay, *Le Pantalon*, pp. 82–84.

17. During the Revolution of 1848, the Saint-Simonians submitted a design for a uniform that included wearing cloth pantaloons. At the same time, in the name of the right "to come and go," the Club des Vésuviennes declared: "Women should work to efface the differences that exist between men's and women's clothing imperceptibly, without, however, exceeding the limits of modesty or becoming ridiculous, nor even abandoning graceful shapes and good taste." *Les Vésuviennes ou la Constitution politique des femmes* (Paris, 1848), p. 26. Later, "bloomerism," a fashion invented by the American Amelia Bloomer, who was active in the women's rights movement around 1850, also proposed a costume with trousers. Though unsuccessful it was the talk of the town. In the nineteenth century feminism was often accompanied by proposals for "sartorial reforms."

18. "Among the garments of Ancient Greece, which considerations of good taste and health ought to convince European women to adopt, there is one which,

to my eternal regret, we have never realized we need. These are lined drawers, the interior of wool and the outside of light silk, which by preventing the passage of air, either while women are simply walking or dancing energetically, would prevent rheumatism and other discomforts. . . . This attire, antique as well as new, if it were adopted, would also have the advantage of freeing them from the trammels of their triple skirts." Dr. Desessartz et de Saint-Ursin, cited by Pierre Dufay, *Pantalon féminin*, p. 8.

19. Thus, according to Laure-Paul Flobert, "Joséphine had only two pairs of drawers, flesh-colored, in her trousseau when she married Bonaparte. The first woman to wear percale pantaloons was her daughter, Hortense de Beauharnais. Leroy, the great dressmaker, supplied her with several of embroidered cloth at twenty-seven francs each." *La Femme et le costume masculin*, p. 8.

20. (*The year 1810*) *Observations sur les modes et les usages de Paris pour servir d'explication aux caricatures publiées sous le titre de Bon Genre depuis le commencement du dix-neuvieme siècle* 42 (1817): 9. Edouard Texier also wrote: "As early as 1822 several *élégantes* of the Chausée-d'Antin tried to introduce the Turkish fashion of the long mousseline drawers worn by children; but an extraordinary thing happened: only courtesans took up this decent fashion; nothing more was needed to discredit it." *Tableau de Paris*, p. 332.

21. "Hygiène et médecine," *Fashion-Théorie* 33, no. 252 (March 1861).

22. Jean L. A. Commerson, cited by Adolphe Ricard, *Les Femmes, l'amour et le mariage*, p. 453.

23. Like the night dress, the pantaloon was too attractive, too seductive, too embroidered. It was perceived as a sign of licentiousness and bad morals, especially during the Second Empire when modesty in this domain required a Jansenistical simplicity.

24. "Whether a housewife or a peasant, a lower-class woman did not generally wear pantaloons," Pierre Dufay could still write in 1906. *Pantalon féminin*, p. 1906. Among the bourgeoisie its absence was no longer tolerated after the 1880s.

25. Today the moral order does not even need clothing to rule; witness the extraordinarily "decent" and puritanical character of the nudism that is becoming general on beaches in the West.

26. *Les Sélections sociales*, p. 315.

27. On the history of the shirt, see the articles of R. Flury von Bultzingslowen, "La chemise et la mode" and "La chemise dans les croyances et les moeurs populaires," *Cahier Ciba* 71 (August 1947): 7–10 and 23–29.

28. Between the Second Empire and the first decade of the twentieth century an important development in the refinement and visibility of women's undergarments took place. We owe this quivering evocation to a visit Octave Uzanne made to a large luxury lingerie shop: "I thought that I was living in an edenic milieu where houris might have dropped their veils of light. . . . Oh! the divine belted and fitted chemises with hemstitched tops, trimmed with wide collerettes that plunged the soul into a disturbing obsession with the shapes that they would cover! Then there were others, no longer lawn or batiste but silk, trimmed with fancy Alencon, English, and Saxony lace, or Venetian guipure whose white or ecru shades blended harmoniously with the fabrics' tones of soft pink, delicate blue, subtle heliotrope, or sulphur yellow." *L'Art et les Artifices de la Beauté*, p. 215.

29. "Hygiène et médecine," p. 1075.

30. Only a few unusual women, who embodied perfectly the period's norms of beauty, dared do without them. If Horace de Viel-Castel's account is to be believed, the Countess of Castiglione, for example, who "carried the weight of her beauty arrogantly" and "ostentatiously displayed proofs of it, ... did not wear a corset, and would gladly pose before a Phidias, should one be found in our benighted time, adorned with nothing but her beauty. Her bust is truly admirable, proudly erect like the bosoms of young Moorish women; the tops of her breasts are smooth, and her two breasts seem a challenge to all other women." *Mémoires* (Paris, 1924), vol. 2 (1851–64), p. 39.

31. On the history of corset forms, see above all Fernard Libron and Henri Clouzot, *Le Corset dans l'art et les moeurs du XIIIe au XX siècle* (Paris, 1893).

32. On the erect postures imposed by the corset and the somatic conceptions and functions that the corset underlay see Georges Vigarello, *Le Corps redressé.*

33. Nevertheless, in the middle of the nineteenth century the binding and suspending of infants still existed, as this document indicates: "Sixty years after Jean-Jacques Rousseau directed his righteous anger at suspending infants, we still encountered, at the gates of Paris, a piteous victim of this torture, whom we removed from his hook to the stupid astonishment of his nurse." Charles Roux, *Contre le corset* (Paris, 1855), p. 8.

34. The whaleboning of the eighteenth-century "body," which descended very low over the stomach, was most impressive. The busks were made of wood or ivory, and the extremely rigid corps could sometimes weigh more than 800 grams.

35. Jacques Bénigne Winslow, "Mémoire sur les mauvais effets de l'usage des corps à baleines," *Mémoires de l'Académie des Sciences* (Paris, 1741).

36. Jean-Charles Desessartz, *Traité de l'éducation corporelle des enfants en bas age* (Paris, 1760).

37. Charles Auguste Vandermonde, *Essai sur la manière de perfectionner l'espèce humaine* (Paris, 1756), 2 vols.

38. *Émile* was published in 1762.

39. Buffon, *Histoire naturelle*, part 3, "Les Mammifères," sec. 1 (Paris, 1749–67).

40. Samuel A. Tissot, *Essai sur les maladies des gens du monde* (Lausanne, 1770).

41. Alphonse Leroy, *Recherches sur les habillements des femmes et des enfants* (Paris, 1772).

42. In 1772 a certain Bonnaud published a brochure in Paris entitled *Degradation of the Human Species by the Use of Whaleboned Corsets, a Work in Which It Is Demonstrated that It Is to Go against the Laws of Nature, Augment Depopulation, and Bastardize So to Speak Man to Put Him to Torture from the First Moments of His Existence, under the Pretext of Shaping Him.*

43. The use of constricting devices has aroused criticism throughout history. But the remarks of Galen, Paré, or Montaigne remained sporadic and imprecise.

44. Not all physicians espoused opposition to standards of elegance considered stiff and rigid and resulting in artificial, painful shapes. Fortified by the reticence of some doctors, corset makers, concerned about the threat to their livelihood, attempted to justify the industry. Thus the Sieur Doffemont (a master tailor) published *Avis très important au public sur différentes espèces de Corps et de Bottines d'une nouvelle invention* (Paris, 1758), which he reissued in 1759, 1763, and 1775. In

1770—the year of Bonnaud's brochure—a women's tailor at Lyon, Reisser the elder, wrote *Avis au sexe ou essai sur les corps baleinés pour former et conserver la taille aux jeunes personnes* (Lyon, 1770), in which Rousseau's argument was completely turned around: "If one examines the figures of country girls," he wrote, "it will be seen that their shoulders generally hunch forward, their chests are narrow, stomachs large and backs rounded. If city girls have better figures the cause must be sought in the use of whaleboned bodies." Pp. 117–118.

His orthopedic radicalism went so far as to recommend putting children in corsets at night:

"Children often assume irregular and cramped positions in bed. This can contribute to malformation, and destroy at night what the stiffened body accomplished by day. This damage should be stopped and even prevented. It can be averted by having stiffened corsets made, but softer than the ones for day wear." P. 76.

45. "L'établissement du sieur Delacrois, chirurgien-mécanicien herniaire du roi," to which Louis Marie Prud'homme's *Le Voyage descriptif et historique de l'ancien et du nouveau Paris* called attention at 18, rue des Vieux-Augustins, is significant in this respect. One part of the building contained machines intended for exercise and body modification, while another part was a workshop for the manufacture of corsets that simulated shapes or hid deformities. Vol. 2 (Paris, 1821), pp. 156–157.

46. *Theory of the Leisure Class*, p. 168.

47. "It [the corset] bruises the hips, creases and hardens the skin. Around the waist it causes a red, inflamed, wrinkled aureole. Some women in the evening, when they undress, are so tortured by burning sensations that they tear their flesh with their pink nails. This is not acceptable." Dr. Daumas, "Hygiène et medecine," p. 1803.

48. "Valérie, standing before the fire, where a log was blazing, was allowing Wencelas to lace her stays. . . . 'Come, come; after two years' practice you do not yet know how to lace a woman's stays! You are too much a Pole!' said Valérie, laughing at him." *Cousin Betty*, trans. James Waring (New York, 1901), p. 411. The scene is set in 1840.

49. "The desirable art of being prepared for anything and of taking into account all social conditions [that is, persons without chambermaids] has invented a mechanical busk that is very useful.

This busk is made of two thin, supple pieces of steel, joined together by a variable number of hooks that a spring placed at the bottom opens or closes at will. This busk is sewn to the corset, which is worn in the normal fashion. If the lady is too tightly or loosely laced, she does not need to relace herself to remedy this. She need only loosen or tighten the cords. Nothing is easier than removing her corset, and without undressing. The hooks of her dress—only those at the waist—are undone, the busk spring is pressed, and the busk separates in two; the loosened corset is slipped off. There are occasions when it is of inestimable value to be able to remove one's corset promptly." Mme S., *Physiologie du corset* (Montpellier, 1847), pp. 75–76.

50. Dr. Collineau, "Corset," *La Grande Encyclopédie*, vol. 12.

51. *Hygiène vestimentaire*, pp. 170–171.

52. *Manuel du bon ton*, p. 99.

53. *De la politesse*, pp. 57–58.

54. *Hygiène vestimentaire*, p. 169.

55. *Hygiene and Physiology of Marriage*, 23d ed. (Paris, 1861), pp. 24–25.

56. Dr. Henri-Victor Bouvier, *Études historiques et médicales sur l'usage des corsets* (Paris, 1853), pp. 32–33.

57. *Traité d'hygiène publique et privée*, vol. 2, p. 252.

58. "Hygiène et médecine," p. 1082.

59. Théophile d'Antimore, *L'Orgueil* (Paris, 1863), p. 51. "The husband who marries her," he continued, "will be dumbfounded when he sees her in her negligée."

60. *Hygiène vestimentaire*, p. 170.

61. Casimir Delmas, "Hygiène et médecine," p. 1082.

62. Michel Lévy, *Traité d'hygiène*, vol. 1, p. 251.

63. *Études historiques et médicales*, p. 34.

64. *Hygiene for Fashionable People* (Paris, 1870), p. 504.

65. *Hygiène vestimentaire*, p. 185.

66. Their particular ways of reporting the development of this accessory is also significant. For Bouvier dedramatization was necessary. After the Revolution, "the former 'body' did not completely perish. The corset, its derivative, and in a way its diminutive, replaced it. With thin stays and the busk in front, it formed the garment still worn. Through a singular anachronism, most physicians, apparently unaware of this transformation, continued to hurl against the corset the anathemas that had been directed against the stiffened bodies of the last century. Is it not obvious that a distinction should be made and that the same reprobations cannot rightly include the ancient armor of Catherine de Medici and the present-day corset." *Études historiques et médicales*, p. 19

Debay noted the metamorphosis but found it no improvement:

"These whaleboned bodies, which from time to time are somewhat modified, have for nearly four hundred years remained an indispensable article of clothing. It took all the enlightenment of the eighteenth century and the great revolution of 1789 to open women's eyes and make them abandon their armor of whalebone. Yielding to the dictates of reason, they grasped the dangers of this fashion, and drawing closer to Greek dress they presented themselves in all the elegance of their natural graces.

But alas! This return to reason did not last long. Around 1810 another kind of stiffened body, the modern corset, again compressed women's breasts, and men were barbaric enough to find a corseted, stiff, stilted woman charming. From then on, to please men, ladies accepted the corset, and, what is worse, challenged one another to see who would lace herself the tightest, deform her bosom, and kill herself the quickest." Debay, *Hygiène vestimentaire*, pp. 163–164.

67. Bouvier, *Études historiques et médicales*, p. 31

68. *Hygiène vestimentaire*, p. 165.

69. The tempo of this literature picked up during the Third Republic and that time did affect practices. The feminist contribution was considerable; a series of women doctors wrote their theses on the corset's pathological costs and helped introduce reforms, some of them decisive, like the brassiere. See Dr. O'Followel, *Le Corset (histoire, médecine, hygiène)* (Paris, 1908). Associations of Catholics, moralists, famialists, and natalists also played a role. See, for example, *Pour la beauté*

naturelle de la femme contre la mutilation de la taille par le corset, with a preface by
E. Haraucourt, published by the League of Mothers (Paris, 1909).

70. "In Spain the minimum waist measurement was forty centimeters; in France
it ranged from forty-eight to fifty-eight, except in Paris, where women seem to be
more slender than elsewhere." Georges d'Avenel, *Le Mécanisme de la vie modèrne*,
4th ser., p. 64.

71. Drohojowska, *De la politesse*, p. 57.

72. Verardi, *Manuel de bon ton*, p. 99.

73. Ibid. From everywhere, accusations poured out against mothers: "How
many young girls and young wives have we seen weakened from sunrise! Young
flowers strangled by a pitiless lacing, to attain or preserve a waist that would be an
object of envy, one achieved at the cost of the cruelest suffering. Foolish mothers,
culpable girls!" Raoul de Lamorillière, *Crinolines et volants*, p. 7.

74. *Considerations on Five Plagues: The Abuse of the Corset, the Use of Tobacco, the
Passion for Gambling, the Abuse of Strong Drink, and Speculation* (Paris, 1857), pp.
30–31,

75. Ibid., p. 14.

76. Dr. A. Debay, *Hygiène vestimentaire*, p. 171.

77. See Jean-Paul Aron and Roger Kempf, *Le Pénis et la démoralisation de l'Occident*.

78. Dubois, *Considérations*, p. 36.

79. Ibid., p. 33.

80. Ibid.

81. *Manuel-Physiologie de la bonne compagnie*, p. 144.

82. Alfred Picard, *Exposition universelle internationale de 1900 à Paris. Le bilan
d'un siècle (1801–1900)*, vol. 4 (Paris, 1906), p. 441.

83. *L'Ouvrière*, p. 229.

84. *Statistiques de l'industrie à Paris* (1864), p. 260.

85. *L'Amour à Paris sous le Second Empire* (Paris, 1896), p. 182.

86. *L'Art de plaire*, p. 61.

87. Casimir Daumas, "Hygiène et médecine," p. 1076.

88. *Gargantua*, book 1, chap. 8; or book 3, chap. 3. Triumphant, ostentatious
codpieces went out of fashion around the end of the sixteenth century. Before then
Montaigne had criticized their immodesty: "that empty and useless model of a
member that we cannot even decently mention by name, which however we show
off and parade in public." *The Complete Essays of Montaigne*, p. 86.

89. During the Second Empire, "culottes could be found only in backward
provinces. They have fallen into such disuse that the name itself is offensive, ill-
bred, so far has prudery seeped into our morals." Edmond Texier, *Tableau de Paris*,
p. 321.

90. "Le coût de la vie à Paris," p. 49.

91. Published under the direction of Raigé Delorme and A. Dechambre, 100
vols. (Paris, 1865–67).

92. *La Médecine des passions* (Paris, 1841), pp. 173–174.

93. *Study of the Action of Flannel in Direct Contact with the Skin* (Paris, 1855).

94. Michel Lévy, *Traité d'hygiène*, vol. 2, p. 297.

95. A Debay, *Hygiène vestimentaire*, p. 297.

96. *Considérations*, p. 16.

97. Ibid., p. 17.

98. Ibid., pp. 17–18.

99. "The right to the body, to nudity, originates in a new standard of appearance that made what was underneath as honorable as the exterior," writes Jean-Paul Aron on present-day briefs. "Des slips et des hommes," *Le Nouvel Obsérvateur* 525 (2–8 December 1974): 70.

100. As Jean-Paul Aron also observed, "sported proudly like a bandoleer, nudity loses its explosive charge. Displayed on beaches, paraded about newsstands, in bookshop windows and on posters outside cinemas, it is evidence of a civilization that suppresses any division between inner and outer, depth and surface, private and public life." L'air du temps, *Playboy* (French ed.), vol. 69 (August 1979): 15.

101. On this subject see Alfred Franklin, *La Vie privée d'autrefois*, vol. 22, pp. 12–19; and especially Norbert Elias, *The Civilizing Process*, pp. 163–165.

102. *The Civilizing Process*, pp. 165–166.

103. "How can one bear the thought of sleeping next to a really naked man?" From this passage in Molière's *Les Precieuses ridicules* and other literary accounts, Edmond Cottinet argues that this practice persisted. See his article "La nudité au lit selon Cathos et l'histoire," *Le Moliériste* (April 1883): 20–25. In the June issue of the same year Dr. Malthamasius upholds the same view; see pp. 86–89. In fact, if the tradition of sleeping in the nude lasted beyond the sixteenth century, it was a case of social and geographical disparities within a general tendency in the opposite direction.

104. Marguérite d'Aincourt, *Études sur le costume féminin* (Paris, 1883), pp. 14–15.

105. Let us note, nevertheless, that peasants did not invariably wear special clothes at night. Guy Thuillier points out that in the Nivernais "practices such as getting dressed in the morning and undressed in the evening were not 'common' until the 1850s: men slept completely dressed and Jules Renard's peasants did not take their clothes off." "Pour un histoire des gestes," *Revue d'histoire économique et sociale* 2 (1973): 244.

CHAPTER X

1. Alexandre Dumas, fils, *Le Demi-Monde* (Paris, 1855).

2. "Of course, the courtesan spends to satisfy her tastes and appetites, but she has another reason for her spending. One should not believe that she surrounds herself with the refinements of luxury and elegance only to appease a need. No, the courtesan with servants and a carriage is obviously the mistress of a wealthy man accustomed to everything that luxurious living requires, a man who, when he spends his leisure hours with her, expects everything to match his life-style. The courtesan knows that she needs a decor approaching that of the man who pays the bills. In other words, she is a player who constantly doubles her ante: she receives a thousand francs from a keeper, spends them on clothes and entertainment, thus usually attracting the attention of a spendthrift who quickly offers her three or four thousand, assuming that such a woman could not cost less. In short, excessive,

exaggerated spending is a necessity for them, especially today, when the men conventionally known as high-livers keep courtesans not for the pleasures they derive from them but out of a ridiculous vanity. For some of them, it is a speculation in vanity; it flatters such a man that society should know that he keeps a fashionable beauty celebrated for never wearing a dress twice, sporting new jewelry daily, and changing horses and carriage monthly. What glory accrues to the happy mortal whose privilege it is to pay for that!" "Courtisane," *Grand Dictionnaire universel du xixe siècle.*

3. *Le Code de la mode,* pp. 9–10.

4. *La Joie du foyer* 5, no. 11 (1 April 1869).

5. Eugène Chapus, *Manuel de l'homme et de la femme comme-il-faut,* p. 137.

6. "Courtisane," *Grande Dictionnaire universel du xixe siècle.*

7. A. Coffignon, *Les Coulisses de la mode* (Paris, 1888), p. 50.

8. Well before a racetrack was built there in 1854, during Holy Week the church at Longchamp attracted princes, lords, fashionable people, *impures* in grand carriages but also behind them, bourgeois in hackney cabs, and common people in carts. The Tenebrae services served as the pretext for this worldly pilgrimage, but people really came to show off as well as hear Mme Lemaure and the chorus of the opera. After the Revolution, the church was deserted and then demolished, but people continued the annual journey, which had become thoroughly secularized. As far as fashion was concerned, however, the races provided the principal motivation.

9. Amédée Achard, "Le Bois de Boulogne, le Bois et le Chateau de Vincennes," *Paris-Guide,* part 2 (Paris, 1867), p. 1236.

10. Ibid.

11. Ibid.

12. *Nana* (New York, 1933), p. 365.

13. Ibid., p. 354.

14. *Paris-Guide,* p. 1236.

15. H. D'Orvalle, *Le Coquet* 2, no. 8 (1 May 1868).

16. *Ces dames du grand monde par une femme qui n'en est pas* (Paris, 1868), pp. 24–25.

17. Edouard Gourdon, *Le Bois de Boulogne* (Paris, 1861), p. 67.

18. Edmond Texier, *Tableau de Paris,* p. 5.

19. Eliane de Serieul, *Le Diable rose* 9, no. 3 (1 March 1868).

20. Comtesse Dash, *Les Femmes à Paris et en province,* pp. 6–7.

21. Amédée Achard, *Paris-Guide,* p. 1242.

22. "Bois de Boulogne," *Grand Dictionnaire universel du xixe siècle,* vol. 2.

23. Edouard Gourdon, *Le Bois de Boulogne,* p. 158.

24. *Le Bois de Boulogne, histoire, types, moeurs* (Paris, 1854), pp. 183–184.

25. The phenomenon was not new: "The reign of 'semiroyalty' of the royal favorites in the eighteenth century approximated what we find today among loose women," wrote Edouard Fournier. "Until contagious displays of vanity, which almost always start below, gained little by little, the real elite scrimped and saved money while it was wasted by the 'demimondaines' who for most of the eighteenth century were known by a near-synonym, *demi-castors.*" *Le Vieux-Neuf,* vol. 2, pp. 246–247.

26. One should note that fashion plates exaggerated what was novel, but their popularity also helped make novelty commonplace because they informed seamstresses and aroused their customers' desires. The history of fashion magazines and fashion plates has yet to be written. Engravings of figurines with commentary were first published in the second half of the seventeenth century with the *Mercure galant*, founded by Donneau de Vizé in 1762. In the eighteenth century these almanacs and collections of plates proliferated. The *Journal du goût ou Courrier de la mode*, for example, appeared in 1760, the *Monument du costume* in 1774, *La Galerie des modes et costumes français* in 1778, and *Le Cabinet des modes* in 1785. During the Directory, La Mésangère published *Le Journal des dames et des modes*, in which the painter Garnerey illustrated the creations of his collaborator, the tailor Leroy. After the Restoration, this magazine began to compete with the *Petit Courrier des dames*, *Psyché*, *Follet*, *Iris*, and above all with Émile de Girardin's *La Mode*. Shortly afterward, there was an explosion of this sort of publication. They were more or less durable, but new ones continued to appear throughout the century.

27. Bassanville, *La Science du monde*, p. 5.

28. Alfred de Meilheurat, *Manuel du savoir-vivre*, p. 99

29. "The society woman who does not eschew the Bois on Sunday affects very simple dress on that day," notes Edouard Gourdon. "With one's carriage bearing a well-known coat of arms only two steps away, with a valet in knee breeches decorated with braid, one can wear a high-neck dress without flounces, and a plain hat." *Le Bois de Boulogne*, p. 187.

30. Mme Émile de Girardin, *Oeuvres complètes*, vol. 4: *Lettres parisiennes*, p. 335 (Letter of 27 April 1839).

31. Vol. 2, no. 14 (1 November 1868).

32. Henri Despaigne, *Code de la mode*, p. 82.

33. Ibid., p. 87.

34. *Souvenirs de la princesse Pauline de Metternich, 1859–1871* (Paris, 1922), pp. 61–62.

35. Histories of dress perpetuate the old and tenacious misrepresentation of the empress as the fashion leader, portraying her, for example, as setting the mode for the crinoline. As we have seen, this shape began before the Second Empire and developed imperceptibly year by year.

36. From the beginning of the Second Empire an abundant medical literature on spas provided scientific endorsement for commercial enterprises. Each spa was credited with therapeutic properties that were at least as fictitous as the illnesses of the people who visited them but that served as pretexts for their trips. "Would Madame like to go to Aix or Savoy? The diagnosis is passive metrorrhagia. Does she prefer a season in the Pyrenees? A careful auscultation will certainly indicate the presence of emphysema after a case of bronchitis. Had she arranged last year to meet someone at the fountains in Spa? A tactful doctor will promptly render a diagnosis of chlorosis.

If the women and 'girls' who take the waters really suffered from their alleged maladies, the fashionable thermal baths would not be enchanting resorts but veritable hospitals offering a most depressing tableau of human infirmities." Charles Brainne, *Baigneuses et Buveurs d'eau* (Paris, 1860), p. iv.

37. On the history of some French thermal baths and seaside resorts from the point of view of urban and architectural studies, see *Monuments historiques*, no. 1 (1978).

38. *La Corbeille* 16, no. 8 (1 August 1855).

39. *De la politesse*, p. 136.

40. *L'Illustration de Bade* cites the following figures:

Year	Number of Bathers
1799	554
1800	1,555
1810	2,462
1820	5,138
1830	10,992
1840	20,122
1850	33,632
1855	49,067
1856	46,457
1857	50,097

During 1857 foreigners visited the baths in the following proportions:

Germans	18,368
French	15,908
English	5,595
Russians	2,955
North Americans	2,447
Dutch	1,727
Swiss	1,094
Belgians	741
Italians	630
Poles	453
Spanish	251

Cited by Brainne, *Baigneuses et Buveurs*, p. 65.

41. Ibid., p. 109.

42. *Fashion-Théorie* 33, no. 258 (September 1861).

43. *La Corbeille* 13, no. 10 (1 October 1861).

44. Alred de Meilheurat, *Manuel du savoir-vivre*, p. 99.

45. *Notes on Paris*, pp. 32–33.

46. Mme Émile de Girardin, *Lettres parisiennes*, vol. 4, p. 336 (27 April 27 1839).

47. Edmond Texier wrote, "I recall seeing not long ago an upright provincial who had arrived the day before on the coach from Caen or Périgueux, whose mother's savings probably made Humann or Dussautoy unattainable and who was not aware of the bargain-priced splendors at Quatre-Nations and La Belle Jardinière. He went to the Temple market and reemerged metamorphosed from head to toe; he had donned the castoffs of an ex-lion, and he had not even thought of removing from the buttonhole the red ribbon of the Legion of Honor left by its former owner." *Tableau de Paris*, p. 148.

48. A. Coffignon, *Les Coulisses de la mode*, pp. 51–52.

49. Comtesse Dash, *Les Femmes à Paris et en province*, p. 280. Stemming neither from the *petits-maîtres*, beaux, merveilleux, *muscadins*, coxcombs, *gandins*, nor lions of the previous periods, the *cocodés* nevertheless appeared as a Second Empire offshoot of this lineage.

50. *Le Magasin des demoiselles* 7 (November 1850).

51. *Le Diable rose* 9 (20 December 1860).

52. Emile Kerckhoff, *Le Costume à la cour et à la ville*, p. ii.

53. In partnership with a Swede named Bobergh, Worth offered her their services in 1860:

"These gentlemen, quite eager to have me as a customer, asked if I would be so kind as to have a dress made by them. I only had to tell them the price I would be willing to pay. . . . The evening dress would be launched at the next ball at the Tuileries Palace. . . . It was made of silver-lamé white tulle (which was new) and decorated with daisies with pink centers placed in tufts of wild grass. The flowers were veiled in white tulle, and a wide white satin belt circled my waist. I had diamonds sewed everywhere—and Worth had his first success!

As soon as the Empress entered the throne room where the diplomatic corps was gathered for the circle, she instantly noticed the masterpiece! When she came up to me she asked who had made this dress so marvelous in its simplicity and elegance. 'An Englishman, Madame, a rising star in the heavens of fashion!' 'And what is his name?' 'Worth.' 'Well,' replied the Empress, 'Let the star have satellites. Please ask him to call on me tomorrow morning at ten!' Worth was launched and I was lost, because three hundred–franc dresses disappeared." *Eclairs du passé, 1859–1870* (Zurich, 1922), pp. 106–107. Diana de Marly's *Worth, Father of Haute Couture*, 2d ed. (New York, 1980) is adulatory and gossipy but valuable for its photographs of Worth dresses.

54. His clientele included the Empress Eugénie, Elisabeth of Austria, Marguerite of Italy, Mme de Castiglione, Mme de Pourtalès, the princess Mathilde, not to mention the great demimondaines such as la Païva, Coral Pearl, etc.

55. Vicomte d'Avenel, *Le Mécanisme de la vie moderne*, 4th ser., p. 74.

56. "Mme Francisque B., a lady of the best society, an elegant woman, went to him last month to order a dress. 'Madame, who is introducing you to me?' 'What do you mean?' 'I mean that I dress no one who is not introduced to me.' She left, bursting with indignation." Taine, *Notes on Paris*, pp. 150–151. Translation slightly altered.

57. Mme Bourdon, *La Machine à coudre* (Lille, 1878), pp. 15–16.

58. During this heyday, the amounts high society spent on clothes defy the imagination. "Three hundred thousand francs go quickly when the simplest outfit costs five hundred francs, not to mention the five thousand francs of Valenciennes trimming for the lace insets, and puffs, and the capes of Venetian lace. Then add eight thousand francs of Alençon lace for a dressing gown, sheets costing two to three thousand francs a pair, and fixed expenses, which include ten or so thousand francs for laundry, five to six for shoes, as much for hats, and ten francs a day for perfume." Nestor Roqueplan, *Parisine*, p. 37.

59. 26 February 1870.

60. "These men concerned with fashion, toilettes, lace—everything that per-

tains to sewing—should be condemned to general contempt, subjected to withering scorn, and punished by fines. These occupations should be left to those that nature formed for the purpose." This was what the Marquis de Vilette suggested in his *Cahiers* (Senlis, 1789), p. 20

61. "Couturier, -ière," *Grand Dictionnaire universel du XIXe siècle.*

62. In 1858 *Fashion-Théorie* indicated that "in certain circles, it is conceded that the simplest dress of a *merveilleuse* is expected to cost six hundred francs! Can anyone wonder that there are so many bachelors?" vol. 30, no. 217 (April 1858). Ten years later the figures had risen appreciably: "Let us assume . . . that in the great fashion houses today a lady needs to pay a minimum of 500 to 600 francs for an ordinary day dress. A complete outfit costs 750 to 900 francs; a pretty evening dress 600 francs, but with flower trimmings or pearl embroidery between 1,000 to 1,500 francs. To be precise: I have seen a green satin dress, trimmed with Chantilly lace, for 1,110 francs, another in moiré brocade, trimmed with hundreds of meters of black and gold imitation blonde, satin, velvet, etc., etc., for 1,600 francs." *Le Coquet* 2, no. 5 (1 February 1868).

63. Cited by Ciffignon, *Les Coulisses de la mode*, p. 135.

64. As Roger Kempf has subtly noted in Balzac, the tailor is the person who enables "the body and clothing to affirm one another mutually, like assets." See "Costumes et hiéroglyphes balzaciens," *Sur le corps romanesque* (Paris, 1968), pp. 94–98.

65. On this subject, see the study undertaken by Pierre Bourdieu and Yvette Delsaut on contemporary high fashion: "Le courturier et sa griffe: contribution à une théorie de la magie," *Actes de la recherche en sciences sociales* 1 (January 1975): 7–36.

66. Taken to the famous dressmaker Chevreuil, the author of *Paris-Viveur* recounts:

"As soon as he saw me, he asked me to turn around, and after a simple glance at the back of my suit: 'You're dressed by Sentis, aren't you?' he said without hesitation. 'Yes, certainly; but how could you have guessed? . . .' 'Your clothes,' he told me, 'have a certain pretentiousness and skimpiness throughout. . . . With a Sentis suit you can look like a lion, but you will never look like an ambassador." Taxile Delor, Arnould Frémy, Edmond Texier, *Les Petits-Paris*, nos. 6–10, pp. 31–32.

67. 1 July 1855, cited by H. Vanier, *La Modes et ses métiers*, p. 158.

CONCLUSION

1. *Democracy in America*, vol. 2, trans. Phillips Bradely (New York, 1945), p. 146.

2. Whatever the type of garment or the sex of the buyer, the 1971–72 figures of the National Institute of Statistics and Economic Studies indicate that the mean expenditure per person reaches its maximum between the ages of fifteen and twenty. See Bernard Feuillet and Anne-Marie Vasseur, *Le Marché d'occasion*, p. 5.

3. Cited by Yvonne Knibiehler, "Le Discours médical sur la femme: constantes et ruptures," *Romantisme* 13, no. 14 (1976): 46.

4. *La Bréviaire de la femme*, p. 167.

5. On this subject see Philippe Julian, *Le Nu 1900* (Paris, 1976); and *Photographies inconvenantes 1900* (Paris, 1978), with commentary by Robert Beauvais.

Bibliography

Anonymous works are alphabetized by title.

Abrantès, Mme Amet d'. "De la mode et du bon goût." *Le Messager des modes et de l'industrie* 1, no. 2 (1853).

Achard, Amédée. "Le Bois de Boulogne, le Bois et le Chateau de Vincenne." *Paris-Guide* (1863): 1228–1265. In *Les Ceintures qui parlent*, pp. 26–27. Paris, 1861.

Adolphe, Joanne. *Paris illustré en 1870. Guide de l'étranger et du parisien.* 3d ed. Paris, 1870.

Aftalion, Albert. *Le Développement de la fabrique et le travail à domicile dans les industries de l'habillement.* Paris, 1906.

Aghulon, Maurice. "La société paysanne et la vie à la campagne." In *Histoire de la France rurale.* Paris, 1976.

Aincourt, Marguérite d'. *Études sur le costume féminin.* Paris, 1883.

Alter, Jean-V. *Les Origines de la satire antibourgeoise en France.* Vol. 2: *L'Esprit antibourgeois sous l'Ancien Régime.* Geneva, 1970.

Amiel, Henri-Frédéric. *Journal intime, année 1857.* Paris, 1965.

Annuaire statistique de la France. Paris, 1910.

Antimore, Théophile d'. *L'Orgueil.* Paris, 1863.

Antonelle, F. de. "Le marché aux vieux linges." In *Nouveau Tableau de Paris au XIXe siècle.* Paris, 1834.

Aragon, Henry. *Les Lois somptuaires en France.* Perpignan, 1921.

Ariès, Philippe. *Centuries of Childhood: A Social History of Family Life.* Trans. Robert Baldick. New York, 1962.

Aron, Jean-Paul. " L'air du temps." *Playboy* (French ed.), vol. 69 (August, 1979).

———. *Le Mangeur du XIXe siècle.* Paris, 1973.

———. "Des slips et des hommes." *Le Nouvel Observateur* 525 (2–8 December 1974).

———, and Roger Kempf. *Le Pénis ou la démoralisation de l'Occident.* Paris, 1978.

Avenel, Georges d'. "Les grands magasins." *La Revue des Deux-Mondes.* 4 (1894): 335–336.

———. *Le Mécanisme de la vie moderne,* 4th ser. Paris, 1898–1900.

B., Madame la Comtesse de. *Du savoir-vivre en France au XIXe siècle, ou Instruction d'un père à ses enfants.* Paris, 1838.

Bailly, Charles. *Traité de stylistique française.* Geneva, 1909. Reprint. 1970.

Balzac, Honoré de, *"At the Sign of the Cat and Racket" and Other Stories.* London, 1944.

———. *César Birotteau.* Trans. Frances Frenaye. New York, 1955.

———. *Correspondances, 1819–1850.* Vol. 2. Paris, 1876.

———. *Cousin Betty.* Trans. James Waring. New York, 1901.

Balzac, Honoré de. *Oeuvres complètes*. Vol. 11: *Ferragus*. Paris.

———. *Illusions perdues, Oeuvres complètes*. Paris, 1843.

———. *L'Illustre Gaudissart*. Paris, 1971.

———. *Oeuvres complètes*. Vol. 16: *Physiologie du mariage*, p. 369. Paris, 1846.

———. *Traité de la vie élégante*. Paris, 1922.

Barbier, Jean François. *Journal historique et anecdotique du règne de Louis XV*. Paris, 1849.

Bardin G. "Machines servant à la confection des vêtements." *Études sur l'Exposition de 1867*, 8th ser. Paris, 1869.

Barthes, Roland. "Éléments de sémiologie." *Communications* 4 (1964).

———. "Histoire et sociologie du vêtement." *Annales E.S.C.* 3 (1957): 430–441.

Bassanville, Comtesse de. *La Science du monde: politesse, usages, bien-être*. Paris, 1859.

Bataille, Georges. *L'Érotisme*. Paris, 1965.

Baudelaire, Charles. *Curiosités esthétiques, Oeuvres complètes*. Paris, 1968.

———. "Mon coeur mis à nu." *Oeuvres complètes*. Paris, 1968.

Baudrillard, Jean l'. *Échange symbolique et la Mort*. Paris, 1976.

———. *For a Critique of the Political Economy of the Sign*. Trans. and with an intro. by Charles Levin. St. Louis, 1981.

———. *La Société de consommation*. Paris, 1970.

———. *Le Système des objets*. Paris, 1968.

Beauvoir, Roger de. "Le Tailleur." *Les Français peints par eux-mêmes*. Paris, 1841.

Bergler, Edmund. *Fashion and the Unconscious*. New York, 1953.

Berque, Jacques. *Le Maghreb entre deux guerres*. Paris, 1962.

Bertall. *La Comédie de notre temps*. Vol. 1. Paris, 1874.

Berthaud, L. A. "Les chiffoniers." *Les Français peints par eux-mêmes*. Vol. 3. Paris, 184.

Bibesco, Princess. *Noblesse de Robe*. Paris, 1928.

Bienaymé, Gustave. "Le coût de la vie à Paris à diverse époques: le blanchissage." *Journal de la Société de statistique de Paris*, January 1903, pp. 20–29; and February 1903, pp. 40–56.

Boehn, Max von. *Die Mode*. 8 vols. Munich, 1963.

"Bois de Boulogne." *Grand Dictionnaire universel du XIXe siècle*. Vol. 2.

Boitard, Pierre. *Manuel-physiologie de la bonne compagnie, du bon ton et de la politesse*. Paris, 1862.

Bonnaud. *Degradation of the Human Species by the Use of Whaleboned Corsets, a Work in Which It Is Demonstrated That It Is to Go against the Laws of Nature, Augment Depopulation, and Bastardize So to Speak Man to Put Him to Torture from the First Moments of His Existence, under the Pretext of Shaping Him*. Paris, 1770.

Boucher, François. "Les conditions de l'apparition du costume court en France vers le milieu du xive siècle." *Recueil de travaux offerts à Clovis Brunel*. Paris, 1955.

———. "Géopolitique du costume." *L'Amour de l'art*. 1er trimestre, 1952.

———. *Histoire du costume en Occident de l'Antiquité à nos jours*. Paris, 1965.

Bouchot, Henri. *Les Femmes de Brantôme*. Paris, 1890.

———. *La Toilette à la cour de Napoléon (1810–1815)*. Paris, 1895.

Bourdieu, Pierre. *Distinction: A Social Critique of the Judgment of Taste*. Trans. Richard Nice. Cambridge, Mass., 1984.

Bourdon, Mme. *La Machine à coudre*. Lille, 1878.

Bourgeau, Th. *Les usages du monde ou ce qui s'observe dans la bonne compagnie*. Paris, 1864.

Bouvier, Dr. Henri-Victor. *Études historiques et médicales sur l'usage des corsets*. Paris, 1853.

Brainne, Charles. *Baigneuses et Buveurs d'eau*. Paris, 1860.

Brantôme, Pierre de Bourdeille de. *Dames galantes*. Lausanne, 1968.

Braudel, Fernand. *Civilization and Capitalism, 15th–18th Century*. Vol. 1: *The Structures of Everyday Life and the Limits of the Possible*. Orig. trans. of Miriam Kochan revised by Sian Reynolds. New York, 1981.

———. *Civilisation matérielle et Capitalisme, XVe–XVIIIe siècle*. Paris, 1967.

———. *Écrits sur l'histoire*. Paris, 1977.

———. "Histoire des sciences sociales: la longue durée." *Annales E.S.C.* 4 (October–December 1958): 725–753.

Brooks, John. "Petite encyclopédie du blue-jeans." *Jardin des Modes* 31 (April 1980).

Buffon, George Louis Leclerc. *Histoire naturelle*. Vol. 1: *Les Mammifères*. Paris, 1749–67.

Burgelin, Olivier. "Mode," *Encyclopedia Universalis*. Vol. 2. 1968.

Cabanes, Dr. *Moeurs intimes du passé, la vie au bains*. Vol. 2. Paris, 1885.

Cabanès, Augustin. *Le Costume du médecin en France des origines au XVIIIe siècle*. Paris, 1921.

Calvin, John. *Sermon, où il est montré quelle doit être la modestie des femmes en leurs habillements*. 1561. Reprint. Geneva, 1945.

Camp, Maxime du. "Les voitures publiques dans la ville de Paris." *Revue des Deux-Mondes* 37 (15 May 1867).

Caraccioli, Louis A. de. *Voyage de la raison en Europe*. Compiègne, 1772.

Catéchisme des grandes filles qui souhaitent se marier. Paris, 1865.

Cavé, Marie-Elisabeth. *La Femme aujourd'hui, la femme autrefois*. Paris, 1863.

Celnart, Mme. *Nouveau manuel complet de la bonne compagnie ou guide de la politesse et de la biénseance destiné à tous les âges et à tous les conditions*. Paris, 1863.

Ces dames du grand monde par une femme qui n'en est pas. Paris, 1868.

Challamel, Augustin. *Histoire de la mode en France*. Paris, 1881.

Chapus, Eugène. *Manuel de l'homme et de la femme comme il faut*. 5th ed. Paris, 1862.

Charlot, Marcel. "Fripier." *La Grande Encyclopédie*.

Chaussinand-Nogaret, Guy. "La Noblesse, Ministère de l'idéal." *Autrement* 89 (April 1987): 88–95.

"Chiffoniers." *Grande Dictionnaire universel du XIXe siècle*. Vol. 4. Paris, n.d.

Claudin, Gustave. *Le Petit Moniteur du soir*. Cited in *Journal des modes de l'homme*, March 1869.

Code de la cravate, traité complet des formes, de la mise, des couleurs de la cravate. Paris, 1828.

Code du cérémonial. Paris, 1868.

Coffignon, A. *Les Coulisses de la mode*. Paris, 1880.

Collineau, Dr. "Corset." *La Grande Encyclopédie*. Vol. 12.

Comtesse de B———. *Du savoir-vivre en France au XIXe siècle*.

"Consideration sur les avantages de changer le costume françois." *La Décade philosophique littéraire et politique* 10. Floréal l'an II, Ier année.

Constantin, Marc. *Almanach des belles manières ou l'Art du bon ton, de la politesse, etc.* Paris, 1854.

Corbin, Alain. *Archaïsme et Modernité en Limousin au XIXe siècle, 1845–1880.* Paris, 1975.

———. *The Foul and the Fragrant: Odor and the French Social Imagination.* Cambridge, Mass., 1986.

Cottinet, Edmond. "La nudité au lit selon Cathos et l'histoire." *Le Molièriste*, April 1883.

"Couturier, -ière." *Grand Dictionnaire universel du XIXe siècle.*

Coyer, l'Abbé. *Année merveilleuse.* N.p., 1748.

Cravatiana, ou traité général des cravates considerées dans leur origine, leur influence politique, physique et morale, leurs formes, leurs couleurs et leurs espèces. Traduit de l'anglais. Paris, 1823.

Creston, René-Yves. *Le Costume breton.* Paris, 1974.

Csergo, Julia. *Liberté, Egalité, Propreté: La morale de l'hygiène au XIXe siècle.* Paris, 1988.

Cuisenier, Jean, ed. *Mille ans de costume français.* Paris, 1991.

Cunnington, Cecil Willet. *Handbook of English Costume.* London, 1952.

———, and Phillis Cunnington. *The History of Underclothes.* London, 1951.

Darwin, Charles, *The Voyage of the Beagle.* New York, 1909.

Darwin, George H. "Development in Dress." *Macmillan's Magazine*, September 1872.

Dash, Comtesse. *Comment on fait son chemin dans le monde.* Paris, 1868.

———. *Les Femmes à Paris et en Province.* Paris, 1868.

Daubert, Paul, *Du port illegal de costume et de décoration.* Paris, 1905.

Daumard, Adeline. *Les Fortunes françaises au XIXe siècle.* Paris, 1973.

Daumas, Casimir. "Hygiène et médecine." *Fashion-Théorie* 33, no. 252 (March 1861).

Debay, Dr. A. *Hygiène des mains et des pieds, de la poitrine et de la taille.* Paris, 1860.

———. *Hygiène et physiologie du mariage.* 23d ed. Paris, 1861.

———. *Hygiène vestimentaire.* Paris, 1857.

Declaration of the King which Permits Women and Girls Who Were Forbidden to Do So by the Edict of the Month March 1700 to Wear Jewels. Given at Versailles the 25th of February 1702. Paris, 1702.

Défense de la Crinoline par un médecin de campagne. Paris, 1867.

Deglaude, Dr. *Dissertation médicale sur les vêtements qui sont en contact immédiat avec la peau.* Paris, 1817.

Delaporte, Yves. "Le Signe vestimentaire." *L'Homme* (July–September, 1980): 109–142.

———. "Teddies, Rockers, Punks, et Cie: quelques codes vestimentaires urbains." *L'Homme* (October–December, 1982): 49–62.

Delord, Taxile, Arnould Frémy, and Edmond Texier. "Paris-Gagne-Petit." *Les Petits Paris.*

———. *Paris Viveur.* Paris, 1854.

Demay, Germain. *Le Costume au Moyen Age d'après les sceaux.* Paris, 1880.

Denis, Diderot. *Regrets on Parting with My Old Dressing Gown.* In *"Rameau's Nephew" and Other Works*, trans. Jacques Barzun and Ralph H. Bowen. Indianopolis, 1964.

"Des usages." *Le Magasin des demoiselles* 9, no. 10 (25 July 1853).

Descamps, Marc-Alain. *Psychosociologie de la mode.* Paris, 1969.

Descuret. *La Médecine des passions*, pp. 173–174. Paris, 1841.

Desessartz, Jean-Charles. *Traité de l'éducation corporelle des enfants en bas âge.* Paris, 1760.

Deslandres, Yvonne. *Le Costume, Image de l'homme.* Paris, 1976.

Despaigne, Henri. *Le Code de la mode.* Paris, 1866.

Devleeshouwer, Robert. "Costume et société." *Revue de l'Institut de Sociologie* 2 (1977).

Dictionnaire encyclopédique des sciences médicales. 100 vols. Published under the direction of Drs. Raigé Delorme and A. Dechambre. Paris, 1865–67.

Discours de deux marchands fripiers et de deux maîtres tailleurs. N.p., 1614.

Doffemont. *Avis très important au public sur différentes espèces de Corps et de Bottines d'une nouvelle invention.* Paris, 1758.

Doncourt, Chevalier A. de [pseudonym of Drohojowska]. *La Verité aux femmes sur l'excentricité des modes et de la toilette.* Paris, 1858.

Donné, Dr. *Hygiène des gens du monde.* Paris, 1870.

Dorchies, Émile. *L'Industrie à domicile de la confection de vêtements pour hommes dans la campagne lilloise.* Lille, 1907.

Drohojowska, Comtesse. *De la politesse et du bon ton ou devoirs d'une femme chrétienne dans le monde.* 2d ed. Paris, 1860.

Duffay, Pierre. *Le Pantalon féminin.* Paris, 1979.

Dumas, Alexandre fils. *Le Demi-Monde.* Paris, 1855.

Dusautoy, Auguste. *Rapport du Jury international de l'Exposition de 1867, 35e classe.* Paris, 1867.

Duveau, Georges. *La Vie ouvrière en France sous le Second Empire.* Paris, 1946.

Echo des tailleurs 8, no. 84 (January 1864).

Eck, Charles. *Histoire chronologique du vêtement (homme) ou, Jadis et Aujourd'hui suivi de l'Art de se vêtir au XIX siècle.* Paris, 1857.

Elias, Norbert. *The Court Society.* Trans. Edmund Jephcott. New York, 1983.

———. *The Meaning of the Civilizing Process: The History of Manners.* Trans. Edmund Jephcott. New York, 1978.

Ellis, Havelock. *Studies in the Psychology of Sex.* New York, 1936.

Empesé, Baron Emile de l'. *L'Art de mettre sa cravate de toutes les manières connues et usitées, enseigné et demontré en seize leçons, précéde de l'histoire complète de la cravate.* Paris, 1827.

Enlart, Camille. *Manuel d'archéologie française depuis les temps mérovingiens jusqu' à la Renaissance.* Vol. 3: *Le costume.* Paris, 1916.

Faraut, François. *Histoire de la Belle Jardinière.* Paris, 1987.

Fargue, L. P. *De la mode.* Paris, 1945.

Faure, Alain. "Classe malpropre, classe dangereuse." *Recherches* (December 1977).

Faust, Dr. B. C. *Sur le vêtement libre, unique et à l'usage des enfants.* N.p.

Favardin, Patrick. "La Villa ou l'avènement d'un nouveau mode d'habitation." *Monuments historiques* 102 (April 1979).

Fay, H. Marcel. *Lépreux et Cagots du Sud Ouest.* Paris, 1910.

Febvre, Lucien. *The Problem of Unbelief in the Sixteenth Century: The Religion of Rabelais.* Trans. Beatrice Gottlieb. Cambridge, Mass., 1982.

Feuillet, Bernard, and Anne-Marie Vasseur. *Le Marché d'occasion de l'électro-ménager et du vêtement*. Mimeographed publication. Paris, 1979.

Feydeau, Ernest. *L'Art de plaire, Études d'hygiène, de goût et de toilettes*. Paris, 1873.

———. *Du luxe, des femmes, des moeurs, de la littérature et de la vertu*. Paris, 1866.

Flobert, Laure-Paul. *La Femme et le Costume masculin*. Lille, 1911.

Flury von Bultzingslowen, R. "La chemise dans les croyances et les moeurs populaires." *Cahier Ciba* 71 (August 1947): 23–29.

———. "La chemise et la mode." *Cahier Ciba* 71 (August 1947): 7–10.

Fohlen, Claude. *L'Industrie textile au temps du Second Empire*. Paris, 1956.

Fontenelle, Julia de. *Nouveau Manuel complet du blanchissage, nettoyage et dégraissage*. 2 vols. Paris, l855.

Fournier, Marc. *La Grande Ville, Nouveau Tableau de Paris*. Vol. 2: *La Rotonde du Temple*. Paris, 1842.

France, Anatole. *Penguin Island*. Trans. A. W. Evans. New York, 1933.

Francos, Ania. *Il était des femmes dans la Résistance*. Paris, 1978.

Franklin, Alfred. *La Vie privée d'autrefois*. Vol. 14: "Les Magasins de nouveautés." Paris, 1894.

Fresne, Mme la Baronne de. *De l'usage et de la politesse dans le monde*. Paris, 1858.

Frémy, Arnould. *Les Moeurs de notre temps*. Paris, 1860.

———. "La Revendeuse à la toilette." *Les Français peints par eux mêmes*. Paris, 1841.

Gaillard, Jeanne. *Paris, La Ville*. Paris, 1977.

Gennep, Arnold. *Manuel du folklore français contemporain*. Part 1. Vol. 2. Paris, 1949.

Giffard, Pierre. *Les Grands Bazars*. Paris, 1882.

Gille, Bertrand. "Recherches sur l'origine des grands magasins parisiens, notes d'orientation." *Fédération des sociétés historiques et archéologiques de Paris et de l'Ile-de-France, Mémoire*. Vol. 7. 1955.

Girard, P. S. *Recherches sur les établissements de bains publics à Paris*. Paris, 1832.

Girardin, Mde de. *Oeuvres complètes*. Vol. 4: *Lettres parisiennes, années 1836–1840*. Paris, 1860.

Glasson, E. "Les origines du costume de la magistrature." *Nouvelle revue historique du Droit français et étranger* 8 (1884).

Goblot, Edmond. *La Barrière et le niveau*. Paris, 1925, 1966. New ed. Paris, 1967.

Goncourt, Edmond, and Charles de Goncourt. *Journal, Mémoires de la vie littéraire*. Vol. 3. Monaco, 1957.

Gorer, Geoffrey, and John Rickman. *The People of Great Russia: A Psychological Study*. New York, 1962.

Goullin, J. A. *La Mode sous le point de vue hygiénique*. Paris, 1846.

Gourdon, Edouard. *Le Bois de Boulogne*. Paris, 1861.

———. *Le Bois de Boulogne, histoire, types, moeurs*. Paris, 1854.

Le Grand Livre de Leroy. Bibliothèque Nationale. Fonds Français 5932.

Guénot-Lecointe, Georges. *Physiologie du gant*. Paris, 1841.

Gummere, Amelia. *The Quaker: A Study of Costume*. Philadelphia, 1901.

Handricourt, André. "Relations entre gestes habituels, forme des vêtements et manières de porter les charges." *Revue de géographie humaine et d'ethnologie* 3 (July–September 1948): 32–48.

Hargreaves-Mawdsley, W. N. *A History of Academical Dress until the End of the Eighteenth Century*. Oxford, 1963.

———. *A History of Legal Dress until the End of the Eighteenth Century*. Oxford, 1963.

Hiler, Hilaine, and Meyer Hiller. *Bibliography of Costume*. New York, 1939.

Hollander, Ann. *Seeing through Clothes*. New York, 1978.

Huart, Louis. "Le tailleur." *Statistiques de l'industrie*.

Huguet, Rev. *Délassements permis aux personnes pieuses appelées à vivre dans le monde*. Lyon, 1856.

Julian, Philippe. *Le Nu 1900*. Paris, 1976.

Kempf, Roger. *Dandies, Baudelaire et Cie*. Paris, 1977.

———. *Diderot et le roman*. Paris, 1964.

Knibiehler, Yvonne. "Le Discours médical sur la femme: constantes et ruptures." *Romantisme* 13, no. 14 (1976).

Kock, Paul de. "Le Dimanche à Paris." *La Grande Ville. Nouveau tableau de Paris*. Paris, 1842.

Koechlin, B. "Techniques corporelles et leur notation symbolique." *Langages* 10 (June 1968).

Koenig, René. *Sociologie de la mode*. Paris, 1969.

Kroeber, Alice L. "On the Principle of Order in Civilization as Exemplified by Changes of Fashion." *American Anthropologist*, n.s., 21 (1919): 235–263.

———, and James Robinson. "Three Centuries of Women's Dress Fashion: A Quantitative Analysis." *Anthropological Records* 5, no. 2 (1940): 111–154.

Kunzle, David. *Fashion and Fetishism: A Social History of the Corset, Tight-Lacing, and Other Forms of Body-Sculpture in the West*. Totowa, N.J., 1982.

La Femme et la Mode. Paris, 1893.

Lachenaud, Mr. "Du paletot." *L'Elégant* 18, no. 214 (1 July 1853).

Lacour-Gayet, Jacques. *Historie du commerce*. Vol. 2. Paris, 1952.

Lamare, Nicolas de. *Traité de police*. Vol. 1. Paris, 1705.

Lamorillière, Raoul de. *Crinolines et volants*. Bordeaux, 1855.

La Mesangère, Pierre Antoine de. *Dictionnaire des proverbes français*. Paris, 1823.

Langlade, Émile. *La Marchande de modes de Marie-Antoinette, Rose Bertin*. Paris, 1911.

Lano, Pierre de. *L'Amour à Paris sous le Second Empire*. Paris, 1896.

Lapouge, Georges Vacher de. *Les Sélections sociales*. Paris 1896.

La Rue, Father. *Sermons*. Lyon, 1719.

Lassiera, R., and J. Plumyène. *Le Complexe de droite*. Paris, 1969.

Laver, James. *Modesty in Dress: An Inquiry into the Fundamentals of Fashion*. London, 1969.

———. Preface to Lawrence Langer, *L'importance d'être vêtu*. Paris, 1959.

———. *Taste and Fashion: From the French Revolution to the Present Day*. London, 1948.

Le Petit, Claude. *La Chronique scandaleuse ou Paris ridicule*. Cologne, 1668.

Leenhardt, Maurice. "Pourquoi se vêtir?" *L'Amour de l'art*, 1er trimestre, 1952.

Legrand du Saulle, Dr. *Les hystériques, état physique et état mental, actes insolites, délictueux et criminels*. Paris, 1883.

Lehoux, Françoise. *Le Cadre de vie des médecins parisiens au XVIe et XVIIe siècle*. Paris, 1976.

Lémann. *De l'industrie des vêtements confectionnés en France, réponse aux questions de la commission permanente des valeurs relativement à cette industrie*. Paris, 1857.

Leroi-Gourhan, André. *Milieux et Techniques*. Paris, 1973.

Leroy, Adolphe. *La Vie des champs comparée à la vie des villes ou la désertion de nos campagnes*. Paris, 1864.

"Les Magasins de Paris." *Paris ou le livre des Cent-et-un*. Vol. 15. Paris, 1844.

"Les marchands de nouveautés." *Nouveau Tableau de Paris au XIXe siècle*. Paris, 1843

Lespinasse, René de. *Histoire générale de Paris, Les métiers et corporations de la ville de Paris*. Vol. 3: *Tissus, étoffes, vêtements, cuirs et peaux, métiers divers*. Paris, 1879.

Lesseli, Claudie. "Employées de grands magasins à Paris (avant 1914)." *Le Mouvement social*. 105 (October–December 1978).

Lévy, Michel. *Traité d'hygiène publique et privée*. 4th ed. vol. 2. Paris, 1862.

Libron, Fernard, and Henri Clouzot. *Le Corset dans l'art et les moeurs du XIIIe au XX siècle*. Paris, 1893.

"Linge de corps et linge de maison." *Ethnologie française* 3 (1986).

Lipovetsky, Gilles. *L'Empire de l' éphémère, la mode et son destin dans les sociétés modernes*. Paris, 1987.

Lo Duca. *L'Amour aujourd'hui*. Paris, 1963.

Lore, Otto. *Catalogue général de la librairie française depuis 1840*. Vol. 8. Paris, 1924.

Ly'onell. *L'Art de relever sa robe*. Paris, 1862.

M., Gr. de. *Histoire philosophique, anecdotique et critique de la cravate et du col*. Paris, 1854.

Macé, Gustave. *Un Joli monde*. Paris, 1887.

"Magasins de nouveautés," In *La Grande Ville, Nouveau Tableau de Paris, comique, critique, et philosophique*. Vol. 1. Paris, 1844.

Maigron, Louis le. *Romantisme et la Mode*. Paris, 1911.

Mainzer, Joseph. "Le marchand d'habits." *Les Français peints par eux-mêmes*. Paris, 1841.

Maître, Eugène Prévost. *Le Procès du Bon Pasteur*. Paris, 1903.

Malraux, André. *Les Chênes qu'on abat*. Paris, 1971.

Mandrou, Robert. *Introduction to Modern France, 1500–1640. An Essay in Historical Psychology*. Trans. R. E. Hallmark. New York, 1977.

Marana, J. P. *Lettre d'un Sicilien à un de ses amis, contenant une agréable Critique de Paris et des Français*. Chambéri, 1714.

Marchand, Louis. *Du costume de l'avocat à travers les âges*. Poitiers, 1919.

Marly, Diana de. *Worth: Father of Haute Couture*. 2d ed. New York, 1980.

Marrey, Bernard. *Les Grands Magasins: des origines à 1939*. Paris, 1979.

Martinet, André. "La fonction sexuelle de la mode." *Linguistique* 10 (1974).

Martinon, J. P. "Mythe du Dandy." *Encyclopedia Universalis*. 1980 supplement.

Marx, Karl. *Gründrisse: Introduction to the Critique of Political Economy*. Trans. Martin Nicolaus. New York, 1973.

Matos Sequeira, G. De. "Le costume défendu." *Actes du Ier Congrès International d'histoire du costume*. Venice, 1955.

Mazrui, Ali A. "The Robes of Rebellion: Sex, Dress and Politics in Africa." *Encounter* 34, no. 2 (February 1970): 19–30.

Meilheurat, Alfred de. *Manuel de savoir-vivre ou l'Art de se conduire selon les convenances et les usages du monde dans toutes les circonstances de la vie et dans les diverses régions de la société*. Paris, 1852.

Mercier, Louis Sébastien. *Tableau de Paris*. Vol. 2. Amsterdam, 1782.

Merton, Robert K. *Social Theory and Social Structure*. 2d ed. Glencoe, Ill., 1957.

Metternich, Pauline de. *Eclairs du passé, 1859–1870.* Zurich, 1922.

——. *Souvenirs de la princesse Pauline de Metternich, 1859–1871.* Paris, 1922.

Mémoires sur Voltaire et sur ses ouvrages, par Longchamp et Wagnière, ses secrétaires. Vol. 2. Paris, 1862.

Michelet, Jules. *The People.* Trans. and with an intro. by John P. McKay. Chicago, 1973.

Miller, Michael B. *The Bon Marché: Bourgeois Culture and the Department Store, 1869–1920.* Princeton, 1981.

Montaigne, Michel de. *The Complete Essays of Montaigne.* Trans. Donald M. Frame. Stanford, 1958.

Montesquieu, Charles Louis de Secondat, Baron de la Brède et de. *The Persian Letters.* Ed. and trans. J. Robert Loy. Cleveland, 1961.

Mortemart-Boisse, François-Jérôme-Léonard de. *La Vie élégante à Paris.* Paris, 1857.

Mousseau, Jacques. *L'Amour à refaire.* Paris, 1969.

Muller, Eugène. *La Boutique du marchand de nouveautés.* Paris, 1868.

Napias, Dr. Henri. *L'Assistance publique dans le departement de Sambre-et-Loire* [*sic*] Paris, 1890.

Nathan, Joseph, and Alex Nicholas. "The Uniform: A Sociological Perspective." *American Journal of Sociology* 77, no. 4 (January 1972).

Neuville, Louis Lemercier de. *Physiologie du coiffeur.* Paris, 1862.

Nietzsche, Friederich. *The Complete Works of Friedrich Nietzsche.* Vol. 12: *Beyond Good and Evil.* Ed. Oscar Levy, trans. Helen Zimmern. New York, 1964.

——. *The Complete Works of Friederich Nietzsche.* Vol. 7: *The Wanderer and His Shadow.* Trans. Paul V. Cohn. New York, 1964.

Nouvion, Pierre de, and Émile Liez. *Un ministre des modes sous Louis XVI, mademoiselle Bertin, marchande de modes de la reine, 1747–1813.* Paris, 1911.

O'Followell, Dr. *Le Corset (histoire, médecine, hygiène).* Paris, 1908.

Oberkirch, Baronne de. *Mémoires.* Paris, 1970. "Physiologie de la toilete." *La Silhouette* 2, no. 11 (June 1830).

Observations sur les modes et les usages de Paris pour servir d'explication aux caricatures publiées sous le titre de Bon Genre depuis le commencement du dix-neuvième siècle. Paris, 1817.

Orvanne, Alfred Bourgeois de. *Bains publics gratuits et à prix réduits.* Paris, 1854.

Pagnol, Marcel. *Le Temps des amours.* Paris, 1977.

Pastoureau, Michel. *L'Etoffe du diable: une histoire des rayures et des tissus rayés.* Paris, 1991.

Perrin, Raoul. "Le commis-voyageur." In *Les Français peints par eux-mêmes.* Paris, 1841.

Perrot, Michelle. "Machine à coudre et travail à domicile." *Le Mouvement social* 105 (October–December 1978): 161–164.

Perrot, Philippe. "Aspects socio-culturels des débuts de la confection parisienne au XIXe siècle." *Revue de l'Institut de sociologie* 2 (1977): 185–202.

——. *Le travail des apparences ou les transformations du corps feminin XVIII–XIXe siècle.* Paris, 1984.

Photographies inconvenantes 1900. Paris, 1978.

Physiologie du gant. Paris, 1843.

Physiologie du tailleur. Paris, 1840.

Picard, Alfred. *Exposition universelle internationale de 1900 à Paris. Le bilan d'un siècle (1801–1900)*. Vol. 4. Paris, 1906.

Poirier, Jean, and Patrick O'Reilly. "L'évolution du costume." *Journal de la société des océanistes* 9, no. 9 (December 1953): 151–169.

Polhemus, Ted, and Lynn Procter. *Fashion and Anti-Fashion: Anthropology of Clothing and Adornment*. London, 1978.

Post, Paul. *Die französich-niederlandische Männertracht einschliesslich der Ritterüstung im Zeitalter der Spätgotik, 1350–1475. Ein Rekonstruktionversuch auf Grund der Zeitgenössischen Darstellungen*. Halle, 1910.

Pour la beauté naturelle de la femme contre la mutilation de la taille par le corset. Paris, 1909.

Prevost, Gabriel. *Le Nu, le Vêtement, la Parure chez l'homme et chez la femme*. Paris, 1883.

Prud'homme, Louis Marie. *Le Voyage descriptif et historique de l'ancien et du nouveau Paris*. 2 vols. Paris, 1821.

Quicherat, Jules-Étienne J. *Histoire du costume en France depuis les temps les plus reculés jusqu' à la fin du XVIIIᵉ siècle*. Paris, 1875.

Rabelais. *Pantagruel*. Book 2. Paris, 1955.

Racinet, A. *Le Costume historique*. 6 vols. Paris, 1875–88.

Rapport du Conseil municipal de Paris, présenteé par M. Georges Villain, au nom de la 2ᵉ Commission, sur diverse pétitions relatives au marchée du Temple. Paris, 1892.

Reiset, Comte de. *Modes et Usages au temps de Marie-Antoinette, livre-journal de Mme Éloffe, marchande de modes, couturière, lingère de la reine et des dames de sa cour*. 2 vols. Paris, 1885.

Reisser, the elder. *Avis au sexe ou essai sur les corps baleinés pour former et conserver la taille aux jeunes personnes*. Lyon, 1770.

Renneville, Vicomtesse de. "Les bals." *La Sylphide*, 20 January 1854.

Ribeiro, Aileen. *Fashion in the French Revolution*. New York, 1988.

Ricard, Adolphe. *L'Amour, les Femmes et le Mariage*. Paris, 1857.

Ricord, Dr. *De Paris à Meaux en passant par Venise, Vienne, Pesth, La Roumanie, Constantinople, Athènes*. Paris, 1873.

Robert, Ulysse. *Les Signes d'infamie au Moyen Age*. Paris, 1881.

Robinson, Dwight E. "Fashions in Shaving and Trimming of the Beard: The Men of the 'Illustrated London News,' 1842–1972." *American Journal of Sociology* 81, no. 5 (March 1976): 1133–1141.

Roche, Daniel. *La Culture des apparences, une histoire du vêtement, XVIIᵉ-XVIIIᵉ siècle*. Paris, 1989.

Roqueplan, Nestor. *Parisine*. Paris, 1869.

Rossi, William A. *The Sex Life of the Foot and Shoe*. London, 1977.

Rougerie, Jacques. "Remarque sur l'histoire des salaires à Paris." *Mouvement social* 63 (April–June 1968): 71–108.

Rouquette, Robert. "Une centenaire: la soutane." *Études* 314 (July–August 1962): 32–48.

Rousseau, Jean-Jacques. *The Confessions*. New York, n.d.

Roux, Charles. *Contre le corset*. Paris, 1855.

Royal Declaration Prohibiting the Wearing of Diamonds, Given at Paris the Fourth of February, 1720. Paris, 1720.

Royal Edict against Luxury Stating Regulations for Fabrics, Braids, Furnishings Dishes, Plates, and Other Silver or Gold Utensils etc., Given the Month of March, 1700. Paris, 1700.

Rudofsky, Bernard. *Are Clothes Modern?* Chicago, 1947.

S., Mme. *Physiologie du corset.* Montpellier, 1847.

Saint-Laurent, Cecil. *A History of Ladies' Underwear.* London, 1968.

Saint-Simon, Louis de Rouvroy, duc de. *Mémoires.* Vol. 12. Paris, 1874.

Saint-Ursin, P. J. Marie de. *L'Ami des femmes ou Lettres d'un médecin concernant l'influence de l'habillement des femmes sur leurs moeurs et leur santé et la nécessité de l'usage habituel des bains en conservant leur costume actuel. Dédié a Mme Bonaparte.* Paris, 1804.

Sédillot, René. *Peugeot—De la crinoline à la 404.* Paris, 1960.

Ségur, Comtesse de. *Les Petites Filles modèles.* Paris, 1858.

Sibbar-Pignon, Leïla. "Mlle Lili ou l'ordre des poupées." *Les Temps modernes* 358 (May 1976): 1796–1828.

Simmel, Georg. "Fashion." *International Quarterly* 10 (1904–5): 130–155; reproduced in *American Journal of Sociology* 62, no. 6 (1956–57): 541–558.

———. *Philosophie der Mode.* Berlin, 1905.

Simon, Jules. *L'Ouvrière.* Paris, 1861.

Sombart, Werner. *L'Apogée du capitalisme.* Trans. S. Jankélévitch. Paris, 1932.

———. *Wirtschaft und Mode, ein Betrag zur Theorie der modernen Bedarfsgestaltung.* Wiesbaden, 1902.

Soulavie, Jean-Louis. *Mémoires historiques et politiques du règne de Louis XVI.* Paris, 1801.

Spencer, Herbert. "Manners and Fashion." In *Essays Scientific, Political, and Speculative,* Vol. 3, pp. 1–51. New York, 1892.

———. *The Principles of Sociology.* Vol. 2. London, 1879.

Starobinski, Jean. *1789, The Emblems of Reason.* Trans. Barbara Bray. Charlottesville, 1982.

Statistiques de l'industrie à Paris resultant de l'enquête faite par la Chambre de commerce pour les années 1847–1848. Paris, 1851.

Statistiques de l'industrie à Paris, resultant de l'enquête faite par la Chambre de commerce pour l'année 1860. Paris, 1864.

Statuts Ordonnances et Déclaration du Roy confirmative d'iceux pour la communauté des courturières de la ville, Fauxbourgs et banlieue de Paris, Verifié en Parlement le 7 octobre 1675. Paris, 1678.

Stendahl. *Oeuvres complètes.* Vol. 36: *Souvenirs d'égotisme.* Geneva, 1970.

Sumner, William Graham. *Folkways: A Study of the Sociological Importance of Usages, Manners, Customs, Mores, and Morals.* New York, 1906.

"Tailleur." *Grand Dictionnaire universel du XIXe siècle.*

Taine, Hippolyte. *Notes sur l'Angleterre.* Paris, 1872.

———. *Notes on Paris: The Life and Opinions of M. Frédéric-Thomas Graindorge.* Trans. John Austin Stevens. New York, 1875.

———. *The Origins of Contemporary France: The French Revolution.* Trans. John Durand. New York, 1931.

Tarde, Gustave. *Les Lois de l'imitation.* Paris, 1890.

Texier, Edmond. *Tableau de Paris.* Paris, 1852.

Thirifocq. "Du costume dans ses rapports avec les moeurs et avec la civilisation." *Journal des modes d'hommes*, no. 1 (January, 1867).

Thuillier, Guy. "Pour un histoire des gestes." *Revue d'histoire économique et sociale* 2 (1973).

———. "Pour une histoire de l'hygiène corporelle." *Revue d'histoire économique et sociale* 2 (1968): 232–253.

———. "Pour une histoire de la lessive." *Annales: Économies, Sociétés, Civilisations.* 3 (1969): 377–390.

———. *Pour une histoire du quotidien au XIXᵉ siècle en Nivernais.* Paris, 1977.

Tissot, Samuel A. *Essai sur les maladies des gens du monde.* Lausanne, 1770.

Tocqueville, Alexis de. *Democracy in America.* Trans. Phillips Bradely. Vol. 2. New York, 1945.

———. *The Old Regime and the French Revolution.* Trans. Stuart Gilbert. New York, 1955.

Tola-Poix, Achille. *Les ceintures qui parlent.* Paris, 1861.

Tramar, Countess de. *Le Bréviaire de la femme, pratiques secrètes de la beauté.* 8th ed. Paris, 1903.

Uzanne, Octave. *L'Art et les Artifices de la Beauté.* Paris, 1902.

———. *Les Modes de Paris.* Paris, 1898.

Vandermonde, Charles Auguste. *Essai sur la manière de perfectionner l'espèce humaine.* 2 vols. Paris, 1756.

Vanier, Henriette. *La Mode et ses Métiers. Frivolités et luttes des classes.* Paris, 1960.

Veblen, Thorstein. *The Theory of the Leisure Class.* New York, 1899.

Verardi, Louis. *Manuel du bon ton et de la politesse française.* Paris, 1853.

Verdier, Yvonne. *Façons de dire, façons de faire.* Paris, 1979.

Verne, Jules. *The Begum's Millions.* New York, 1958.

Verron, A. "La cravate, emblème politique." *Cahier Ciba* 3, no. 31 (September 1950): 1071–1076.

Les Vésuviennes ou la Constitution politique des femmes. Paris, 1848.

"Vêtement et sociétés, Actes du colloque national CNRS, Vers une anthropologie du vêtement." *L'Ethnographie* 92–94 (1984).

Vidal, Pierre. *Histoire de la corporation des travailleurs d'habits, de la ville de Paris d'après des documents orignaux.* Mimeographed publication. Paris, 1923.

Viel-Castel, Horace de. *Mémoires.* Paris, 1942.

Vigarello. Georges, *Concepts of Cleanliness: Changing Attitudes in France since the Middle Ages.* Trans. Jean Birrell. Cambridge, 1988.

———. *Le Corps redressé.* Paris, 1978.

Vilette, Marquis de. *Lettres choisies.* Montargis, 1790.

Violette. *L'Art de la toilette chez la femme.* Paris, 1885.

Wagner, Richard. *Lettres de Richard Wagner à Minna Wagner.* Paris, 1943.

Webb, Wilfred Mark. *The Heritage of Dress.* London, 1907.

Weber, Max. *Economy and Society: An Outline of Interpretative Sociology.* Ed. Guenther Roth and Claus Wittich. Berkeley, 1978.

———. *The Protestant Ethic and the Spirit of Capitalism.* Trans. Talcott Parsons. New York, 1958.

Weill, Alexandre. *Un Fléau national, les grands magasins de Paris et les Moyens de les combattre.* Paris, 1888.

Wilhelm, Jacques. *Histoire de la Mode*. Paris, 1955.

Winslow, Jacob B. "Mémoire sur les mauvais effets de l'usage des corps à baleines." *Mémoires de l'Académie des Sciences*. Paris, 1741.

Woolf, Virginia. *Orlando*. New York, 1928.

Worth, Gaston. *La Couture et la Confection des vêtements de femme*. Paris, 1895.

Wright, Lawrence. *Clean and Decent: The Fascinating History of the Bathroom and the Water Closet*. London, 1960.

Yonnet, Paul. *Jeux, modes et masses*. Paris, 1985.

Young, Agnes Brooks. *Recurring Cycles of Fashion 1760–1937*. New York, 1966.

Zola, Émile. *Ladies' Delight*. Trans. April Fitzlyon. London, 1957.

———. *Nana*. New York, 1933.

———. *Pot Bouille*. Paris, 1957.

———. Preparatory dossier for *Au Bonheur des Dames*. Manuscript. Bibliothèque nationale, Nouvelle Acquisitions françaises, N° 10278.

Index

working class, 8; and bourgeois dress, 73;
and dirtiness, 74
World War I, 11, 21, 27, 77, 190
Worth, Charles Frederick, 4, 40, 51, 67, 167,
184–187, 250nn. 53 and 54, 250n.53

yashmak, 7
Young, Agnes, 23

Zola, Emile, 60, 61, 62, 63, 67, 168, 171–
172, 190, 214n.5, 215–216n.23